An Invitation to
Ethnomethodology

An Invitation to Ethnomethodology

**Language, Society
and Social Interaction**

David Francis

and Stephen Hester

SAGE Publications
London ● Thousand Oaks ● New Delhi

First published 2004
Reprinted 2006

SAGE Publications Ltd
1 Oliver's Yard
55 City Road
London EC1Y 1SP

SAGE Publications Inc.
2455 Teller Road
Thousand Oaks, California 91320

SAGE Publications India Pvt Ltd
B-42, Panchsheel Enclave
Post Box 4109
New Delhi 100 017

British Library Cataloguing in Publication data

A catalogue record for this book is available
from the British Library

ISBN-10: 0-7619-6641-2   ISBN-13: 978-0-7619-6641-8
ISBN-10: 0 7619-6642-0 (pbk)   ISBN-13: 978-0-7619-6642-5 (pbk)

Library of Congress Control Number: 2003103982

Typeset by C&M Digitals (P) Ltd., Chennai, India
Printed and bound in Great Britain by Athenaeum Press Ltd., Gateshead, Tyne & Wear

Contents

1

Social Interaction, Language and Society

This book is about how society is accomplished in and through social interaction, how language is central to this accomplishment and how the interactional nature of social life may be investigated. We invite the reader to share in not only a particular vision of social life, as constituted in and through language and social interaction, but also a form of sociological inquiry that is consistent with and follows from this vision. This form of inquiry is known as ethnomethodology. In this chapter we outline the nature of our conception of social life by considering in turn its three key ideas or components: social interaction, language and society. In the next chapter we explain what we mean by ethnomethodology. In the chapters to follow, various aspects of social life are considered from the point of view we propose. We present analysis and discuss studies consistent with this approach and explain how they implement the form of sociological inquiry that we are recommending. Our overall aim is not just to show what is involved in doing ethnomethodology, but also to invite the reader to try for him- or herself this way of doing sociology.

Social interaction

What we refer to as 'society' is made up of social activities of many different kinds. What makes these activities 'social' is that they are done with or in relation to others. Some activities are collective activities – these are done by several or many persons acting together. Examples of such collective activities are a family meal, a business meeting, a football match or a political election. Other activities may be done by a single individual but with reference to others, or in a context that involves and is made possible by other people. Examples of this are getting dressed in the morning, walking along the street, reading a book or writing a letter. Such activities can be referred to as 'individual' activities so long as it is remembered that, like collective activities, *what* is done and *how* it is done is shaped by the fact that the activity is part of a shared social life, a life that we lead with others.

This is confirmed by the fact that such individual activities are recognizable as the activity they are, not simply to the person who happens to be performing them but to other members of society. In other words, for something done by an individual (or by a number of persons acting together) to be identifiable and describable as 'this' activity (for example, waiting at a streetcorner, reading a newspaper, running to catch a bus) means that the activity in question forms part of a 'grammar' of activities known by and recognizable to the society's members. Consequently, using the term 'individual' to refer to activities done by a single person acting alone does not mean that such activities are somehow less social than others done by persons acting together. Even if an activity is being done by an individual acting entirely alone, it is none the less a social activity in the sense that we intend here.

Another way of putting this is to say that our activities as members of society are fundamentally interactional in character. By this we mean not simply that much we do is done through face-to-face interaction with others, nor even that we do many things through 'mediated interaction', for example, talking on the telephone, communicating by letter or e-mail. More than this, our point is that even things we do alone are informed by our membership of society and our social relationships with others. As we have already indicated, the very possibility of recognizably engaging in this or that activity is provided by such membership. Furthermore, the circumstances in which we are able to be alone and do things by ourselves are socially organized and the things we are entitled to do by ourselves are socially sanctioned. Not only this, but we have learned how to do things – from speaking our native language to using the Internet – through interaction with other people. We can be held accountable by other people for how we do these things, whether we do them in socially acceptable ways or in appropriate circumstances. In this sense everything we do, from the most obviously collective actions to the most 'individual' ones, are made possible by the interactional nature of our social lives. In relation to this point, then, it is not an incidental fact about us that we are members of society, rather it is a fundamental one with regard to who we are and what we do – to *all* that we are and *everything* we do.

Later in this chapter we expand upon what we mean by 'membership of society'. For the moment we will observe that social interaction takes place in many settings: on the street, in the home, at work, in institutions such as hospitals, schools and prisons, and in the corridors of government and the boardrooms of transnational companies, to name but a few. In all these settings, and many more, persons interact with one another to get social activities done. The activities may be as ostensibly simple and commonplace as asking the time or for directions to the railway station, or as complex and momentous as deciding the interest rate of the Bank of England (and therefore the national level of interest rates in the UK). Nevertheless, whether the participants to the interaction are strangers on a city street or the members of the Monetary Policy Committee, their interaction has some general features. Two of these features common to all social interaction are the structured character of interaction and the contextual availability of meaning. We discuss these two features in turn.

The structured character of interaction

It is often assumed that interaction between people can be explained in terms of individuals and their characteristics. Indeed, this view has a long and illustrious history in theories of human behaviour. Anyone who has not studied social interaction could be forgiven for thinking that the course of any interaction depends entirely on what the persons involved decide to do or say, based on their individual desires, intentions and predispositions. Since interaction takes place between persons, it is tempting to think that there is nothing more to it but what individuals happen to do. Therefore interaction, one might think, is simply a product of individuals and the 'choices' they make, where these choices are to a degree unrestricted. After all, much interaction has a highly spontaneous character; one does not know what someone is going to say or do until they say or do it. To call interaction 'social', on this view, is to refer simply to the fact that it occurs between individuals. It implies nothing about the *organization* of what is done.

Through much of its history as a discipline, sociology has sought to establish the inadequacy of such an individualist account of human behaviour. Typically it has done so by arguing that behaviour is nowhere near as unrestricted as individualist accounts assume. Sociologists have insisted that how persons act towards one another is constrained in significant ways by their membership of society. In other words, and putting things very simplistically, whereas individualist theories locate the determinants of behaviour 'inside' the individual, sociological theories traditionally have located them 'outside' in the structure of society. Social interaction, from this point of view, is an arena within which the social forces that constrain individuals and shape their behaviour are played out.

The view we argue for in this book differs from both of these conceptions. Both the individualist and traditional sociological approaches are to be rejected, since each treats the interactional character of human behaviour as 'epi-phenomenal', that is, as the product of some more basic factors and therefore of secondary interest. In both approaches, whatever order is to be found in social interaction is explained as the result of something else. Both its origin and character comes about either because of the 'inner' make up of individuals or the 'outer' determinants of society (or some combination of the two). Social interaction has no intrinsic orderliness in its own right; it only has the orderly features that are imposed upon it by such inner or outer factors.

Against this view we will argue that all social interaction is 'intrinsically socially structured'. What we are referring to as social interaction involves any situation in which a person produces an action addressed or directed towards another and/or which invites or makes possible a response from another. All such actions are 'structured' in the sense that the character of the action produced by Person A 'conditions' what can be done in response to it by Person B. Let us look at some simple examples:

Example 1
A: Hi, my name's Brian.
B: Hi, I'm John.

Example 2
A: Excuse me?
B: Yes?

Example 3
A: [*wringing his hand*] SHIT!
B: Are you OK?

Note the links between the first utterance and the second in each of the examples. In Example 1 A introduces himself to B, whereupon B produces a return introduction. The two actions go together as a pair; they constitute an 'introduction exchange'. This exchange exemplifies what conversation analysts call an 'adjacency pair', in that A's utterance performs a first action which makes relevant a responding second action by B in the next utterance. (We will discuss adjacency pairs in more detail in Chapter 3). In Example 2 the structure is a little more complex. Again the two utterances form an adjacency pair, but here the structure extends into the third (not as yet produced) slot. A's 'Excuse me?' is responded to by B with a 'Yes', which does two things. First, it indicates that B has heard it as what we might call a 'pre-question marker', and second it responds to A's utterance as such a marker by returning the interactional floor to A with 'permission' to ask the question or make the request that A has in mind. In both these first two examples person B is 'selected' to speak by person A addressing an utterance to him/her. Example 3 illustrates how an action that is not actually addressed to another (A's 'SHIT' is an expletive on hurting his hand) can nevertheless occasion an interactional response. Although B is not 'selected' to speak by speaker A, it is clear that B's response is the proper ('natural') one in the circumstances. When someone near to us suffers a sudden hurt or injury a response such as B's is the expectable (and expected) one. Ironically, were B to have not acted in response to A's hurt, he/she would most likely be found to have acted improperly by ignoring someone in trouble. Thus Example 3 also illustrates how not responding to another can be a kind of action – 'doing nothing'.

To say that interaction is intrinsically socially structured, then, is to note that the actions of the participants are 'tied' together in intelligible and appropriate ways. An action *projects* the kind of thing that can or should be done next, while this in turn, in so far as it is recognizable as a responding action, *fits* with what has been projected. The structures involved are not invented on the spot by the individuals that happen to be engaged in this particular interaction, but neither are they reproduced 'mechanically' by such persons. One's social competence consists in the ability to use these structures in producing and making sense of social interaction.

The contextual availability of meaning

What the examples above also show is that mutual intelligibility is fundamental to interaction. Obviously for person B to respond in an appropriate way to person A, it requires that B understands what A has said or done. For persons to interact with one another requires that each has some grasp of what the other is doing or saying. Once again, the individualistic perspective might suggest that the meaning of persons' actions is highly problematic. Presumably the only person who knows definitively what is meant by something said is the individual saying it. Along not dissimilar lines, some recent sociological theorizing, associated with postmodernism and radical reflexivity, holds that all meaning is problematic and relative and that therefore 'common understanding' is at best arbitrary and at worst impossible. In so far as common understandings obtain in social life, such sociologies suggest that they do so largely as a result of the exercise of power. Of course, we would not disagree that the meaning of a word, an action or a situation can be problematic. Thus, we have all experienced situations where someone has said or done something and we have been unsure what they meant by it. But equally, we are all familiar with occasions where it is perfectly plain what someone means. Furthermore, it is a massively observable fact that members of society interact with one another with little apparent difficulty in mutual understanding.

In our view, any adequate account of such mutual understanding has to recognize the role that 'context' plays in the comprehension of meaning in interaction. Taken out of its context of use, just about any phrase or sentence can be viewed as puzzling or ambiguous. Within that context, however, what is meant is normally quite transparent. Thus, while even the most plain and clear meaning can be rendered problematic if one so chooses, such problematizing of meaning involves removing the contextual specifics that make meaning clear. Those sociologists and philosophers who argue for the 'indeterminacy of meaning' do so on theoretical grounds that have little to do with how members of society actually comprehend the meaning of what is said or done. Furthermore, it is only within the confines of academic discourse that the possibility of questioning every common and plain understanding is a legitimate activity. In ordinary social life, in actual contexts of interaction, persons are not given license to systematically doubt the meanings of words and actions. In this sense, then, the skeptical character of postmodernism and radical reflexivity would seem to have little relevance for how people understand one another in everyday social life.

We have hinted above that the individualist view of interaction is associated with a 'mentalistic' view of meaning. According to this view, meaning is something created in the mind of the individual. Proponents of this mentalistic view of meaning argue that since one does not have access to the mind of the other, one can never really know what is meant by their actions. There are three noteworthy problems with this mentalistic view of meaning. The first is that problems of understanding are not ubiquitous: they are the exception rather than the rule. Second, when we experience a problem about what someone means, it is almost never an 'open-ended' difficulty (that is, where one has no idea at all what could be meant). Usually the problem of understanding is quite specific – one is not sure whether what is meant in this context is this or that. Third, when we have such a problem we have ways of dealing with it – by asking for explanation or clarification. For example:

Example 4
Mother: Who else is going to this party?
Teenage daughter: What do you mean?

Here the daughter asks her mother to explain what she means by the question about the party. What might the problem of understanding be here? Is it that the daughter has no idea what her mother means by the question, in the sense that she has no notion of what the words mean? This seems a remote possibility. A more plausible one is that the daughter's problem concerns her mother's motive in asking the question. Grasping the motive provides a way of understanding what is being asked and thus what an appropriate kind of answer might be. For example, is the mother asking for a list of all those who are due to attend the party? But what reason could she have for wanting to know this? Asking who will be present at a party can be one way of judging what kind of party it will be. Perhaps the question is not about *all* who will be at the party, but just certain specific persons. The speaker is, after all, a mother, and what is more, a mother of a teenage daughter. Typically, mothers of teenage daughters are known to be concerned about who their daughters associate with, wanting to avoid her getting 'in with the wrong crowd'. This possibility suggests that the daughter's problem may not really be to do with understanding at all, but is more about the mother's right to ask such a question. 'What do you mean?' may be used to express not a problem of comprehension but of entitlement: what right has the mother got to question her daughter about who she associates with?

Of course, with ingenuity (and a tolerance for implausibility) one could come up with an infinite list of possible things that the mother in the above example might have meant by what she said. One can construct these possibilities by introducing other contextual features and thereby attributing all sorts of (weird and wonderful) possible motives to her. For example, perhaps she is really asking because she would like to come to the party herself: she is jealous of her daughter's teenage status and would like to relive her own adolescent years. Alternatively, perhaps she is an extreme evangelical Christian and sees the party as a possible opportunity for religious activity: she is interested to know who will be at the party because she is thinking of coming along to distribute religious literature and appeal to the non-Christians present to 'see the light'. The reader may invent other possibilities for him- or herself.

In the absence of any actual contextual information supporting these interpretations, they amount to idle, groundless speculation. However, participants in social interaction seldom have the freedom to engage in this kind of idle speculation about the motives behind the actions of others. The fundamental constraint that operates in all interaction is that persons should, wherever possible, take things 'at face value'. In other words, one should respond to the actions of others on the basis of what those actions seem, obviously or most plausibly, to be. If something seems quite obviously to be a question addressed to oneself, then respond to it as such. The same holds for the meaning of what is said. If the meaning of the question is clear, then respond to it on that basis.

Against the mentalistic theory, then, we suggest that there is no general problem of meaning or understanding in interaction, therefore nothing for a general theory to explain. Rather, problems of understanding are 'occasional'. They arise in specific interactional contexts, and the particular difficulties they involve exist by virtue of that context. It is the contextual availability of meaning that provides the background against which specific actions may on a specific occasion be found puzzling. The occasioned nature of problems of understanding has implications for how meaning is conceptualized. Ever since the writings of Weber, it has been common for sociologists to emphasize the importance of meaning by talking about the 'interpretive' nature of interaction. The term 'interpretation' is useful in emphasizing that participants in interaction have to make sense of what others are doing. Interaction is not a mechanical process of stimulus and response. However, the use of the term 'interpretation' as a general description can misleadingly suggest that interaction involves persons in a kind of continual puzzle-solving: that everything anyone does has to be 'interpreted' before one can decide how to respond to it. We suggest the opposite – most of the time what others are doing is 'transparent'. This does not mean that persons do not make sense, but that most of the time such sense making is massively routine and unproblematic.

Language

So far we have talked about the nature of social interaction. But as the examples we have given above make clear, interaction is overwhelmingly conducted through language. It is in and through language that most of the actions we perform are done. Through language we ask and answer questions, request help, give instructions, report problems, make jokes, explain who and what we are, and so on. Language is fundamental to everything that is done in social life: as members of society we live our social lives by talking to and with others. This is true of the 'insignificant' activities we engage in as well as the 'significant' ones. For example, through language we are able to do things like chatting with a friend or asking the time, but also things like answering questions in a job interview or proposing marriage. However, it is not just the activities of individuals that are dependent upon language. The institutional structures of society that you have read about in sociology textbooks – such things as economic organization, the legal system, political and educational structures – are also made possible by language. Such institutions themselves consist of activities of various kinds – business meetings, courtroom trials, parliamentary debates and classroom lessons – which are conducted through the use of language.

In short, social life is permeated by language at every level. As members of society, we use language to describe, question or explain what is going on around us, as well as to perform actions that others may then describe, question or explain. The relationship between language and social life is thus a mutually constitutive one. Without language there could be no social life, at least as we human beings live it. Conversely, without social life there would be no need of language, since it is communication that lies at the heart of language. Through language persons are able to communicate with one another; we need to communicate because we lead social lives together and it is linguistic communication that makes social life what it is.

There are various interests that one could have in language. Our focus in this book will be on language-in-use; we are concerned with the ways that language is used in social activities. Our approach to language contrasts, for example, with the predominant approach taken in the discipline of linguistics. Here the concern is with language conceived as a grammatical system. Linguistic theory seeks to explain the principles by which grammatically well-formed sentences are generated, hence the approach is called 'generative linguistics'. These principles are assumed to be part of any speaker's mental apparatus. The task of the linguistic theorist, therefore, is not to describe 'performance' – how persons actually talk – but to reconstruct the linguistic 'competence' that each one of us, according to the theory, possesses in our minds. To this end, linguistic theorists such as Chomsky (1975) study language in abstraction from its actual use, examining sentences that have been invented by the theorist.

The view of language taken here differs in several fundamental respects from this generative linguistic approach. First, our concern is not with language as an abstract system but as a practical vehicle of communication. From this point of view it is notable that, contrary to what generative linguistics might lead one to think, persons much of the time do not speak in grammatically perfect sentences, or even in sentences at all. Yet the ungrammatical character of much language-in-use does not typically create communication difficulties; persons seem quite able to understand one another without prioritizing grammatical correctness. Second, our concern is not with the individual speaker and his or her internal linguistic knowledge, but with the ways that persons achieve 'interpersonal understanding' through language. Whereas linguistic theorists like Chomsky conceive language as an individual and mental phenomenon, language-in-use is a social phenomenon; it 'exists' in the communicative relations between persons. This leads to a third difference, of a methodological kind. Unlike the isolated, invented sentences of the linguistic theorist, the data for our inquiries has to be the actual things that are said by real people in social interaction. Our interest is in how persons use language together to accomplish the social activities that they are engaged in.

What about the view of language taken within sociology? Here too one finds that the dominant approach differs from the one advocated here. The first point to make is that, for much of its history, sociology paid little attention to language and failed to see it as a significant phenomenon. Given the essential and paramount role of language in social life, it is perhaps surprising that sociology for so long took little interest in it. With the exception of the later writings of Durkheim, one will find no mention of language in the works of the founding fathers. During the period of sociology's expansion as an academic discipline, language was marginal at best to its research interests. What could account for this neglect? One possibility is that the very ubiquity of language, its pervasiveness in everything we do, makes it easy to overlook its importance. It is so much a part of what we do that it requires effort not to take it for granted.

We suspect that there is also a theoretical reason for this neglect. The predominant tendency in sociology has been to focus upon the results or outcomes of social activities without asking how language is used to accomplish such results. For example, sociologists traditionally have paid much attention to 'rates of behaviour' – crime rates, suicide rates, rates of industrial or political action of various kinds – and typically have sought to explain these in terms of other kinds of measures. The availability of such rates as sociological data is made possible by the activities of those who have assembled the records from which the rates are compiled, such as police officers, coroners, civil servants, employers and so on. These activities are conducted through language: it is by means of language, for example, that decisions are made as to whether to count an event as a case of this or that statistical type. Yet the linguistic activity that has gone into the production of official records disappears from sight when the rates are treated as free-standing, 'anonymous' phenomena.

In so far as sociologists have paid attention to language, this has often taken the form of theorizing language as just another variable that requires sociological explanation in terms of its relationship with other social factors. Language is often taken to be a 'mediating variable', providing a causal link between general features of society and the fates of individuals. The form of such explanations is twofold: first, socially distributed aspects of language use such as dialect, vocabulary and idiom are explained by other social factors, for example social class, gender or race. Second, these linguistic features are held to account for the life chances of individuals, involving such things as marital patterns and occupational career paths. We will briefly mention two examples of this approach to language.

The first concerns the relationship between language and educational achievement. A theory of educational achievement that was very popular in the 1970s holds that a critical factor in determining class differences in children's school performance is the linguistic code, or style of speech, that they have acquired as a result of their family background (Bernstein, 1975). Children from middle-class families, the theory proposes, arrive at school equipped with an elaborated code of speech that fits well both with the expectations of teachers and the communication demands that formal education makes upon the child. Children from lower-class backgrounds, however, are said to arrive at school equipped with a restricted code that leads them to be viewed as less able by teachers and which creates difficulties for them in meeting the demands of schooling.

More recently, numerous studies have argued a relationship between language and gender. In the work of Tannen (1990), for example, it is argued that differences between women and men in the style of their conversational interaction reflect basic differences in the social personalities of women and men. Tannen argues that as a result of childhood socialization, men and women are motivated by quite different general orientations in interaction: men towards hierarchy and competition for position, women towards solidarity and mutual support. This individualist/collectivist gender difference is then reflected in how talk is conducted. In their turn, such differences can be seen to reproduce and to have an impact upon the relative life chances of men and women. Tannen claims that women, by virtue of these learned personality characteristics and the linguistic patterns that follow from them, are at a systematic disadvantage in the male-dominated world of work, thus perpetuating occupational inequality.

In these ways language is incorporated within explanations of specific aspects of society. Now, it is not our intention to argue that learned ways of speaking cannot have educational consequences or implications for gender relations. Indeed, that there may be a link between how one speaks and one's chances of educational success or occupational advancement is something that novelists and other writers have noted long before it became thematic within sociology. However, while such connections between language and social relations may be evident, our point is that sociological theories that conceive it solely in terms of causal connections between social structural variables and linguistic interaction take an excessively narrow view of the social nature of language. The causal approach is inadequate because it crucially misses the 'constitutive' nature of language in social life; language is not just one variable among many, nor does it simply play a role in this or that aspect of social life. Rather, it constitutes the very possibility of social life in the first place. Thus, in relation to schooling, language is not simply (if it is) a basis for teachers' judgements of children's abilities; it is through the use of language that the fundamentals of schooling within which such judgements are embedded are produced in the first place. Without the use of language there could be no such things as lessons and therefore no teacher's questions or pupil's answers. Similarly, that gender is both massively observable in and widely relevant to the activities that make up ordinary social life is largely constituted in and through language. One expression of this is that men and women are conventionally given different names such that if one knows a person's name a reasonable inference can be made about that person's gender.

In recent years the constitutive character of language in social life has come to be recognized to a certain extent in social thought. In place of the causal approach just described, many sociologists nowadays regard language as comprising a system of representations or signs in and through which all social phenomena are realized. Society is a 'semiotic' reality in this view: every aspect of social life shapes and is shaped by language, conceived as structures of linguistic signs. Such structures, or 'discourses' as they are often called, amount to organized sets of linguistic representations that give meaning to social phenomena. The key point made by proponents of this approach is that linguistic representation is never neutral, never simply corresponds *to* the extra-linguistic nature of that which it represents. Thus meaning does not flow from object to sign, but rather the other way round: signs *impose meaning upon* that which they represent. Thus different discourses represent things in quite different ways. Furthermore, discourses themselves differ in their social distribution. While there may be a variety of discourses within society, some are used more widely and propagated more effectively as representational systems than others. Some discourses are apparently 'expert' or 'authoritative' ways of representing an aspect of social life. On this basis, one can speak of 'dominant' (and of course 'subordinate') discourses in society. The more widespread and/or authoritative a discourse is, the more it dominates the way in which social phenomena are thought about and acted towards by members of society.

This semiotic approach to society has become enormously popular and influential in present-day sociology, underpinning studies in areas of inquiry as diverse as media, education, health, work, crime and the family, to name but a few. Across these fields of research studies display strong analytical similarities. Such studies tend to be geared towards identifying the features of this or that discourse and tracing its influence upon the definition and treatment of social issues and problems. As such, the analyses they present invariably have a critical cast, explicitly or implicitly. The semiotic notion that meaning is 'imposed' upon phenomena provides the basis for conceiving socially accepted definitions of issues and problems as irremediably tendentious: they are imposed by some groups upon others in the service of social interests. Where once social domination was accounted for in terms of the control of society's economic resources, now it is held, by discourse analysts at least, to consist in control of society's semiotic structures. By revealing the social origins and the arbitrary character of such structures, sociological analyses are held to point towards more rational understandings of social life and 'emancipation' from such domination.

While the political ends that inform contemporary discourse analysis may be laudable, the conception of language it assumes is highly questionable in several respects. First, it presupposes an extremely cognitive view of language. We referred earlier in this chapter to a 'mentalistic' conception of meaning, namely the view that mean consists of ideas in the mind. The conception of meaning that lies at the centre of the semiotic approach is just such a mentalistic view. Meaning is conceived in terms of the relationship between a textual or aural vehicle and an idea in the mind (a 'signifier' and a 'signified' in the terminology of semiotics). However, unlike the individualist theory discussed earlier, semiotics conceives of such meanings as socially shared. On the basis of this assumption, to describe the system of signs is by definition also to describe the organization of people's ideas. Thus language is held to shape and restrict the very possibilities of thought. However, since the system itself resides at an unconscious level, the discourse analyst argues that the semiotic shaping of social experience is not something that members of society are aware of. From the viewpoint of ordinary members of society the discursive formations in terms of which phenomena are perceived and understood are invisible. Furthermore, their 'hegemonic' character means that the meanings they give to phenomena are experienced as objective and natural. Given the assumption of the semiotic approach that persons are only able to conceive phenomena through the discursive frameworks available to them, it is difficult for them to step outside such frameworks and comprehend them independently. It follows that the contingent and historically relative character of the way of thinking and the forms of practice that the discourse provides remains beyond the member of society's ordinary comprehension. Only sociological analysis has the capacity to reveal the structure and operations of discourse.

The cognitivist presuppositions of the semiotic approach entail a gulf in understanding between the sociologist and the ordinary member of society. For reasons that we will explain presently, the notion of such a gulf is inimical to the approach we recommend in this book. The important point to note here is that the view that how members of society think can be read off from a semiotic analysis of the structure of language deflects sociological attention from the detail of people's actual conduct. This neglect of situated action in favour of decontextualized analysis of the meaning of signs is reinforced by a distinction, fundamental to the whole semiotic approach, between the structure of language and its use. As expressed by the founder of semiotics, Ferdinand de Saussure, the difference between '*langue*' and '*parole*' concerns two distinct dimensions of language (Saussure, 1983). On the one hand is *langue*, the systematic relations between signs, while on the other is *parole*, the actual ways in which persons use language to communicate in concrete situations. This distinction is not dissimilar to Chomsky's (1965: 4) distinction between 'competence' and 'performance'. Like Chomsky, in Sausurre's view no scientific analysis of language is possible at the level of *parole*: how persons actually use language is subject to too many random factors for any generalizations to be possible. But this is no particular loss for Saussure; since the structure of language corresponds to the organization of thought, the analysis of *parole* would in any case tell us little about how people understand their experience.

Language-in-use

The semiotic approach is right to stress the constitutive role of language in social life. Language is not merely a factor or variable to be understood in relation to theoretically-defined problems and issues, but first and foremost is the means by which all aspects of social life are conducted. The key word here is 'conducted'. Members of society use language to do the social activities that make up their lives together. As we have already suggested, everything we do, from the most extraordinary and significant things down to the most insignificant and ordinary ones, including the trivial and uninteresting parts of our lives, are done in and through the use of language. However, though the uses made of language may sometimes be trivial, the fact that language is a mundane feature of all social life is anything but trivial. Furthermore, in our view, by ignoring how people actually use language in social interaction, sociologists both misunderstand the social nature of language and lose sight of the detail of social life. The key point that both the causal and the semiotic approaches to language fail to appreciate is the 'situated' nature of language use. We noted above that context is fundamental to meaning in interaction. In using language to perform activities, members of society shape the words they use to the situation at hand, and use the situation at hand to understand the meaning of words. When persons speak to one another, they do not simply recite pre-determined linguistic formulae, independent of the circumstances of their speech situation. There are, of course, some 'ceremonial' speech situations, in which a ritualized form of words must be precisely recited in order for the desired outcome to be achieved – marriage ceremonies, courtroom oath-taking and the bestowing of knighthood would be examples. However, these occasions confirm the point, for the sense of the required expressions is tied to the particular ceremonial occasion. Overwhelmingly, however, ordinary speech does not involve the use of pre-set linguistic expressions. Rather, persons spontaneously produce talk that 'fits' the situation they are in, including the talk of others. They do so, then, not in some predetermined way but because the words used display a particular understanding of what is happening 'here and now'.

A simple way to illustrate the situated nature of language use is by considering how descriptions are constructed. Descriptions are a universal feature of social life: pretty much everything that is done in any walk of social life involves describing things – events, objects, places, persons, actions and so forth. If language use was not situated, it would be reasonable to expect that whenever a given object or event was referred to in talk, by whomsoever for whatsoever reason, it would be described in the same way – perhaps in the way that had been established as the most 'accurate' description. But clearly this is not how description works. How something is described varies according to the circumstances in relation to which the description is produced. As we will see in Chapter 3, the same object or event may be described in very different terms according to who is describing it to whom and for what reason. The issue about the description often is not accuracy but relevance or appropriateness: is this the appropriate kind of description for this occasion or purpose? For example, a spouse who asks 'What sort of day have you had?' to a partner just home from work might find it puzzling to receive a lengthy description of a quite routine journey to work or a detailed account of a telephone call concerning a minor and uninteresting business matter. Similarly, a parent telephoning their student son might be nonplussed to receive, in answer to the question 'What have you been up to?', a description of the night-club that he had attended the previous evening and a detailed account of the numerous 'mixes' that the DJ played. The strangeness of such talk lies in its situational inappropriateness rather than its factual status. In other words, the problem the recipient has in such cases is not 'Is this true?' but 'Why are you telling *me* this?' In experiencing such a puzzle, what is being oriented to is the 'recipient designed' nature of talk. Let us explain what we mean by this notion.

We noted earlier that interaction involves fitting actions to their context and that meaning is understood contextually. A key contextual feature of such understandings is the identity of the participants. Persons do not talk to one another as anonymous 'actors', but as occupants of situationally relevant identities or membership categories. These concepts will be explained in subsequent chapters. For now, we simply note that one of the ways such identities are made relevant is through the construction of descriptions that are geared to 'this person' with whom one is interacting. The term 'recipient design' has been coined to describe the ways in which speakers gear their talk to the relevant identity of the person with whom they are interacting. In other words, it is a general feature of conversational talk – as well as talk of other kinds – that speakers will 'design' their talk to take account of the person to whom they are speaking in the circumstances in which they are being spoken with. Recipient design involves taking into account such things as the knowledge and interests of the other person, the relationship in which one stands to them and, perhaps most importantly, what it is that the other person has just said.

The key point to note here, then, is that language use in interaction has a 'local character'. The situated nature of language use means that what is said in any interaction is being said here and now in *this* situation, with *these* circumstances in mind and *this* interactional task at hand. The form of words that a speaker employs is tied to and displays the character of the local situation at hand.

Society

We suggested at the beginning of this chapter that the notion of the individual as an entity separate from society is incoherent and fails to recognize the all pervasive character of social life. Yet so far we have said little about the concept of 'society'. As students of sociology, readers will be aware that according to the textbooks it is the study of this phenomenon, 'society', that sociology is all about. Therefore it seems reasonable to expect that sociology will provide a clear account of what this phenomenon consists of. However, on consulting the above-mentioned textbooks, the student of sociology will discover something rather peculiar: that the question 'What is society?' is treated as a theoretical puzzle. It will also become apparent that sociology's prevailing assumption is that solving this puzzle requires a theory that will explain what kind of entity society is, and provide some clue as to its significant features. Reading on in the textbooks, the student will find that there are many candidates for such a theory, that what society is like has been conceived in many different ways. For example, society can be regarded as a kind of 'social organism', on the model of a living creature, with needs that must be met for it to survive. Other theoretical conceptions view society in architectural terms, as involving a 'base' that gives shape to the whole and a 'superstructure' that rests upon the base. Alternatively, society can be viewed as a 'system' of some kind, perhaps on the model of a mechanical system like an engine or – as in the semiotic approach – as a symbolic system like morse code. The history of sociological thought consists in large measure of debates amongst the proponents of such theoretical conceptions and the programmes of inquiry through which they are applied and their detail worked out. Furthermore, it would be no exaggeration to say that research in contemporary sociology consists overwhelmingly in the empirical implementation of such theoretical conceptions. So pervasive are such conceptions of society that the student can be forgiven for concluding that sociological inquiry cannot be done any other way. However, several reasons can be adduced for thinking that a different approach to sociological analysis may be worthy of consideration.

To begin with, the assumption that understanding society is dependant upon possession of a theory has several unfortunate consequences. The first is that it generates the kind of gulf mentioned earlier between professional sociological accounts of social life and the understandings possessed by those whom the sociologist studies. It is commonly argued that ordinary members of society do not possess the theoretical concepts of sociology. The implication is that those aspects of social life that can only be understood by virtue of these concepts are unavailable to ordinary understanding. Persons may be members of society, but precisely what it is that they are members of is assumed to be beyond their ability to fully grasp. By comparison with the understandings that can be derived from the theories of the sociologist, whose accounts are taken as a benchmark for assessing the value of knowledge, the understandings of the ordinary members are regarded as second rate; they are both incomplete and faulty. Lacking the theoretical concepts of sociology, the ordinary member of society is unable to transcend the limitations of ordinary understanding. The sociologist, in contrast, uses theoretical concepts to reveal aspects of social life that are 'hidden' from the ordinary person.

From this widely accepted point of view, then, the sociology task is a corrective one *vis-à-vis* the things that ordinary persons think and believe about social life. The stance that sociology usually adopts towards ordinary social life, therefore, is best described as 'professional skepticism'. It is a mark of sociological professional expertise that ordinary assertions, claims, beliefs that are made by members of society about this or that aspect of social life should be regarded skeptically, and therefore as requiring either replacement or explanation. The knowledge that members of society possess and use to conduct their activities typically is deemed to be irrational, ungrounded and in various other ways arbitrary and inadequate. Despite these perceived failings, however, the fact of the matter is that these activities continue to be accomplished. Social life, it would seem, carries on regardless of the deficiencies of understanding allegedly pervading it, deficiencies that are extensively documented by sociologists.

This fact might lead one to question the validity of the conventional sociological denigration of ordinary life and ordinary understandings. Furthermore, it might suggest that the theories of society put forward by sociologists are irrelevant with reference to ordinary social activities. The clear implication of sociology's professional skepticism is that social life would be better organized and more successfully conducted if things were done in accordance with sociology's theories. But why should members of society accept this prejudice? Why should one suppose that members of society require any theory of social life in order to accomplish their activities? It is a sociological assumption that social life is only adequately understood through theory. Perhaps ordinary persons do not have a theory of their social life and the activities that comprise it because they do not need one to carry those activities out.

In contrast to conventional sociological assumptions, then, it may be more reasonable to suppose that ordinary persons are quite well equipped to engage in their social activities without possessing anything like a professional sociological theory of those activities. Of course, this is not to deny that members of society, in the course of their ordinary activities, engage in theorizing about aspects of their social circumstances. But such theorizing, as we will see in the later chapters of this book, overwhelmingly is ad hoc, practical theorizing. Therefore, from the point of view adopted in this book, such theorizing is simply another social activity; that persons construct and use theories about this or that puzzling feature of their experience does not mean that they find social life itself a theoretical puzzle. In other words, there is a fundamental difference between the kinds of theorizing that members of society actually engage in and the kind of theorizing they would have to perform in order to match up to the presuppositions of theoretical sociology. Instead of that kind of presupposed knowledge we will show that what members of society actually possess is a practical, working knowledge of how to do the social activities that make up the organization of society.

If members' knowledge is not theoretical knowledge, then what kind of knowledge is it? Persons act on the basis of what they know and understand: about the relations between themselves and others, the circumstances of their situation, the relevant norms and rules to which they should attend in carrying out their activities, and many other things. They know these things not as theoretical objects or topics but as practical matters. The philosopher Alfred Schutz (1962) argued that the understandings through which persons conduct the activities of ordinary life have a fundamentally practical character. What this means is that members' knowledge is knowledge-in-use. Persons employ what they know in the course of acting in the world, not in reflecting upon society from some detached and independent standpoint. For theoretical sociology, this might be seen as confirming the inadequacy of members' knowledge: how can it be expected to be as accurate, valid and so on as sociological knowledge when it is 'pre-theoretical' and driven by practical requirements? However, there is another way of looking at this: that members' knowledge is pre-theoretical and practical means that it is of a different order to the theoretical knowledge sought by the sociologist. It is 'designed' for a different purpose – that of getting things done. If we want to understand it, therefore, we should not assume that it is some lesser version of sociological theory, but a different phenomenon altogether.

For the above reasons, then, the notion that theory must occupy a primary place in sociological inquiry if we are to learn anything worthwhile or interesting about society can be questioned. In contrast with the prevailing assumption that social order is revealed via the practice of sociological theorizing, then, the view taken in this book is that social order is available to ordinary members of society as both a precondition and a product of their activities. In other words, whereas conventional sociology regards the member of society as someone who lacks sociological expertise and therefore adequate grounds for understanding, we will emphasize that the members of society know society from within. We will suggest that they possess working sociological knowledge, that is, knowledge of how society works and how social life is done. It is this knowledge that they use and rely upon and presume others to use in producing social activities. Far from there being no social order other than that revealed through sociological theorizing, for members the orderliness of social life is a taken for granted and an ever-present reality.

The above argument has important methodological implications. If theory is not required by members of society in order to perform their activities, then why should one assume that it is necessary for the sociologist who seeks to understand how those activities are done? We will argue that, instead of seeking such a theory, what is required is close attention to the knowledge that members possess and how they use it in producing their activities. Accordingly, instead of asking the question 'What explains social life?' and answering it in terms of some theory of society, we propose to ask 'What do persons relevantly know and how is this knowledge employed in making sense of social life and in carrying out their activities?' Rather than trying to describe such knowledge in general in a decontextualized way, our focus will be upon how such knowledge is employed in specific instances. The radical step, then, involves putting on one side the assumption that sociological understanding is only to be gained through theory. It follows that questions such as 'What is society?' will also have to be put aside. Instead of asking 'What kind of thing is society?', we will ask instead 'What it is that people use to do their social activities and how can these activities be investigated?' In so far as addressing these questions might also produce an answer to the preceding question – about the nature of society – it will be an answer of a radically different kind to that which is provided by sociology's programmes of theoretical analysis.

Many sociologists, of course, would argue that such a focus fails to adequately address what is often referred to in sociological circles as the 'bigger picture', namely the larger or wider social context or social structure within which the production of social activities takes place. We will take up this question in the concluding chapter of this book. For now, we simply point out that for us the question is one of how such a notion of a wider social context can be reconciled with the approach taken in this book. Our answer is that such a reconciliation is indeed possible but not via the conventional route of positing and synthesizing different levels of analysis, that is, the local or situated (often conceptualized as the level of 'micro' social phenomena) on the one hand and the broader structural level (standardly referred to as 'macro' analysis) on the other hand. For us, such a dualistic conception is set aside because it reifies what is, after all, a distinctly sociological conception of social context, namely one that follows from the adoption of a peculiar theoretical attitude towards social life. The distinction between the micro and the macro is, in other words, a particular sociological device for making sense of social life. Our task, rather than presuming and imposing such a theoretical artifact and thereby investigating the social world through the cloudy lens of sociological theory, is to illuminate as clearly as possible how the members of society themselves produce social life in and through their activities.

We emphasize that our focus upon social activities does not mean that social context is insignificant. However, its significance from the point of view taken in this book is at the level of members' orientations and not that of theoretical inventions. Accordingly, then, our reconciliation of a 'sense of social structure' with a focus on members' social activities is afforded by 'respecifying' so-called larger contextual phenomena as 'members' phenomena'. In other words, our interest is in how members of society employ their knowledge of the social world in which they live to fit their actions to the relevant context. This means that social context becomes investigable as something to which members of society are themselves oriented and which they invoke in their social interaction with each other, rather than as something the sociologist invokes by theoretical fiat.

Conclusion

In this chapter we have outlined a vision of society as consisting of social activities conducted through social interaction with respect to which the use of language is crucial. The key point of this vision is to highlight a domain of phenomena, namely the practices involved in producing social activities. Since social life consists of social activities, the illumination of what these practices consist of will, we suggest, provide us with a more adequate understanding of society than that provided through the theoretical speculations of orthodox sociology. However, there remains the question of how this project is itself to be conducted and put into practice. In other words, what kinds of investigations follow from the vision of social life we have outlined? In the subsequent chapters of this book, we answer this question by presenting exemplary studies of various aspects of ordinary social life. The approach to sociological inquiry that such studies involve and exemplify is called 'ethnomethodology', to distinguish it from the theory-driven approach that is more frequently taken in sociological investigations. In Chapter 2 we will explain in more detail what we mean by ethnomethodology and how it is methodologically distinctive.

Further reading

A. Duranti and C. Goodwin (eds) (1992) *Rethinking Context: Language as an Interactive Phenomenon.* Cambridge: Cambridge University Press.
P. McHugh (1968) *Defining the Situation: the Organisation of Meaning in Interaction,* 'Defining the situation and the traditions of sociology.' New York, NY: Bobbs-Merrill. Ch. 2.

2

Doing Ethnomethodology

In the first chapter we outlined a conception of sociology, based on a particular way of thinking about society, language and social interaction. This conception has implications for how to study social life. It recommends the sociological approach known as ethnomethodology (or ethnomethodological sociology). Its concerns are with the 'observability' of ordinary social life, and its principle method of investigation is that of observation. Its focus is upon the methods by which observable social activities are produced. It seeks to investigate how social activities are accomplished by members of society (or 'members' for short).

Ethnomethodology was founded by Harold Garfinkel in the 1950s and 1960s and first came to general notice with the publication in 1967 of his book *Studies in Ethnomethodology*. Its key assumption is that the production of observable social activities involves the local or situated use of member's methods for doing such activities. With respect to these methods, the mastery of natural language is paramount. Thus, ethnomethodology conceives of society, language and social interaction along the lines that we have outlined in Chapter 1. We do not have the space here to go into detail on the origins and development of ethnomethodology; if the reader wishes to know more about this there are several useful accounts available (for example, Heritage, 1984; Sharrock and Anderson, 1986). We simply note that its origins lie in Garfinkel's engagement with the thought of Talcott Parsons, the leading sociological theorist of the mid-twentieth century. This engagement led Garfinkel to turn to the writings of Alfred Schutz (for example, Schutz, 1962) and seek to apply the lessons of Schutz's phenomenological studies to the problem of social order as discussed in the work of Parsons. Schutz had emphasized the need for sociological analysis to attend to and be grounded in the ways in which persons, as members of society, experience social life. Garfinkel took this experiential focus and refined it to pose the question of how members of society produce 'from within' the observable features of social life.

Over the past forty years or so, ethnomethodology has developed and diversified, in ways that will become apparent in the later chapters of this book. At this point, we simply sketch some of the main developments. First and most notably, ethnomethodology has given rise to the approach known as conversation analysis. This originated in the work of Harvey Sacks and his colleagues at the University of California in the early 1960s, where Garfinkel also was located. Sacks took seriously Garfinkel's notion of the local production of social activities and sought to realize this conception by studying the most mundane social activity of all, ordinary conversation. The reason for focusing upon ordinary talk was that it could be recorded and transcribed, and thereby made available to be inspected over and over again. Such a method had considerable advantages over more traditional ethnographic methods. By examining in close detail the constitutive features of conversational interaction, Sacks and his colleagues identified what they referred to as 'conversational objects', that is, structures that were oriented to and used interactionally by participants to conversations. Over the years, conversation analysis has tended to generate two distinct analytic themes with respect to these conversational objects. On the one hand 'sequential analysis' is concerned with analysing the sequential organization of talk, how one utterance or other conversational item is tied to and part of a larger sequential structure. On the other hand, 'membership categorization analysis' is concerned with the organization of common-sense knowledge in terms of the categories members employ in accomplishing their activities in and through talk. In line with the basic approach of ethnomethodology, both 'sequences' and 'categories' are conceived as members' methods for doing social life.

The sequential and categorical aspects of talk do not, however, exhaust the discoverable organizational features of social activities. A more recent development within ethnomethodology is what is known as the 'studies of work programme'. This programme seeks to investigate members' methods and competencies involved in the production of complex activities. While such activities typically involve talk and therefore involve structures of sequential and categorical organization, attention to the detail of complex activities reveals additional structural features and other layers of locally accomplished organization.

Ethnomethodology and ethnography

It may seem strange that we should suggest that a focus on the observability of social life and the use of observation as a method of inquiry recommends an ethnomethodological approach. Surely it is through 'observation' that much sociological investigation has always been done? Sociologists, especially those of a 'qualitative' research inclination, have long argued the importance of first-hand observation of people's social activities and relationships as a central part of sociological inquiry. Indeed, a major approach to social research, ethnography, emphasizes the technique of 'participant observation' to study people and their social lives. Advocates of this approach argue that only through such first-hand observation can the sociologist appreciate the points of view of the subjects under study and thereby construct adequate accounts of their activities and shared culture. In what follows we will discuss the ethnographic tradition and indicate how ethnomethodology differs from it.

Ethnography has a long and respected history within sociology and its sister discipline, social anthropology. In sociology, its origins date back to the 1920s and the pioneering studies of urban life by sociologists at the University of Chicago. In the 1960s and 1970s it became associated with the theoretical perspective of symbolic interactionism, which in part developed out of the Chicago tradition. Symbolic interactionists emphasized observation of naturally occurring social life, using the method of participant observation in conjunction with interviewing and other techniques. For a long time this interactionist ethnographic tradition was a minority one within sociology, denigrated by more scientific approaches for producing findings that were deemed loose and impressionistic. Nevertheless, it produced many important and useful studies, especially ones that were informative about the ways of life of social groups existing outside the mainstream of society. Among these were classic studies of urban occupational groups, such as janitors, taxi-drivers and waitresses, and of deviant groups such as drug users and various types of career criminals. The strength of such studies was twofold. First, they provided insight into ways of life with which most people are unfamiliar, indeed their 'newsworthiness' derived in part from the fact that the ways of life depicted were not ones of which most readers of sociological studies had experience. Second, they frequently showed that the practices involved in such ways of life had a hitherto unrecognized rationality when viewed in their social context. The findings of such studies served a valuable function in debunking conventional stereotypes and normalizing the strange and deviant.[1]

In recent years the tide has turned, methodologically speaking, in the social sciences. With so-called scientific approaches to social inquiry coming under sustained critical attack, ethnography has grown in popularity and influence as a research method. It has long been the method of choice in social anthropology, but has become so also in much contemporary sociology. Where once the survey method and statistical analysis dominated social research, nowadays ethnography has become the most popular approach to inquiry. It is widely and increasingly used beyond the confines of sociology, in related fields such as management studies, education studies, social psychology, and new fields such as computer supported co-operative work (CSCW). This popularity is marked by the plethora of textbooks in ethnographic method that nowadays occupy the social science shelves of bookshops. The main reason for this turn to ethnography, it seems to us, is recognition of the importance of the role of subjectivity in social life, or what sociologists in the Chicago/interactionist tradition used to refer to as 'the point of view of the actor'. In other words, researchers accept that the concepts and findings of social inquiry, if they are to explain social action, need to be grounded in an understanding of the meanings and perspectives taken by the participants in such action.

This emphasis on subjectivity is to be welcomed and has obvious relevance for the approach we are recommending. Nevertheless, the observational character of ethnomethodology as exhibited in this book differs in important ways from the ethnographic tradition. We will mention two key differences: first, ethnomethodology's quite different take on the idea of observation; and second, and as a result of this, the different direction that its inquiries then take. With reference to the first point, in ethnography observation is conceived as a sociological technique for gathering data. It is a means by which to discover sociologically significant things about people and their social relations. Ethnographic observation, then, is a method of discovery, by which the researcher builds sociological knowledge of the persons or groups under study. In this sense the ethnographic tradition is based upon a distinction between observer and observed. Even though the ethnographer may be a participant in the setting or activity under study, he or she is always an outsider in the sense that whatever he or she is doing as a participant is as a means to something else. The activity of observing sets the sociologist apart from other people; the observer necessarily stands over and above that which is being observed. Despite this, however, it is clear that the observations that the ethnographer makes depend massively upon ordinary observational competences. As a 'participant observer' the sociologist trades upon his or her ordinary membership of the society in order to see and understand what people are doing in the situations being observed. No amount of methodological self-consciousness and professional systematization can alter the fact that the sociological observer is utterly dependent on his or her ordinary observational competencies in order to see what 'anyone can see' is happening.

It is upon this ordinary observational competence that ethnomethodology focuses. As persons go about their ordinary lives as members of society, they are continuously making observations of what is going on around them. Not only do they engage in the activity of observation, but also in various ways they are *required* to do so. Competent participation in any social setting demands that those involved pay attention to, and make sense of, what is happening around them. Consequently, observation is not so much a special sociological technique as an inevitable and necessary part of everyday social life. Observation, in this sense, is a constitutive feature of the collaborative actions and interactions that comprise social life. Ethnomethodology starts from the assumption that observing what is going on in the social world is something that anyone can do, and indeed it is something that everyone does as a matter of course, and then it seeks to explain how this is possible.

Ethnomethodology, then, is an approach that takes seriously the implications of the routine observability of social activities. It starts from the fact that sociologists are, first and foremost, members of society like anyone else, equipped with the same kinds of social competencies that any member of society can be presumed to possess. However, where conventional ethnography draws upon such competencies as an unexamined resource for doing sociological description, ethnomethodology turns its attention to such competencies as topics of inquiry in their own right. Its focus is upon the methods by which members of society are able to observe and recognize what is happening around them, and thereby know what they should do to fit their actions together with the actions of others. Another way of putting this is to say that the difference here between conventional ethnography and ethnomethodology concerns the latter's focus upon the 'possibility' of observation. What does it mean to say that our interest as ethnomethodologists is in the 'possibility' of observations? For us this means two things. First, how it is that an observer, be it a sociologist or anyone else, is able to make sense of what they are seeing as this or that phenomenon. Second, how the observed phenomenon is produced or assembled in such a way that it is observable as the phenomenon it observably is. Ethnomethodology consists in observational studies of what is observably the case. It takes ordinary observations of social activities and asks how is what is observably the case in respect of them produced?

We have here, then, the two sides of sense-making: members of society make sense of what they observe and they produce talk and action in ways that enable definite sense to be made of what they are doing. These two aspects are really one: sense-making is not something detached from action, rather sense is made in action, in the very situations that members of society find themselves in and with which they have to deal by acting in this or that way. What we are suggesting by the notion of 'production' is that social activities have intelligibility by virtue of the ways they are done by whomsoever is doing them. In this regard, our attention is focused on how the sense of social activities is produced from within. This raises, for us, the question of just what this production consists of. In other words, how do people make sense of and produce sensible social activities? What, specifically, do they use to do this?

Asking this question directs inquiry towards the 'methodicity' of members' social activities. It refers to ethnomethodology's conception of social activities as methodically accomplished. It is a conception articulated in the following remarks of Sacks (1992a: 10–11):

> And now when you, or I, or sociologists, watching people do things, engage in trying to find out what they do and how they do it, one fix which can be used is: Of the enormous range of activities that people do, all of them are done with something … What we want to find out is, can we first of all construct the objects that get used to make up ranges of activities, and then see how it is those objects do get used.

And again (1992a: 11):

> Some of these objects can be used for whole ranges of activities, where for different ones a variety of the properties of those objects will get employed.

And we begin to see alternative properties of those objects. That's one way we can go about beginning to collect the alternative methods that persons use in going about doing whatever they have to do. And we can see that these methods will be reproducible descriptions in the sense that any scientific description might be, such that the natural occurrences that we're describing can yield abstract or general phenomena which need not rely on statistical observability for their abstractness or generality.

What this Sacksian approach recommends is a focus on the methods and resources that members of society employ in producing their activities. Activities don't just happen, they are made to happen; similarly, they don't just happen to make sense, their sense is an achievement.

Ethnomethodology in practice

So far, we have outlined how ethnomethodology is distinctive in terms of its focus and subject matter. If ethnomethodology has a distinctive focus for its inquiries, it also has a distinctive investigative attitude. Where everyday social life is normally taken for granted, the ethnomethodologist turns this into an object of reflection. Specifically, it is treated as a practical accomplishment along the lines we have outlined above. This attitude is not necessarily easily adopted precisely because, as members of society, our ordinary, everyday way of relating to the social world is to take the social world for granted. It therefore can require some effort to turn the everyday into a topic of inquiry. Having adopted the appropriate attitude, however, the ethnomethodological sociologist may make use of particular aids in order to investigate the constitution of social activities in their detail. These aids range from simply taking notes of what one is observing to audio and video tape recording of instances and sequences of activity. In addition to these aids to data collection, there are analytical procedures that may be followed in order to 'make visible' the phenomena of interest. In other words, such procedures have to do with ways of making methods and resources available for inspection and analysis. The procedures involved will be explained in detail and illustrated in later chapters. In this way, the chapters that follow are designed not only to report the findings of ethnomethodological sociological investigations, but also to offer the reader a practical guide for his or her own studies. For now, it is important to grasp that ethnomethodology means starting out with what anyone can observe about some situation or activity and then turning 'what is observably the case' into a topic for analysis, where the observable features of social life are treated as 'productions' of the parties to them. Accordingly, doing ethnomethodology involves taking three methodological steps:

1   Notice something that is observably-the-case about some talk, activity or setting.
2   Pose the question 'How is it that this observable feature has been produced such that it is recognizable for what it is?'

3 Consider, analyse and describe the methods used in the production and recognition of the observable feature.

For example, on entering some setting one may easily observe that some persons are engaged in the activity of having a conversation. In terms of the above methodological steps, one would then ask how what it was that the persons were doing, such that it had the recognizable appearance of a conversation. In turn, one would then attempt to describe in detail the methods (or at least some of them) that were used in the production of the observable conversation. In other words, then, ethnomethodology starts out with what might be called the 'common-sense appearances of the social world' and then seeks to describe how they will have been produced 'from within' such that they do indeed have the appearances they have. Observations, then, are not the product of specialized sociological techniques, they are the 'available observations' that anyone can, and expectably does, make. Observations are not an end of inquiry, they are the starting point for what might be called 'constitutive analysis'.

The three-step method of ethnomethodology can be applied in various ways. In this book we explain three such modes of analysis: self-reflection; analysis of recorded talk and action; and what we will call 'acquired immersion'. What is common to all these three modes is the presumption that analysis is premised upon immersion in the activity under study. In the words of Rawls (2002: 6):

> Ethnomethodologists generally use methods that require immersion in the situation being studied. They hold it as an ideal that they learn to be competent practitioners of whatever social phenomena they are studying. The ideal is referred by Garfinkel as 'unique adequacy'.

The emphasis upon immersion is necessitated by the aim of ethnomethodology, that is, to explicate the methods used to produce 'from within' a given activity. In other words, what the ethnomethodological sociologist is seeking to explicate is the practitioners' knowledge and competence involved in accomplishing the activity under investigation. Not all activities, however, are equivalent in this regard. As Rawls (2002: 6) goes on to point out:

> When the subject of research is something that most persons participate regularly, like ordinary talk, the game of tic tac toe, driving, walking, etc., the unique adequacy can be assumed for most persons (persons with disabilities, who may lack ordinary competence, may nevertheless have revealing understandings of these common tasks). However, with regard to practices that have specialized populations, like science or policing, unique adequacy can be very hard to achieve. An ethnomethodologist pursuing unique adequacy within a specialized population may spend years in a research site becoming a competent participant in its practices, in addition to collecting various sorts of observational, documentary, and audiovisual materials. Ethnomethodologists have taken degrees in law and mathematics, worked for years

in science labs, become professional musicians, and worked as truck drivers and in police departments in an effort to satisfy the unique adequacy requirement.

In light of this, our first mode of analysis, self-reflection, refers to a mode of inquiry in which the researcher's own understandings and activities provide the phenomena for analysis. Thus in Chapter 3 we use self-reflective analysis in examining our own everyday understandings and considering the methods involved in their production. In other words, we treat *our own* understandings of the activity in which we are immersed as data. Our second mode of analysis involves the use of recordings of naturally occurring talk and action. Again, drawing on our own competence as conversationists and speakers of natural language, we use the three-step method of observational sociology to analyse the talk and action of others through the use of recording and transcription of talk. This is the preferred method of conversation analysis, and we will show how conversation analytic procedures can be deployed in relation to naturally occurring social activities. Where conversation analysis focuses upon structures of talk, our third mode of application of our method involves the study of complex activities where talk and physical behaviour both play a part. More specifically, we seek to analyse activities that are removed by some distance from ordinary conversation. To understand such activities requires 'acquired immersion', because such understanding demands that the analyst possess something of the particular knowledge and competence taken for granted by practitioners. In other words, we call this mode of analysis 'acquired immersion' to point out the fact that some complex activities require the researcher to acquire specialized knowledge and competence not ordinarily available. Whereas conversation analysis trades upon and topicalizes ordinary competencies possessed by any competent conversationist, the analysis of the activities involved in, for example, laboratory science or air traffic control, demands a grasp of skills beyond those of everyday conversational expertise. By virtue of their specialized character, such activities tend to be inaccessible to the ordinary person in two senses: they are done in restricted environments to which non-qualified persons do not have access, and what is being done by the participants is not fully understandable without possession of the requisite knowledge. It is for these reasons that acquired immersion is a prerequisite for analysing and reflecting upon the production of such specialized activities.

The three modes of analysis we have outlined are not mutually exclusive, nor are they unrelated. As we shall see, they can usefully be combined. Indeed, the separation of them into distinct modes is somewhat arbitrary, useful for purposes of introductory explication. In a sense they are related developmentally. All three involve the analysis of methods and competencies, where such analysis is always 'from within'. In other words, the activities under study have to be understood in terms of the participant's orientations and this in turn means that doing ethnomethodology requires that the researcher is always part of the phenomenon of inquiry. The differences between the modes of inquiry have to do with the kinds of competencies that are involved and that the ethnomethodologist seeks to describe. Thus in the self-reflective mode of analysis the methods to be analysed are those of the researcher him- or herself, where it is assumed that these methods are employed by 'any' member of society. Conversation analysis seeks to describe the methods involved in the production of talk-in-action. The structures involved are relative to the kinds of conversational activities that are being done. The researcher trades upon his or her ordinary knowledge of such activities to describe and analyse them. In the third mode of inquiry, the researcher cannot presume that ordinary conversational competencies will be sufficient to provide the basis for an adequate understanding – that is, an understanding in participant's terms – of what is being done. In order to understand and correctly describe what one is observing demands 'insider' knowledge. It is only through immersion that the researcher can become as familiar with the methods involved in the production of these activities as he or she is with the methods of ordinary conversation. Thus, the acquisition of such knowledge requires that the researcher makes him- or herself part of the phenomenon of inquiry, just as much as with the previous two modes. In each case the point is to produce data upon which one may reflect and analyse using our three-step procedure for doing observational sociology.

Principles of ethnomethodological analysis

The three-step procedure points one towards where to look to find the methods in and through which social activities are done. In contrast to the tendency in sociology to treat abstract phenomena such as culture, world view and ideology as decontextualized sources of members' actions, ethnomethodology seeks instead to investigate 'culture in action'. This means that the members' methods of understanding, reasoning, co-ordinating, decision-making and so on are to be found in, and only in, the situated activities themselves: they are part and parcel of those activities, not separate from them. In following the three-step procedure, ethnomethodology is guided by several methodological principles for the conduct of analysis.

The principles we outline below are used to structure the kinds of analyses and descriptions that are then offered to the reader. There are four principles, as follows:

1   The demonstrable relevance of sociological descriptions.
2   The consequentiality of members' orientations and understandings.
3   The situatedness of talk and action.
4   The inspectability of data.

The first principle – the commitment to demonstrable relevance – refers to the requirement to ground sociological descriptions of social phenomena in members' orientations and understandings. In other words, ethnomethodology treats as its phenomena those phenomena to which members are oriented and which are relevant for them in the specifics of their situated talk and action. It thus rejects the widely prevalent tendency to view social activities through the lens of pre-defined sociological categories.

The issue of members' orientations and relevancies places, then, considerable methodological constraints on the analyst. He or she just cannot presume the omni-relevance of some category of identity, rather those categories have to be demonstrably relevant for the parties to the scenes witnessed and analysed. These constraints we refer to have been articulated with considerable acuity by Schegloff (1987, 1991). He emphasizes the dangers involved in a premature incorporation of social structural notions with ethnomethodological and conversation analytic inquiry. As Schegloff (1991: 51) says:

> Now let us be clear about what is and what is not being said here. The point is not that persons are somehow not male or female, upper or lower class, with or without power, professors and/or students. They may be, on some occasion, demonstrably members of one or another of those categories. Nor is the issue that those aspects of the society do not matter, or did not matter on that occasion. We may share a lively sense that indeed they do matter, and that they mattered on that occasion, and mattered for just that aspect of some interaction on which we are focusing. There is still the problem of *showing from the details of the talk* or other conduct in the materials that we are analyzing that those aspects of the scene are what the parties are oriented to. *For that is to show the parties are embodying for one another the relevancies of the interaction and are thereby producing the social structure.*

The second principle is to attend to the consequentiality of member's orientations and understandings. This means that it is incumbent upon the analyst to show how a particular orientation or understanding enters into the production of a social activity. In other words, for some phenomenon to qualify as a members' phenomenon it has to be capable of being shown to have been taken into account and used as grounds for the production of that activity. Current turns at talk, for example, embody and display the speaker's analysis of prior talk which, in so far as its content is taken up, can then be said to be procedurally consequential.

The third principle is to respect the situatedness of talk and action. As we have emphasized, persons fit their actions to the immediate circumstances that they find themselves in. Therefore, the analytic task is not to describe what persons might take account of in general or in the abstract, but rather what they are orienting to specifically and how they use their knowledge of the situation to produce courses of action that fit the particular features of that situation. For example, the meaning of a particular word or expression is understood in relation to the specific occasion of its use – meaning is 'indexical' in Garfinkel's words. Therefore, as we pointed out earlier, in contrast with conventional ethnography, which views meaning as something generalized and disembodied, ethnomethodology treats meaning (that is, sense) as locally produced and understood.

We said that the ethnographic tradition typically uses its observations as a means to finding something else. This something else is generalized descriptions of social life and culture. Thus, the point of view of the actor typically is described in terms of a decontextualized perspective that is shared by the members of a social group. The ethnographic tradition has emphasized the idea of a common culture among the members of a social group. Such a culture, it is argued, provides a group's members with shared ways of understanding their situation and shared patterns of response to common problems. The aim of conventional ethnography is to build up through observation a description of such common cultures and then offer that description to the reader as an explanation of the patterns of thought and action which have been reported. Thus common culture is conceived as 'lying behind' the detail of persons' talk and action. While sociologists in the ethnographic tradition have recognized the importance of such things as 'common-sense knowledge', 'shared meanings' and 'social rules', they have tended to address these things in an abstract and decontextualized way, allocating to them an explanatory role in relation to social behaviour.

Ethnographic studies therefore describe such things as 'the janitor's view of the tenant' (Gold, 1973), 'the police officer's perspective on violence' (Westley, 1970) or 'the jazz musician's attitude to the audience' (Becker, 1963). Such descriptions consist in generalized characterizations of how the members of the group think about some aspect of their situation. The perspective is an analyst's construct, extracted from things said and done by group members in specific situations and at specific times. The analyst constructs the perspective by treating specific actions as expressions of a unified underlying phenomenon. Thus, for example, something said by one person in one situation is treated, analytically, not simply as expressing the same view as something else said by a different person on another occasion, but as another manifestation of a cognitive entity – a shared meaning – common to all members of the group. This entity is decontextualized in the sense that it does not explain how the *action of saying what was said* is tied to the specific circumstances *in which it was said*.

Ethnomethodology, in contrast, seeks to avoid such decontextualized generalizations; it attends to the ways in which things said and done are situated within the occasions of their saying and doing. Thus rather than treating some utterance as a manifestation of an underlying attitude, the observational sociologist asks what is being done here and now by saying it. From this point of view, then, the concern is with how cultural knowledge is displayed and used in the specifics of social situations and activities, so as to accomplish those situations and activities. Thus shared culture is not something that lies behind people's talk and action, neither should it be conceived as a disembodied system exercising explanatory force over that talk and action. Rather, shared culture is accomplished in and through the making of observations of sameness and difference. Persons 'recognize' their sameness with others by seeing that others think or act in the same sorts of ways as themselves. Culture, therefore is an accomplishment of talk and action, not a determinant of it. Thus the point is not to construct theories of the relationship between, for example, culture and behaviour or social rules and their application, but to investigate the cultural methods and resources persons actually and observably employ in getting done whatever it is that they are doing.

The fourth principle – the inspectability of data – requires the analyst to show that members' phenomena and members' methods are available in the talk somehow, and to then make that availability inspectable by the reader. This principle involves a fundamental methodological difference between ethnomethodology and conventional ethnography. Characteristically, ethnographic studies present the reader with typifications and summaries of observed activities, with a view to identifying patterns and regularities in those activities. Thus whilst observation is emphasized as a research technique, such ethnographies fail to make the detail of reported observations available to the reader, with the consequence that, while general characterizations are given of this or that activity, relationship, or cultural event, there was no way that the original detail on which such observations were based can be examined. The reader of such studies had to take the ethnographer's word for it that the things observed had the typical or general form ascribed to them, but – apart from one or two illustrative descriptions – has no way of knowing whether this is the case, nor *how* particular instances display the described form. In contrast, ethnomethodological studies seek to make available the detail of persons' talk and action. In part the reason for this is to provide the reader with the very data itself upon which any analysis is based. Thus, unlike traditional ethnographic inquiry where the reader has to trust the ethnographer's word that descriptions of scenes are adequate, for ethnomethodology the data upon which analytic descriptions are based and to which they refer must be available for inspection by the reader. It is only in this way that the reader will be in a position to check the claims of the analyst. In other words, the *readers* of any analysis should be able to check any analytic rendition of the text or talk's form or content against the original data. More fundamentally, the preference for first-hand naturally occurring data is because ethnomethodologists are committed to the view that it is in the detail of situated talk and action that the methods for producing and recognizing social activities are to be found.

The contents of this book

The contents of this book are arranged in a developmental sequence. In Chapter 3 we exemplify the self-reflective mode by considering our own understandings of three news texts taken from the mass media. As we have said, however, we assume that the understandings that we make and have methodically produced are ones that any reader or viewer of these texts would have no difficulty in making. In Chapters 4 to 8 we shift our attention to social interaction between persons in settings with which all of us are familiar: family life, going to the doctor, getting an education, working in an organization and so on. Our data here primarily is of a different order. The task of investigating social interaction demands data that expresses participants' methods and orientations and captures the detail of their interaction. We move, then, from self-reflection on our own understandings to the examination of transcripts of talk-in-interaction. As we will see, the familiarity of the activities in these settings provides us with phenomena that we can easily topicalize. In the latter part of the book we move into unfamiliar territory. The emphasis placed upon the ordinariness and familiarity of social activities raises the question of how ethnomethodology works in respect of activities that are relatively unfamiliar, specialised, esoteric and so forth. In Chapters 9 and 10 we consider how our third mode of inquiry, immersion, can be deployed in investigating complex activities that we ourselves, as ordinary members of society, are unfamiliar with. We thus apply our method for doing ethnomethodology to the relatively unfamiliar activities of managing high technology systems in the workplace and conducting scientific experiments in the laboratory. For the participants in these settings, of course, the activities involved are perfectly familiar, but their investigation requires the acquisition of such familiarity on the part of the ethnomethodological sociologist before 'what is observably the case' can be appreciated. The same question is asked about these esoteric, 'expert' activities as has been asked about more familiar ones: how are they accomplished in and through language and social interaction and by what methods are they produced as the activities they observably are?

To sum up, then, in the chapters that follow our aim is to present a particular way of doing sociology that involves a focus upon ordinary social life and how it is done. It involves the observation of social activities 'as they happen' in two senses. We mean, first, as they happen in the real world, not in some theoretically constructed version of the social world. Second, we mean that these activities are observable at first hand, not just by professional sociologists but by anyone. Social life is made up of many different activities and these are available to be recognized and understood for what they are by ordinary members of society. In fact, of course, that such activities are available in this way is what makes social life, indeed 'society', possible.

Our starting point is to ask what can be discovered about how the social world is organized by reflecting upon it and upon what you know about it. The use of the word 'discover' needs to be clarified. We are not suggesting that by observing in the way we will recommend you will suddenly come across activities that you were not aware existed – that people who you thought did 'x' and 'y' actually do 'a' and 'b'. This might be the case were you to observe situations that you had never encountered before or groups of people entirely new and strange to you. But we will be asking you to observe very ordinary situations involving people just like yourself. It would be very surprising if you were to suddenly discover an entirely new bunch of things going on in such situations, things never before noticed or suspected. No, in the main we will be focusing on activities that are quite familiar and 'obvious'.

What, then, is the point? What can be learnt about social life from observing ordinary, familiar situations and activities? The message we hope to get across is this: even the most mundane, ordinary activities – ones that we (members of society) normally take for granted and have little or no problem with and which one might therefore assume to be simple and uninteresting – turn out on closer inspection (when we put on our sociological hat) to be complex and skilful accomplishments. To see that this is so, the trick, sociologically speaking, is to reflect on these activities in such a way as to bring out their complex interactional character. The key step is to begin with the 'recognizability' of activities – the fact that you (the member of society) can see what is happening (who someone is and what they are doing) simply by looking. But instead of simply taking this recognizability for granted, you should then switch to your sociological mode and reflect upon how this recognizability is accomplished, that is, how the activity is done such that it is recognizable. Think of the most ordinary things that people do as being done so as to be understandable to others; they are 'produced' to be recognizable for what they are. From your standpoint as a sociologist, therefore, you can begin to consider just what the 'work' of producing a recognizable activity involves. This is what we mean by sociological observation; our aim is to show you how to do this kind of observation for yourselves.

Further Reading

H. Garfinkel (1967) *Studies in Ethnomethodology.* Englewood Cliffs, N.J.: Prentice Hall.
J. Heritage (1984) *Garfinkel and Ethnomethodology.* Cambridge: Polity Press.
H. Sacks (1992) *Lectures in Conversation,* Vols. 1 and 2. Oxford: Basil Blackwell.

Note

1 However, we note that for some these strengths of the ethnographic tradition were also a source of weakness. The concern with the strange and often deviant distracted attention from the more mundane features of the ways of life studied. By focusing excessively on what was 'different' and esoteric, ethnographers in

the Chicago tradition could be accused of neglecting what was ordinary, mundane and familiar. Perhaps unjustifiably, this left such studies open to charges of voyeurism and sensationalism. Thus symbolic interactionist ethnographies were sardonically described by some critics as having a preoccupation with 'nuts, sluts and perverts' (Liazos, 1972).

3

Ethnomethodology and Self-Reflection

Once upon a time in sociology 'armchair theorizing' was a phrase used to caricature a particular kind of sociological practice, one that seemed to be out of touch with the realities of people's lives in society. The description 'armchair theorist' referred to a sociologist who preferred to speculate about societies in the abstract rather than investigate what actually occurred in people's lives. The image of the armchair theorist was of a sociologist who sat around in an armchair and thought about the social world in terms of his or her preconceived notions without ever venturing out into the world to find out what actually went on. The armchair theorist had little interest in what members of society actually did and what things meant to them. Armchair theorizing came to denote not only a failure to observe what was actually going on in the social world but also the excesses of the sociological imagination to which sociologists sometimes were tempted.

In this chapter and as a feature of our first steps in the development of expertise in ethnomethodology we would recommend that this judgement of the armchair theorist not be amended in any way, nor do we want to be understood as advocating any kind of rehabilitation of armchair theorizing. However, we do want to begin by recommending the entirely different practice of armchair *research* in sociology. We want to suggest that the beginning sociologist (and the more practised one also) does not have to leave the comfort and surroundings of his or her own armchair in order to begin to think and observe sociologically. Indeed, in our view there is far too little armchair research in sociology, using the method we outline in what follows. Sociology has developed elaborate and specialized techniques for gathering information that will enable it to describe and explain the social world. Such techniques presuppose that the social world is out there awaiting discovery. However, as we have emphasized earlier, the researcher is as much a part of the social world as anyone else. In an important sense, therefore, the social world is as much 'in here' as it is 'out there'. Accordingly, it seems reasonable to us that the beginning of social inquiry can be the researcher's own experiences and activities, and self-reflection upon these. After all, the first and most accessible thing for observation is yourself. Furthermore, as members of society we are already immersed in the social world and in the course of our daily lives we become immersed in a succession of activities. We engage in them with our own taken-for-granted social knowledge. If we are competent members of society, accomplishing social activities, then why not treat our own activities as topics of inquiry? If inquiry requires data – as we believe it does – then why not take our own experiences and actions as our data? All you need is ready to hand – your capacity for self-reflection.

To self-reflect is not simply to think about yourself. It is to turn yourself, or more particularly your experiences and actions, into topics for analysis. You can take anything about yourself, from your daily routines to your emotions, and turn it into a topic for analysis. Following on from what we indicated in Chapter 1, the method of self-reflective analysis involves three main steps. First, focus on some action or experience as a candidate phenomenon for self-reflective investigation. Second, find a way to turn the (often) fleeting and ephemeral experience or action into something that can be systematically examined – by, for example, writing down or otherwise recording one's feelings or activity. Third, attempt to account for the production of the recorded feelings or actions in terms of the methods involved in their production. The upshot of these analytic procedures will be, we suggest, an account of the methods that provide for or make possible a given experience or action.

What, then, might we expect to learn from using this method of self-reflection? As we pointed out in Chapter 2, our particular 'take' on the relationship between our everyday action and experience and our membership of society is to view our experiences and our actions as 'productions'. For example, in relation to experiences, we recognize a person, understand what is meant by what they say, feel sorrow or joy at their actions, feel guilt or remorse in relation to our own actions and so forth by virtue of our membership in society. Likewise, we are able to request a favour or return one, recognize a joke and also tell one, laugh on cue when told a joke by someone else, agree or disagree with a stated opinion or argument and so forth by means of our social competence. We can do these things because we have acquired the knowledge of how to do them through our immersion in them. How it is that we are able to have appropriate experiences and competently produce actions is, for us, a methodical matter. More particularly, as we have suggested, experiences and actions are produced by us with the use of something. We have referred to this something as 'methods' or, alternatively, 'resources'. The task of ethnomethodology is to identify and describe the use of such methods. Such a task, as subsequent chapters will demonstrate, involves making observations of people's talk and action. However, we have found it instructive to begin not with observations of others, but with observations that may be made of ourselves, since we are members of society just as they are. In other words, we want to recommend beginning with the practice of self-reflection.

We will then focus on two examples of self-reflective analysis that we are confident that anyone can do. Each involves an activity that can be done whilst sitting in one's armchair. Whilst we may engage in a wide variety of social activities in such a context, the activity we will analyse is that of 'sense-making' and the experience of 'understanding'. The data that provides the object of this activity are drawn from newspaper and television media. Thus, given that the mass media of newspapers and television are available to everyone in our society, one does not have to leave one's armchair to be informed about what is going on in the world. One can be a 'well-informed citizen' about places, people and events one has not witnessed personally, simply as a result of watching the television or reading the newspaper. This means, of course, that the resources for doing self-reflective analysis are ready to hand in relation to the media. One does not have to leave the comfort of one's armchair to engage in self-reflective media research. Of course, we cannot speculate about the relevance of this fact for the popularity of media studies amongst professional sociologists. Our first example consists of an investigation of sense-making in relation to a newspaper headline, our second concerns a television news story. In each case following our procedure we will start with what is observably the case concerning our sense, experience and understanding, and then subject this to analysis.

Analysing a newspaper headline[1]

The reading of specific news items will make available to us via the method of self-reflection our own engagement in sense-making. We ask the reader to imagine that you have picked up the newspaper and on the front page you find the following headline:

Mother charged in death of child[2]

We further ask that you do no more than read this headline; you do not at this stage attempt to read the article or story that would follow. We start by observing that headlines such as this are readily understandable and intelligible. The sense or understanding that is readily achieved provides what we call a 'reading' of the headline that then affords us an opportunity for sociological analysis. The first step, then, in this form of analysis is to make sense of the headline 'unreflectively', if we can put it that way. We mean by this that sense should be made initially in the way that it is ordinarily made. One reads the newspaper headline and typically without puzzlement or special effort a sense is made of it. In other words, we understand it without difficulty. It is only when we have made our ordinary sense of the headline that we will then be in a position to begin self-reflective sociological analysis of our sense-making procedures or methods.

Accordingly, then, we and presumably you read this particular newspaper headline to mean that a mother killed her child and as a result was arrested and charged by the police. The child was probably a baby or young infant and was most likely killed by suffocation or neglect. The question for us is, how do we 'know' this? None of the above is stated in so many words in the headline. The headline does not provide all the details, and at least on the surface several other readings are possible. Yet we, as readers, seemingly have no problem in understanding what the headline is describing. Somehow we assemble a sense of the headline. Let us first, then, spell out our own understandings of the headline. Once we have done so, we can begin to reflect on the methods by which they are produced. It seems to us that the understandings involved amount to something like the following:

- that the mother is the mother of the dead child (and not someone else's mother);
- that the mother was charged by the police (and not someone or something else);
- that the child was killed by its mother (and not by someone else);
- that the death of the child was intentional (and not accidental);
- that the mother was charged because she killed her child (and not because of some other matter); and
- that the child was most likely a baby or young infant (and not, for example, a teenager).

The fact that we can understand all this is because, we want to suggest, of our everyday knowledge of 'membership categories'. More precisely, it is because of our engagement in an activity that is referred to as 'membership categorization analysis'. This originated in the work of Sacks (1967; 1972; 1974; 1992a) and has been defined (Hester and Eglin, 1997: 3) as follows:

> The focus of MCA (Membership Categorisation Analysis) is on the use of membership categories, membership categorisation devices and category predicates by members, conceptualised as lay and professional social analysts, in accomplishing (the sociology of) 'naturally occurring ordinary activities'. MCA directs attention to the locally used, invoked and organised 'presumed common-sense knowledge of social structures' which members are oriented to in the conduct of their everyday affairs, including professional sociological inquiry itself.

Thus, the activity of membership categorization analysis can be understood in two senses. First, it is an activity that we, as ordinary members of society, engage in when, for example, we make sense of things like a newspaper headline. Second, it refers to the analyses that we, as professional researchers, produce *of* the analyses of the ordinary members of society.

So, in the headline above, we can notice that 'mother' and 'child' are mentioned. These are examples of membership categories or, more specifically, 'personal' membership categories. As members of society, all of us belong to various membership categories, such as male or female, father, mother, student, teacher, southerner, hockey player, chorister, sailor and so on. However, we have to be careful here. The sense in which we 'belong' to these categories needs to be clarified. It is very important to make a distinction here between those categories that we may say are correct descriptions of who we are and those that are 'operationally relevant' descriptions in the specific context of social interaction that we currently find ourselves in. So, whilst in some sense we (or at least most of us) are always either male or female there are numerous occasions in our lives when our gender is simply not relevant. One of the major difficulties with what is referred to as 'variable analysis' in sociology is that the analyst standardly presumes the relevance of categories of membership for some set of persons without establishing that they are in fact relevant for them with respect to the activity, problem or attitude under investigation. In contrast, the position of ethnomethodology is that if we are to sensibly talk about the role, influence or impact of a category then what we say has to be grounded in data that reveals that the people we are talking about are actually oriented to that category with respect to their own talk and action. Not only then are the operative categories to which we may belong and in terms of which we act enormously varied, they are also 'situational' or 'local' in character. By this we mean that we can only discover what categories persons are demonstrably oriented to by inspecting the detail of the talk and action that they are engaged in at a particular interactional moment. From this point of view, depending on the activity that a person may currently be engaged in, a person's membership category may be telephone caller, current speaker, complainant, advice seeker, sulker, litterer or dog walker and so forth. Even more specifically we may be someone who has just been smiled at, told off, humiliated, questioned, kissed, insulted and so on. Our incumbency of these membership categories fluctuates; our current interactional circumstances make relevant some category memberships and not others.

In general terms, the significance of these membership categories, on one level, is that they provide a means for us to make sense of the social world. It is in terms of such categories, at least in part, that our knowledge of the social world is organized. Such categories, as Sacks (1992a) points out, are 'inference rich'. This means that when we know what category applies to a person, then we know something about them. We can predict what kinds of attributes they may have, what their obligations and entitlements are and, perhaps most importantly – at least for our purposes here – what kinds of activities they properly and typically engage in, and hence how they may act here and now. In the news headline under consideration we can observe that some specific incumbents of these membership categories are mentioned. Reflecting on our own experience or sense of the headline we suggest that they are usable in analysing in the headline in such a way as to make sense of it. We will reflect upon each of the six components of our sense of the headline and analyse the use of categories involved in the production of each component.

Reading the mother as the mother of the dead child

We note first that the headline does not involve mothers and children in general but a particular instance of a mother and a child. Furthermore, our understanding of the headline, as we indicated above, is that these are not just any mother and any child, rather they are related to one another. They appear to go together naturally as a pair. Of course, they might not be such a pair, as our bracketed alternative reading above suggested, but it seems natural for us that they are so related. By 'natural' here we mean 'in terms of our common sense' as it pertains to everyday life. The hearing of mother and child as going together as a pair is, one might say, our first and unthinking hearing, a presumption on our part that unless otherwise indicated they are indeed related as a pair.

Sacks speaks of membership categories 'going together' and by this he was referring to the organization of our common-sense knowledge. Membership categories that refer to types of person are, or at least can be, according to Sacks, organized into collections of categories. One example of such a common-sense collection is 'family'. Thus, as everybody knows, the collection 'family' is ordinarily and conventionally understood to include categories such as mother, father, son, daughter, aunt, uncle, grandmother, grandfather and so on. Of course, in the case of any particular family not all of these categories may be actually present; some families are without a mother or a father or children or aunts and uncles. However, such particular omissions do not mean that as far as our common-sense knowledge of society is concerned such categories of person are not conventional, proper and expectable members of families. Indeed, the very noticeability of the absence of one or more of these categories from particular families serves only to confirm that, conventionally speaking, families may and typically are composed of such categories of person. Thus we speak of 'single mothers' and 'single fathers' and thereby imply the absence of a father or mother in the family unit.

Furthermore, 'mother' and 'child' are not only hearable as co-incumbents of the category collection 'family'. They also seem to go together as a particular pair of categories. Sacks (1972) referred to this type of pair as the 'standardized relational pair'. There are many such pairs, for example, doctor–patient, teacher–student, boyfriend–girlfriend, husband–wife, parent–child and so on. To say that such pairs are standardized means that it is known what the typical rights, obligations, activities, attributes and so forth are of the one part of the pair with respect to the other. These typicalities, or 'predicates', constitute the character of their relation or relationship. For example, it is a standardized feature of the doctor–patient relationship that the doctor has the specialized knowledge to diagnose the patient's illness, that the patient goes to the doctor because they have a medical problem and that the doctor has the capacity to prescribe a course of remedial treatment. These features are 'standardly' built into the doctor–patient relationship. Furthermore, mention of one part of such a pair is to imply the other – to have the other programmatically present. So, when one thinks of or mentions, say, 'husband' one thinks of, or makes relevant the other part of the pair of which husband is the first part, namely 'wife'.

The organization of categories into collections, including standardized relational pairs, in this way provides persons with conventional ways of talking and in particular describing events and persons. In this connection, Sacks directed our attention to 'rules of application' for the use of categories. One of these, the 'consistency rule', refers to how, if one uses a category from a particular collection to describe a first member of the population of persons, then one may use a further category from the same collection to refer to additional member of that population. It is from this consistency rule that a 'hearer's maxim' is drawn as a corollary. This states that if a hearer can hear two consecutively (not necessarily immediately adjacent) categories as going or belonging together then: hear them that way. In other words, don't doubt that they are related if that is how you hear them, unless you have good reason for doing so. By the notion of the hearer's maxim, Sacks is trying to get at how we experience the world, and especially the descriptions that we encounter within it.

Accordingly, then, by following the hearer's maxim we are able to hear 'mother' and 'child' as belonging together not only in the collection 'family' but also as the occupants of a particular standardized relational pair, namely 'mother and child'. It is via this method, then, that we are able to produce the sense of this particular component of the headline.

Reading the mother as having been charged by the police

A second observation is that the headline does not say that the mother was charged by the police, but we hear it that way. This is because of a second method for sense-making, namely our 'orientation to category predicates'. Originally, in the work of Sacks (1992a), the focus was on 'category-bound activities'. These are those activities that are expectably and properly done by persons who are the incumbents of particular categories. A category-bound activity of, for example, judges is that of passing sentence, of teachers, instructing the class, and of babies, crying. Subsequently, researchers investigating what may be common-sensically presumed of categories reached the conclusion that category-bound activities comprise just one class of 'predicates' which 'can conventionally be imputed on the basis of a given membership category' (Watson, 1978: 106). Others include rights, obligations, knowledge, entitlements, attributes, skills and competencies. In the case at hand, 'charging' is an activity that is routinely, expectably and properly tied to, that is, predicated of, the membership category 'police' or more precisely 'police officer'. It is an activity that we not only expect them to do (under certain circumstances) but it is also something that they quite properly do. It is a part of their job within the criminal justice system. Accordingly, we are completely unsurprised when we hear mention that someone was 'charged by the police'. Our lack of surprise, we suggest, is a result of our common-sense assumptions about this particular membership category, namely that bound to it are particular category-bound activities and other predicates.

It is also easily recognized that the word 'charged' can have a number of different meanings. Someone may, for example, be charged for being overdrawn at their bank. Alternatively, in the context of a bull ring a bull-fighter may quite properly be charged by a bull. However, we have no difficulty in understanding the sense in which this word is being used in this headline, that is, someone is being charged with a crime or offence. This is because we assume that in this case the activity is being done by the incumbents of a membership category to which it is bound. Our assumption, furthermore, involves the use of a further maxim or method, a 'viewer's maxim'. This states that if an activity can be seen as being done by an incumbent of a category to which it is bound, then 'see it that way'. Accordingly, against our background knowledge of the relationship between categories and predicates, we can confidently assume that 'charged' refers to being 'charged by the police' rather than to some other kind of charging, hence observation.

Reading that the child was killed by its mother

The third component of our reading of the headline consists in our sense that the child was killed by its mother and not by someone else. Upon reflection, we find the source of this reading to lie in the fact that we have already taken it that the mother is the mother of the dead child and that the police have charged someone who is the mother. If the police have charged the mother of the child, rather than someone else, then it seems reasonable that it is she who has killed her child, rather than some unnamed category of person. This is so because the police, as we presume, charge people because they have committed offences. We derive our sense that the mother killed her child from our understanding of charging as bound to the category 'police'. Additionally, we suggest that we can understand the mother of the child as the killer of the child because of our orientation to standardized relational pairs which we mentioned earlier. The pair in this case is 'killer and killed' (or victim). As with other such pairs, if one part of the pair is present then the other is programmatically so. Thus, if there is a person present (in the description) who could be the incumbent of the programmatically present category, then we hear that person as the incumbent. Clearly, then, given that the mother is the mother of the child and given that she has been charged by the police then it is perfectly reasonable to assume that she is the killer, rather than someone else. Thus, our third understanding is accounted for.

Reading that the death of the child was intentional

The fourth component of our reading is that we have understood the headline to mean that the death of the child was deliberate; the child died as a result of a killing and not of natural causes. How do we arrive at this piece of sense-making? We suggest that it is because of the fact that the mother was charged by the police. From what we presume about the work of the police we take it that they have a responsibility to charge persons with offences only when they are confident that such charging will result in a conviction in the courts. Otherwise, they will waste not only their own time but also that of the courts. A vital element, furthermore, of confidence consists in the demonstrable intentionality of the offence in question. In other words, we might put it this way: offences with which persons are charged have the attribute 'intentional' bound to them. Accordingly, we have a method to account for our fourth observation.

Reading that the mother was charged because she killed her child

We also read the headline to mean that the mother was charged because she killed her child. Clearly, she could have been charged because of some other matter. For example, she could have been an accessory to the killing or she could have been charged with obstructing the course of justice with respect to someone else who had killed the child. We don't hear it that way and we suggest that this is so because we already know that she is the killer. Since this is so, we can say that it is a 'category-paired action' that she has now been charged. In other words, just as killer and victim go together as a pair of categories, the one implying the presence of the other, so also do the actions 'killing' and 'charging'. These actions are paired predicates of the categories. So, by a similar course of reasoning as pertains to standardized relational pairs, the presence of one part of a 'predicate pair' provides for the presence of the other part. Given that she killed, it stands to reason (by virtue of these categorical relationships) that she was therefore charged. This, then, accounts for the methodical production of our fifth understanding.

Reading that the child was a baby or young infant

We have also understood the headline to mean that the child in question is a young child, in all likelihood a baby or an infant. Of course, children remain the children of their mothers throughout their lives, so why is it that we assume that the child is a younger rather than an older child? On reflection, our answer is that this is because of what we 'know' about the death of children at the hands of their mothers. In other words, our sense involves what we can refer to as the common-sense 'grammar' of child-killing. As Eglin and Hester (1992: 3) note with respect to a different kind of act, namely the act of suicide:

> As an action 'committing suicide' also has its conceptual grammar, its category-tied predicates. It is done for conventional reasons, in certain psychological

states, arising out of conventional interactional and structural social circumstances, with conventional methods, and so on.

The grammar for child-killing involves our common-sense assumptions about the nature and causes of such crimes. Like the 'normal crimes' oriented to by lawyers (Sudnow, 1965), the grammar of child-killing marks a constellation of assumptions and presumptions that may be brought to bear on a particular event. They provide for a kind of default reading of the situation. Of course, they are always subject to revision in any specific instance but as common-sense understandings of the nature of such crimes they invoke the conventionality of child-killing. So we take it, until further notice, that this child-killing will be similar in the range of its identifying detail to previous child-killings we have heard of or read about. As with suicide, child-killing is done for conventional reasons (poor parenting skills, poverty, resentment, jealousy, cruelty, misunderstanding of the motives for children's actions such as crying and so on), in certain psychological states (exasperation, loss of temper), under certain circumstances (poverty, where the child is not the 'natural' child of the killer), by conventional methods (starvation, neglect, beating), and where the victim is typically young and defenceless. It is in terms of conventional understandings such as these that we understand the child to be a baby or an infant.

By considering a simple newspaper headline, we have been able to bring into view some of the resources that Sacks suggested were used by members of society to assemble the sense of descriptions. Thus, our use of a newspaper headline should not be read as meaning that the kind of analysis done here is limited to the analysis of such phenomena. The significant thing about a headline is that it is a description of an event or topic, one that is intended to be understandable to anyone who reads the newspaper in which it appears. But, of course, newspapers are not the only place in which descriptions can be found. As we pointed out in Chapter 1, as members of society going about our daily lives we encounter descriptions all the time. Not only that, but we ourselves produce descriptions in conducting our dealings with others, ones that we assume will be understood by them in the way we intend. Thus we both make sense of the descriptions we encounter and produce descriptions that make intelligible sense for others with whom we interact. Sense-making, therefore, is fundamental to social life, in two independent ways: on the one hand, we make sense of the things that others say and do, while on the other hand, we produce our own activities in such a way that what we are doing (and saying) makes sense to other people. Thus, newspaper journalists and editors, in constructing headlines and newspaper stories, draw upon the same common-sense knowledge and interpretive practices as they presume of their readers. They write a headline, for example, in the anticipation that the reader (whoever that happens to be) will be able to understand it in the manner intended.

Making sense of television news

We now ask the reader to imagine that he or she has turned on the television to watch the lunchtime news. Our second example of sense-making is taken from a BBC television news programme at 1 p.m., anchored by Anna Ford. The programme in question, broadcast in April 2002, consisted of a number of items ranging from a report on developments in the Middle East conflict between Israel and the Palestinians to a story about mistakes in the breast cancer screening system at a London hospital. Each of these items comprised several components. In each case, the initial telling of the news story was by the newsreader in the studio. This initial telling was followed by other segments in which the story was elaborated, typically by means of reporters in the field and statements by other parties involved in the story. Among the items contained in the programme was one concerning the death of an elderly woman, which was introduced by the newsreader in the following way:

AF: A 77-year-old woman who was mugged for her fish supper has died in hospital. Marie Watson was outside a chip shop in the Heaton area of Newcastle when she was attacked 11 days ago. She suffered a broken shoulder and extensive bruising to her face. Police have appealed for witnesses to the attack.

As Ms Ford read this story, a picture of a badly injured elderly woman was displayed in the corner of the screen. Following this introduction, the item cut to a reporter in the field who elaborated the story, and this was followed by an extract from a police press conference in which a senior detective appealed for public help in finding the attacker.

As with the previous example of the newspaper headline, it is the initial description of the event that we wish to consider. Therefore we will focus on the newsreader's introduction to the story, as reproduced above, rather than on its subsequent elaboration. The introduction will suffice with respect to generating the data that we need to reflect upon the intelligibility of this story. Once again, in presenting a self-reflective analysis of these materials, we will take our own understandings as the phenomena to be accounted for. We take it, however, that these understandings are not ours alone, but are shared by the reader. Following the procedure identified earlier, then, we can note first that we have no difficulty in understanding what this news story is about. Nor do we have any problem in seeing how it reports something newsworthy. The task of examining the methods by which we make sense of it as we do, though, requires again and firstly that we spell out in some detail what our ordinary understanding consists of.

We note first of all that our extract is composed of four sentences. These are not understood as disconnected but as comprising a story – a connected series of events. Thus, in the first sentence, a membership category – '77-year-old woman' – is mentioned and is said to have been the victim of a mugging for her supper. In the second sentence, a proper name is used – 'Marie Watson' – to describe someone who 'was outside a chip shop in the Heaton area of Newcastle when she was attacked 11 days ago'. We have no trouble in hearing the 77-year-old woman and Marie Watson as one and the same person. Likewise, we have no difficulty in understanding the mugging and the attack as referring to the same event, nor do we have any trouble in hearing that the woman's death in hospital was the result of the attack, even if the injuries mentioned in the third sentence, namely 'a broken shoulder and extensive bruising to her face', might seem less than life-threatening. Finally, we have no difficulty in hearing that the attack with respect to which the police are appealing for witnesses to come forward is the attack on the woman. How, then, following our procedure for analysis, are these various hearings possible? Specifically, then, we can itemize our understandings as follows:

- that the 77-year-old woman and Marie Watson are one and the same;
- that the mugging and the attack are the same event;
- that the death was a result of the attack (and was not caused by something else);
- that the attack the police are seeking witnesses to is the attack on the victim of the mugging (and not some other crime);
- that the story is a tragic one (and not a cause for celebration); and
- that the mugger was probably a young man, possibly a teenager and possibly a drug addict.

Hearing that the 77-year-old woman and Marie Watson are one and the same

With respect to our first observation, namely that the '77-year-old' and 'Marie Watson' are the same person, it would seem that this is provided for by the hearer's maxim, derived from the consistency rule, which we mentioned in our earlier analysis of the newspaper headline. That is, if two or more membership categories can be heard to belong to the same collection or membership categorization device, then: hear them that way. Here we suggest, however, that it is not membership of a collection that is provided for, rather it is incumbency of a membership category. The '77-year-old' is not heard just as an elderly woman, she is described as a victim of a mugging. We assume that 'Marie Watson' is also an incumbent of this membership category. Marie Watson could, of course, be someone other than the 77-year-old female victim. When she is mentioned at the start of sentence two, she could be anybody. She could, for example, be a witness to the attack on the old woman. However, her identity is clarified when she is said to have been attacked outside a chip shop. In hearing that the attack and the mugging are one and the same, so the 77-year-old woman and Marie Watson are identical. Hence, our first understanding.

Hearing that the mugging and the attack are the same event

We have presumed that the mugging and the attack are the same event, and that presumption has been used to hear the 77-year-old woman and Marie Watson as the same person. Yet how is it that we hear the mugging and the attack as the same? One answer, it seems to us, involves our assumption that the victim is the same person in each case. Of course, she could have been a victim of more than one violent attack but there is no indication of this in the story, and so in the absence of instructions to the contrary we assume that only one event is being talked about here. It also seems to us that our sense of the mugging and the attack as one and the same involves an application of the hearer's maxim. Thus, in this case, if two categorizations of an event can be heard as categorizations of the same event, then: hear them that way. We also suggest that our hearing can be produced via the orientation to category predicates. Thus, 'attacking' can be heard as predicated (indeed constitutive) of mugging since, after all, mugging is robbery with violence.

We also note that the first sentence of the report can be heard to name a topic, namely the mugging of the 77-year-old woman. Topics, as Sacks (1992a) points out, provide for the selection of items that remain consistent with the topic. For example, say a person begins speaking about cigars, then a topically consistent object for a next speaker to talk about might be pipes or cigarettes. There is, it seems, a preference for consistency in so far as changes of topic have to be specifically accounted for. In the case at hand, the story of the mugging makes relevant a collection of items that are hearably 'on topic' unless the storyteller indicates otherwise. The first two sentences are thus assumed to be parts of a collection of sentences comprising the story. It is assumed that they go together; they are about the same event and person(s) involved in it. So, we have no reason to suppose that the second sentence might be about some entirely unconnected person and event.

Sentences comprising stories can be related in various ways. In Sacks' (1974) classic analysis of 'The baby cried. The mommy picked it up' it is assumed that each of the two sentences describes an event and that the events occurred in the order in which the sentences are positioned. In our example, however, the relationship between the first two sentences is rather different. The first sentence is hearable as a kind of headline covering the whole story from attack to death. The second sentence begins to elaborate the events mentioned in the first sentence. The elaboration begun in sentence two is then carried on in sentences three and four, and we hear them, like 'The baby cried ...' as reporting a chronology of events: attack, injury and police action. The chronology or local history of the mugging provides a topical collection, such that the attack can be then heard as a member of that collection and not as a member of some other, unrelated, collection. Hence, our second understanding.

Hearing the death as a result of the mugging

We have also observed our lack of surprise at the report that the woman died as a result of the attack. The injuries mentioned – a broken shoulder and bruising – appear at first sight to be less than terminal. However, when combined with her incumbency of the category '77-year-old' it is possible to find that an attack producing such injuries could have caused her death. We suggest that this is because of what we know about 77-year-old women. This sort of category is conventionally associated with such attributional predicates as frailty and vulnerability. Therefore, in contrast to other categories, 77-year-old women are assumed to be less able to withstand the impact of a physical attack of this kind, and we can easily imagine the trauma that may result from the shock of the attack as well as the actual physical injuries. So, it is the woman's categorial membership that provides for our being readily able to understand the attack as the cause of her death. Had the attack been on a 25-year-old male we might have been surprised to learn of their demise and require some additional explanation. In the case of the elderly woman we have far less difficulty in this regard. Accordingly, we have a method for understanding the death as a result of the mugging.

Hearing the attack that the police are seeking witnesses for as the attack on the woman

The story also exhibits what Sacks (1992a) has referred to as the 'character appears on cue' rule. Thus, here it is utterly unremarkable that the police appear in the fourth sentence of the story. They appear 'on cue', as it were. But what is the nature of this cue? Sacks indicated that in the case of a story describing a person speeding in their car and then getting arrested, the appearance of the police does not have to be explained or specially provided for. Offender and law enforcer go together as a pair of categories in a normative relationship, such that the appearance of an incumbent of the first category not only makes relevant the appearance of an incumbent of the second, but makes that appearance an event which can be properly anticipated. So, in our materials, it is utterly unsurprising that the police should appear in the story when and how they do because they are paired with offender in a normative (and standardized) relationship.

Just as the police appear on cue, so also do the witnesses. We suggest that we can understand this because the story of the mugging sets up a particular category collection or membership categorization device, namely 'parties to a mugging'. Following what we have said earlier about the consistency rule and the hearer's maxim, if consecutively used categories can be heard as belonging to the same collection, in this case the collection 'parties to a mugging', then we hear them that way. The witnesses, then, like the police, are one part of the story's cast of characters and, like Marie Watson, the victim, if the police and the witnesses can be heard as categories which belong to this category collection then we hear that way. This, then, accounts for our understanding that the attack that the police are seeking witnesses for is the attack on the woman.

Finding the tragedy and moral repugnancy in the story

Additional observations are afforded by other aspects of our experience of the story. Thus, the story is also interesting because it allows us to consider or reflect upon our emotional experiences and thereby upon the grounds of their production. We find that the story is one that easily generates an emotional and moral response. It seems an especially tragic kind of crime. Our sense of tragedy is generated, we suggest, because of the nature of the victim. We know she was elderly, and therefore relatively defenceless against a powerful (and we assume young) mugger, but we also sense that she must have been minding her own business, just going to the fish and chip shop. As an apparently harmless person, nearing the end of her life, not only did she not deserve such an attack but it seems tragic that she could not end her days in a peaceful and gentle way rather than as a result of a violent attack. The tragedy, in other words, would seem to emanate, for us, from the category membership of the victim.

Furthermore, not only does the story report a tragic crime, the crime is a particularly heinous one, such that feelings of disgust, sympathy and outrage are appropriate responses. We have, we suspect, much in common with our readers in reacting to this story with moral repulsion. Why is this so? We suggest that these feelings are not simply individualistic emotions; rather, they are social facts in the sense that they are both available to anyone and they are socially appropriate. Indeed, a response to this news that did not display any such emotion would invite a charge such as heartlessness. In part, it is so because the victim is hearable as elderly, frail and vulnerable. Such persons need care, not attack. The morally repugnant character of the attack is generated by the category membership of the victim. It is not simply because robbery is illegal that makes this case so objectionable. It is the fact that the victim is old, frail and vulnerable, which makes the mugging especially cowardly and callous.

We would also suggest that there is a further moral feature of the attack that provides for our feeling appalled by it. This involves the motivation for the attack that the story provides. We refer here to our ways of understanding criminal motivation. There are some murders, even if they are otherwise horrific, that are in some sense understandable, even rational, given the motivation of the killers. One example that occurs to us is the case of so-called suicide bombing. However, in this reported attack the act appears senseless, given that the mugger only obtained a fish supper. It might have been more understandable had the victim had in her possession large amounts of money, but to attack an elderly woman for something so trivial as a fish supper appears beyond the bounds of 'civilized' conduct.

As has been noted elsewhere (Eglin and Hester, 2003), when it comes to making sense of and responding to social phenomena we are, to put it plainly, not just sociologists. We are also fathers and sons, husbands and lovers, friends and foes, professors and colleagues, amongst a whole host of other memberships. Few, if any, of these memberships are omnirelevant. Rather, they *become* relevant. Certain arrangements, relationships, actions and events make them relevant. Furthermore, as incumbents of these various categories, we are entitled and obliged to engage in activities predicated of them, to display associated and/or constitutive attributes and perhaps to have certain attitudes, beliefs, opinions, thoughts and feelings.

More particularly, for a given members' characterization of an event there are normatively arranged, organizationally provided for, categorically built, paired responses. Such responses appear on cue, just like the characters who appear in this story. Indeed, their non-appearance is an accountable matter. We suggest, then, that the category of news implies the character of the response to it. The response to good news is conventionally different from that to bad news. It seems at least intuitively the case that certain kinds of good news will be received in a congratulatory manner. A: 'I'm getting married.' B: 'Really? Congratulations!' the sequence might go, or A: 'I passed my exams.' B: 'Great. Well done.' In contrast, we know that the grammar of bad news makes relevant acts of commiseration. The conventional response to news of a death in the family, for example, is an expression of sympathy, as in A: 'My mother died.' B: 'Oh, I'm sorry to hear that.' Alternatively put, the category of news proffered makes relevant different (membership) categories of response. To the recently engaged we are congratulators, to the bereaved we are commiserators, to the distraught we are comforters, and so forth.

The receipt of tragic news is appropriately in the form of commiseration rather than nonchalance or indifference. The non-appearance of commiseration is a noticeable and accountable matter. The non-commiserating recipient of tragic news is rendered vulnerable to description as possibly unsympathetic, insensitive or worse. Likewise, we are naturally appalled at the news of a horrific accident accompanied, say, by pictures of gore, carnage, rubble and broken bodies. Expressions of shock appear on cue. 'How terrible' we say. The alternative, 'how wonderful', would be odd indeed except perhaps when we take the victims who are categorized as the 'enemy', but then that is another story. We take it then that our sense of tragedy, sympathy and moral outrage is a normal, 'natural' one, given who we are.

Finding an identity for the mugger and a motive for the mugging

On hearing the news report we also observed that the mugger was most likely male and young, and that he was possibly a drug addict or an opportunist habitual mugger. How do we know this? Our answer, as in our analysis of the newspaper headline, is that it is because of our common-sense grammar of crime and, specifically, our common-sense grammar of mugging. This grammar pertains to motives, personal profiles, circumstances, psychological states and so on, which we assume are present unless we are otherwise notified. In particular, then, we understood the mugging to have been committed by someone with a particular common-sense profile – he was young and male – because such a profile is what we have come to know about muggers. The common-sense grammar of mugging also enables us to picture a possible motive for the crime. In our case, we thought it highly likely that the perpetrator was a drug addict seeking money to sustain a drug habit. Given our conventional grammar of drug addiction, then, such a crime, and therefore this particular mugging, would make sense.

Besides allowing us to speak of criminal motivation, the story also affords topical talk about the wider significance of the mugging, namely the current 'societal state of affairs' and how that might have contributed to the offence in question. Thus, the selection of the news item also provides for such next activities as reflecting and commenting upon the wider social significance of this event. Thus, one may be provoked into considering 'what society is coming to' when elderly women cannot go to get a meal from their local fish and chip shop without being brutally attacked. It is easily imaginable that questions of this kind may be prompted in households where this story has been viewed. Indeed, as viewers of this story (and other comparable crime stories) we find ourselves engaging in speculation about how events such as this could occur and about their implications for our own and other people's lives. The crime has been perpetrated on one elderly woman, at a particular place and time, but it is available to the viewer of the news programme to take this singular event as indicative or emblematic of more general circumstances. Indeed, we suggest that it is a feature of news items such as this one that they invite members of society to engage in theorizing about their wider implications and significance. In this case, we found ourselves talking about the moral fabric of society and the breakdown of moral relations between people. In other words, we could be said to have engaged in sociological theorizing. We did so, however, not in the capacity of professional sociologists but simply as members of society who happened to have watched the lunchtime news. We take it that one of the consequences of news programmes is that they provide viewers with materials for such everyday sociological theorizing.

In relation to crime, we note finally the fact that persons draw inferences about their own situation from things that have happened to others, as reported on the news. Reports such as the one we have been discussing here may provide, through category co-identification, for what has been referred to as the 'fear of crime'. That is to say, other incumbents of the category 'old women', or more generally 'elderly person', may well draw the inference from this event that they themselves face similar risks when they go out to the shops. That such inferences typically may be drawn is itself a fact known, for example, to the police and provides therefore the grounds for police 'reassurances' to elderly people and other members of the general public.

Conclusion

In this chapter it has been our aim to initiate the reader into ethnomethodology via the activity of 'armchair research' using the method of self-reflection. Our claim has been that all of us, as members of society, possess knowledge and competencies that we bring to bear to understand the situations, events, objects and persons that we encounter in and as comprising our daily lives. This knowledge and these competencies are normally taken for granted – we rely upon them but do not typically reflect upon them. Yet these phenomena are fundamental to social life; without them we would not be able to understand others, nor they us. Self-reflection, then, is a method for bringing into focus this taken-for-granted domain. By reflecting upon our own understandings, we can begin to examine and appreciate the accomplished nature of social phenomena, and analyse the methods in and through which ordinary life is done. Having sought to explicate our own orientations in relation to the activity of sense-making, we now turn in the next chapter to the rather more tricky business of understanding the orientations of others. We will do so by considering the organization of ordinary conversational interaction in family settings.

Student activity

1 Identify some description, such as a newspaper headline or television news story.
2 Record (write down) the ordinary or common sense which you, as the identifier of the description or reader of the headline, make of the headline or story. What does it mean to you? This sense or 'reading' now comprises your data.
3 Examine your interpretation of the headline or story and ask: what methods of membership categorization did you employ to arrive at the sense you made?

Further Reading

S. Hester and P. Eglin (eds) (1997) *Culture in Action: Studies in Membership Categorisation Analysis*. Lanham, MD: University Press of America and the International Institute for Ethnomethodology and Conversation Analysis.

L. Jayyusi (1984) *Categorisation and Moral Order.* London: Routledge and Kegan Paul.

J. Lee (1984) 'Innocent victims and evil doers', *Women's Studies International Forum,* 7: 69–73.

H. Sacks (1974) 'On the analysability of stories by children', in R. Turner (ed.), *Ethnomethodology: Selected Readings.* Harmondsworth: Penguin Books.

Notes

1   Before considering a particular instance of news-reading, we can note the following general features of reading the newspaper as a social activity. First, it is something that pretty much anyone – the severely mentally disabled notwithstanding – can do competently in that, for example, people can and do talk about the things they have read in the newspaper. Whilst it is quite clear that different newspapers are geared towards different sections of the population and that therefore the content of a newspaper may take into account its readership, it nevertheless appears safe to assume that 'reading the news' is an unproblematic activity. Second, it is clear that the overall structure of a newspaper has an observable order to it; newspapers, it would seem, are constructed to be read in certain ways. Readers know that there is a relationship between the positioning of a news item within the newspaper and the nature and content of that item. Thus, for example, readers with an interest in sport stories know to turn to the back pages because that is where such stories will be located. Similarly, unless they have wider significance, stories concerning business firms will be found in the financial section of the newspaper. Readers also know that a story which appears on the front page does so because it is deemed particularly important and newsworthy – it is a story of national or international significance and thus a 'front page item'. Third, stories are constructed via the use of standard components. In particular, pretty much all news stories involve two basic components: a headline and a story that elaborates upon the headline. Furthermore, these components are constructed to be read in a definite sequence: first one reads the headline and then, if the reader's interest is aroused, the story beneath it. We take it that newspaper stories are constructed with just this order in mind. When we read newspapers, in other words, we read them in a way that reflects and exhibits our membership of society.

2   For an earlier version of this analysis, see Hester and Eglin (1992).

4

Family Life and
Everyday Conversation

In Chapter 3 we showed that by using self-reflection an appreciation can be developed of some of the methods that persons use in making sense of media texts, specifically a newspaper headline and a television news story. We also suggested that such methods are not limited to the activity of reading the news. Rather, the methods we described are quite pervasive in their utility; their deployment is central to any instance of sense-making. Such methods and the sense whose production they facilitate comprise a key component of our culture and social competence. We will now turn to some further instances of these phenomena. Again, self-reflection is involved but the context for observation is different. Our phenomenon in this chapter is not the solitary activity of reading the news, rather it involves the joint activity of ordinary conversation. Furthermore, we will not just be concerned with how sense may be made of conversation, but also with how conversation itself as a social activity is achieved.

Ordinary conversation is an activity with which, we assume, any speaker of natural language is familiar. In other words, it is another activity, like sense-making, that we feel we can safely presume that people immerse themselves in on a daily basis. When we speak, then, of ordinary conversation we simply refer to what everybody knows is conversation. We do not mean the kind of talk that may be used to conduct ceremonies or debates, or the specialized kinds of talk that occur when parties to some workplace setting engage in tasks that are specifically kinds of work talk, as in doctor–patient interaction or lawyer–client consultations. Of course, such parties may in the course of their work activities engage each other in conversation, and we trust that readers would be readily able to tell the difference. Indeed, such differences between ordinary conversation and other kinds of talk-in-interaction have afforded studies of the variations in the organization of talk-in-interaction in different settings, and in later chapters in this book we will have occasion to focus upon some of the organizational differences that have been found by such studies. For the moment, however, we want to restrict our attention to some features of the activity of ordinary conversation. In keeping with our approach in this book, we will do so not in the conventional way of summarizing the literature (this would take a book in itself) but rather via a consideration of some data.[1] The conversational data we will consider is drawn from ordinary domestic life. In the first half of the chapter we analyse two brief exchanges, both of which are taken from conversations at the breakfast table. The first is between a parent and a child and the second is between two adults who are partners. In the second half of the chapter we turn our attention to a conversation in a different kind of familiar domestic occurrence, namely the return home of a child from school.

In the course of our discussion we will not only be considering the kinds of categorial topics that we introduced in Chapter 2, we will also be focusing on some 'sequential structures' to which the parties were observably oriented and used in organizing their talk-in-interaction. When we speak of the sequential organization of conversation we refer to the easily observable fact that one item of talk follows from and is placed before another item of talk and that there are discernible connections between these items. They are ordered into sequences. Speakers make use of these sequential structures when they talk together. A major task of conversation analysis is to identify, analyse and describe these sequential structures, their properties and uses in specific instances of talk-in-interaction. As we indicated in Chapter 1, one type of sequential structure is the 'adjacency pair'. There are numerous others that are put to an infinite variety of uses in conversation. The key point about them is that they embody an orientation on the part of speakers to the positioning or placement of conversational 'objects' within talk. As we have seen, the production of one kind of conversational object, a question, makes relevant the production of another, namely an answer in the next conversational slot or turn. The question and the answer comprise a sequential structure in terms of which asking questions and providing answers is organized by the parties to conversation. The aim of conversation analysis is to identify the sequential structures in talk, to analyse their properties and to explore the character of their interactional usage. At the inception of conversation analysis the key question is: why is a particular conversational object produced in the position that it is? The answer that is sought involves establishing the object's relationship to other objects in the conversation.

It is, of course, readily observable that the use of sequential structures is linked to the membership categories of the speakers involved. Such a link has provided, in part, for the development of a line of inquiry into the use and operation of 'speech exchange systems' in different settings. Comparison of the organization of talk in various institutional contexts reveals systematic differences between ordinary conversation and other kinds of talk. We will be discussing such differences in later chapters.

Before examining our data, there is one final point that we must make. We have selected the data that we have because we believe that they are the kinds of talk with which anyone involved in family life will be familiar. However, the organizational features that we identify in these exchanges are not restricted to these particular conversations. These single episodes are particular instances of both sequential and categorial features of conversational organization but these features are also, we suggest, easily observed in other instances of ordinary conversation. Indeed, the particular sequential structures and categorial relations on which we focus have been extensively described and exemplified in conversation analytic investigations. So, the kinds of observations we make about the conversational exchanges we have selected are ones that anyone could also have made, and could make, about many other exchanges, not only in family households but in other contexts of ordinary conversation. Thus, it would seem to be a universal feature of all conversations that participants take turns to speak, and that speaker turn-taking is organized on an utterance-by-utterance basis. Fundamental to this is the fact that utterances are sequentially structured and co-ordinated. This achievement involves speakers in analysing utterances as actions of various kinds, and such analyses are exhibited in the actions that they themselves perform in and through their 'next turn' at talk. Thus utterances are sequentially ordered as sequences of actions. The sequential structures on the one hand are themselves general in character, whilst on the other the way in which they are realized in a particular conversation is tied to and exhibits the local features of that conversation. In this sense, then, conversation analysts refer to sequential structures as both 'context-free' and 'context sensitive'.

Talking over breakfast (1)

If we can take our reader back to his or her television room, we invite you to suppose, for a moment, that you put down your newspaper, rise from your armchair and make your way into the next room where the other members of your family are having breakfast. You have two children (David and Lucy) and they are seated at the table, your partner (Angela) having prepared breakfast for them is now reading her newspaper. It's a fried breakfast, brunch really. There's fried egg, sausage, bacon, baked beans, sliced brown bread and French bread. In particular, each child has a couple of sausages on their plate. In the middle of the table is a further plate with two additional sausages. In the normal way, you take these to be there for a second helping, if required. After a few minutes, once one of the children has finished his breakfast (or at least his first helping), he (David) helps himself to the two additional sausages. There then occurs the following exchange between David and your partner, Angela:

Angela: Doesn't Lucy want any sausages?
David: She's already had French bread.

We will approach this short exchange with our basic orientation in mind. Thus, as we stated in Chapter 1, it is useful to begin with what is recognizable.

In other words, our starting point is with what is observable. Once we have done this, we can then turn our attention to how the thing or the things that are observable are produced. We will begin by looking at the turn-taking that is observable in this pair of utterances. Thus, a first thing that is discernible about this exchange is that Angela and David take it in turns to talk. First Angela speaks and then David speaks. As such the exchange exhibits two grossly apparent features of ordinary conversation, namely that overwhelmingly one party speaks at a time and that speaker change recurs. Furthermore, there is no discernible gap or pause between these two utterances, neither is there any overlap between them. The first occurs, closely followed by the second. These, again, are widely prevalent and easily observable features of everyday conversation. Of course, sometimes pauses do occur and occasionally more than one speaker speaks at a time, but these occurrences tend to be less frequent than the kind of orderly transition from one speaker to the next that we can see here. Indeed, when overlaps occur, it is routinely the case that the floor, as it were, will be relinquished by one or more of the parties to the conversation in favour of a single speaker.

How are we to account for these observations? In what follows, we draw on the work of Sacks (1992a; 1992b) and Sacks, Schegloff and Jefferson (1974). In the case at hand we suggest that David's positioning of his talk at this point, rather than before (thus overlapping with Angela's talk) and rather than after an extended pause or gap, exhibits and reveals several important methodical phenomena. The first of these is David's 'analysis' of the completion of Angela's turn at talk. He has monitored Angela's talk and is able to identify it as 'hearably complete'. The second is his orientation to what we might call a 'no overlap rule'. The third is his orientation to what we might call a 'no gap rule'. In other words, for both Angela and David the completion of Angela's turn is a 'turn-transition relevance point', namely a position in the conversation where changing from one speaker to a next becomes relevant, possible and appropriate.

A second observable feature of this exchange relates to the fact that the second speaker, David, hearably speaks because the first speaker spoke to him, and produces an utterance that responds to what has been said to him by Angela. The sequence is, in other words, initiated by the first speaker and the second speaker speaks in response to this initiation. Alternatively put, it is an instance of the use of a particular method or technique for organizing turn transitions, namely 'current speaker selects next speaker'. Such selection can be consequential for the conversationists in at least two ways. First, it is conventionally the case that the person selected to speak has the right, as it were, to talk; they have been allocated by the previous speaker a slot in which they may now take their turn to talk. Indeed, such allocation can be said to confer a kind of ownership of the next turn onto the person who has been selected. Evidence for this is demonstrated by what happens when other persons, having not been selected by current speaker, instead attempt to select themselves. They get accused of interrupting, or speaking when they haven't been spoken to, and may be told to wait their turn.[2] Further evidence takes the form of the 'noticeable absence' of the selected speaker's turn at talk. We will look at this topic later in this chapter.

Of course, sometimes it is perfectly acceptable for persons to select themselves to speak. Indeed, when Angela asked the question, 'Doesn't Lucy want any sausages?' she did so without having been previously spoken to. So, we have two kinds of occasion where people get to take a turn at talking: either persons are selected to speak or they select themselves to speak. What is especially important to notice about these techniques is that they are ordered in terms of a set of rules. That is to say, it appears that the first technique, current speaker selects next speaker, takes precedence. Thus, if the current speaker selects the next speaker then the person so selected has the right to speak, and no one else. The technique of selecting oneself to speak may only operate if the first technique has not been deployed. Sometimes people are neither selected nor do they select themselves to speak. When this happens a third rule operates, namely that the current speaker may continue talking. These rules provide the normative environment for moving from one turn to the next. We take it that these organizational rules, evident in this data extract but also general in character, are easily observable with respect to conversational interaction.

A third observable feature of the exchange is that Angela's utterance could be heard as a question since, grammatically speaking, it takes the form of a question. As such, the utterance could be heard to require an answer from its addressee. Thus, one might imagine that it could receive an answer such as 'Yes' or 'No' or 'Why don't you ask her?' We can imagine such a response because of something very powerful indeed about the organization of conversation, namely not only that one party talks at a time but also that the production of a first utterance can make relevant the production of a particular kind of next utterance. Conversation analysts, as we indicated in Chapter 1, have referred to these kinds of utterance pairs as 'adjacency pairs'. They are a special class of utterances within which current speaker selects next. In these terms Angela's utterance could be heard as a question. We can also see that the status of David's answer as an answer requires a prior analysis of Angela's utterance as a question, and David's answer indicates his analysis of it as such.

Questions and answers, like other kinds of adjacency pairs, have the following properties. First, they are ordered relative to one another: the first occurs and is followed by the second. Second, the production of the second is conditionally relevant upon the production of the first pair part. Another most important feature of these pairs is their normative arrangement. By this is meant that once a first part of a pair is produced, its recipient is normatively required to produce the second part of the pair, such that when it is not forthcoming it is hearably and noticeably absent.

Interestingly, though Angela's question generates a response from David, it is observably and recognizably rather more than simply an answer to a question. We do not have information on what preceded the data except to say that the preparer of the food (Angela) was reading a newspaper when her partner sat down and began to speak to her, and then David helped himself to the sausages. In response to this, Angela selected herself to speak. Whilst it is possible to understand that Angela and David are simply engaged in a question–answer sequence, we feel confident that those of you who are members of this culture, and who in all probability will have come across such scenes or something like them, will also understand that there is rather more to it than a simple question–answer pair. This directs our analytical attention to what it is that persons are understood to be doing with their words rather than their simply grammatical form. Thus, in this case it is hearable that Angela is 'accusing' David of taking the sausages somewhat prematurely. Surely Angela can be heard to say that David has helped himself to the extra sausages rather too hastily and without due consideration and politeness with respect to Lucy? In the light of this, David can be heard to offer an explanation or an account for his actions. Furthermore, his account indicates his analysis of the question as an accusation.

So far, we have considered this first instance of 'breakfast talk' in terms of its sequential organization. The exchange also displays some categorial organizational features. A first categorial aspect of this exchange is that Angela's question is hearably a parental one, the kind of thing that we might expect a parent to say to a child. In other words, the questioning can be heard as an activity that is bound to or predicated of the category 'parent'. Furthermore, it is not merely the questioning in itself that is recognizably category bound, rather it is the question's character as a means of addressing an issue of fairness among the members of the family that makes it hearable in this case as a parental action. Thus, we note first that it is the parent, Angela, who has cooked and more importantly distributed the food to the members of the family. As an incumbent of the category 'parental food provider' it would be unsurprising that Angela would attend to issues of fairness in relation to the distribution of the food. We take it that family members orient routinely to such matters and therefore can recognize, for example, circumstances in which one person receives more than their fair share. Thus, if a parent fails in this regard, children can conventionally be relied upon to remind them of their distributive responsibilities. If the distribution of the food is observably unfair, children can and do complain to the parent.

In the case at hand, it would appear that the issue is not simply the overall distribution of items of food of equal value. Rather, David can be understood to be claiming an equivalence between Lucy's allocation of French bread and his taking of the extra sausages. From David's utterance, it can be inferred that he was not given any French bread; rather, it all went to Lucy. In this respect, his taking the sausages can be understood as 'evening up the score'. Consequently, we can see here that the operative categorial collection is not simply 'food' because it is clear, at least from David's expressed point of view, that some foods have a special character and are more desirable than others.

In so far as the question can also be heard as an accusation issued under the auspices of parent–child relations, it also exhibits the close connection between sequential organization and categorial organization. Its recognizability as an accusation serves to illustrate that different categories may have as their predicates different kinds of turns at talk, at least under certain conversational circumstances. Parents conventionally exhibit in their talk an orientation to rights to speak to children in particular ways and these ways conventionally are different from how they might speak to other adults. Accordingly, they have been described as 'asymmetrical' rights because they are bound to one category but not to the other category or pair of categories. These asymmetrical rights and responsibilities are observable features of the organization of social interaction between adults and children. As Speier indicates, children have restricted conversational rights. As he puts it (1976: 101):

> The manner in which they can participate in conversations with adults is internally controlled by an asymmetrical distribution of speakers' rights, wherein adults claim rights of local control over conversation with children, and children are obliged to allow them that control.

Speier indicates that children have restricted rights in adult–child conversation in six respects. We do not have the space to discuss his analysis in detail but we reproduce his data, with brief comments, under each of the restricted rights to which they pertain below.

Rights to enforce silence

[A teacher (T) in a second-grade classroom giving a geography lesson. B and F are second-graders.]

```
T:  What is that province, Brian?
B:  B.C.
T:  What is that one?
F:  Alaska.
T:  That's close, but it's a state.
T:  Simon, I'm going to ask you to leave if you don't
    keep your mouth closed. You talk too much out of
    turn.
```

Rights to intervene

[Guy, 7, Steve, 8, Brooke, 6 and Leanne, 7 are playing with an electric train in front of a house.]

```
G:  Will you girls get out of here! Who, we never said
    you could come in, we wanted to play alone. Now
```

you guys have to come butt in – don't turn it on,
don't turn it on until the girls go!

S: How do you put this in reverse?

G: You can't put this one in reverse.

Mo: Listen, Guy, they don't have to get out.

G: Well they're in the way too much, you guys just
watch.

Mo: Let them play too, let them play.

G: You guys just watch, just go up there and watch
for a while.

B: Guy!

Mo: Listen, that's not fair.

G: I said I would give them their turn to control it.

Mo: Well, you don't have to act like such a boss. Let
everybody enjoy it, Guy.

Thus, where adults appear to have rights to intervene in children's conversation at any time, Speier suggests (1976: 101) that children 'must not intervene without some care to display politeness rituals as acceptable *pre-intervention behaviour.*'

Rights to require politeness

[Two mothers having coffee at mother A's home. She (A) tells her children, Dougie, 3, and Brenda, 4, to go into the playroom, as does mother B to her daughter Susie, 5.]

MoA: Will you kids please get into the playroom.
Dougie, I told you not to bring that in here. You
have to be quiet. Daddy's sleeping, you know.

S5: Crayons at home.

MoB: That means you, too, Susie.

S5: I want a donut first, huh.

MoB: Not until you ask politely. And don't yell, you
two!

Thus, adults have rights to require children to display politeness in front of others.

Rights to terminate children's talk

[This is a gathering in the television room in the home of a family. Members of another family are also present in the room. The participants include the father (A) of the house and his 8-year-old girl (S). Their guests include father (B) and his two children, a 7-year-old boy (T) and a 5-year-old boy

(R). The mothers of these three children are in another part of the house. The three children are sitting watching television while father A and father B are just entering the room.]

S:	Oh-oh, here comes dad!
T:	Yeah. Mine always watches hockey and we never.
Fa(A):	OK kids?
T:	Yeah. See?
R:	Aw, gee.
Fa(B):	See what, T?
S:	Aw, it's just like always, Mr B. Why can't … ?
Fa(A):	Come on, kids. 'It's Hockey Night in Canada'.
Fa(B):	Heh, heh.
R:	Aw, dad. This is *our* show!
Fa(B):	R, why don't you go and see what mommy's doing?
Fa(A):	Yeah, S. Go ask mother for some ginger ale. Would you like some pop, R?
Fa(B):	Sure you would. Wouldn't you, Tiger?
R:	Gee, and we got here *first too!*
Fa(B):	That's enough.
R:	Aw, gee.

We take it that the right to terminate children's talk is self-evidently manifested in this extract. Two further features, closely tied to termination rights for adults, are 'dismissal rights' and 'removal rights'. However, Speier does not provide illustrations of instances of the exercise of these rights by adults. We assume that the reader will not find it troublesome to locate instances of such phenomena nor to see how they may be accounted for in terms of how they are categorically grounded and sequentially manifested.

Talking over breakfast (2)

We will now turn to our second short breakfast exchange. Here a woman, Claire, and her partner, John, are sitting at the kitchen table. John has just finished eating a bowl of cereal when the following exchange occurs:

Claire:	Do you want a croissant, baby?
	[*John visibly hesitates/considers the offer*]
Claire:	Fifty per cent less fat.
John:	In *that* case …
	[*John reaches over and takes a croissant*]

Again, we want to begin by noticing some sequential features of this exchange. First, Claire's utterance is recognizably a question and John's utterance is clearly an answer. However, this exchange, while apparently simple in this regard, also has some interesting complexities that we can notice. To begin with, unlike the previous breakfast exchange, here the answer does not follow immediately upon the production of the question. Claire's question is followed by a pause of one second in the conversation, after which she speaks again. Only after this second utterance by Claire does John speak, producing something that looks like the beginning of a positive response to the question. However, it seems to us that John's utterance is more than simply a delayed reply to Claire's initial question in which he recognizably considers the question. In saying 'In that case', John can be heard to be responding not just to the initial question but to both parts of Claire's talk. In other words, instead of a two-part sequential structure consisting of question followed by answer, we have here instead a four-part sequential structure that consists of: a question; a noticeably absent answer; an elaboration of the question; and an answer.

How are we to account for this four-part structure? A first observation, as we have said, is that it begins with Claire's question. Second, we can appreciate that Claire's question, as the first part of an adjacency pair, provides for an appropriate answer from John in response. Third, since this is not forthcoming and therefore noticeably absent, Claire repeats (and at the same time elaborates) her offer/question. Indeed, it is easily observable that repetition, either elaborated or non-elaborated, is a standard response to the non-production of answers. John then responds, in the fourth part of the sequence, with an answer/acceptance.

Additionally, we note that Claire's question can be heard as an offer. Offers are a particular type of first pair part of adjacency pairs. By this we mean to say that they provide for alternative second pair parts. Where some adjacency pairs do not have this feature – for example, question and answer, greeting/ return greeting – offers allow for either acceptance or declination. Accordingly, they share organizational characteristics with such first pair parts as invitations, proposals, requests, demands and so forth, where in each case the recipient of the first pair part has a choice as to the form of response. Furthermore, research in conversation analysis (Sacks, 1992a; Sacks, 1992b; Pomerantz, 1984) has indicated that adjacency pairs of this type exhibit a phenomenon called 'preference'. This is not a matter of liking or disliking, but one of structural organization. That is to say, if one examines how the alternative second pair parts are constructed, then one can notice that they are built differently. Adjacency pairs containing invitations, for example, as their first pair part, display a preference for acceptance over declination in the sense that acceptances are produced immediately after the invitation, whilst declinations are standardly 'delayed' in the responsive turn that follows. Such delay consists of the use of various turn constructional components, such as 'partial acceptance', 'apology' and 'account' *before* the declination. For example:

A: Would you like to meet for coffee after work?
B: Well, that'd be nice, but sorry I can't, I have to get back because of the dog.

With reference to our breakfast exchange between Claire and John we cannot say whether there is a 'preference for acceptance' because John does not actually decline the offer, and since a declination is not actually produced we are unable to inspect the arrangement of its component parts. However, what we can say is that Claire, in her follow-up offer ('Fifty per cent less fat'), may be understood to treat the absence of a clear declination from John as a possible acceptance. That is to say, she can be heard as having analysed John's silence as indicating that he may possibly accept. Her repeat of her offer, then, is responsive to this environment. The third part of the sequence can therefore be understood as a response to this apparent hesitation or equivocality to accept the offer of the croissant. In saying 'Fifty per cent less fat' Claire can be heard to be persuasive, adding an extra inducement to John to accept the offer. Such inducement can be heard as the basis of John's reply, 'In that case'. That is, he can be heard to be responding to that extra inducement. In this way, John's utterance can be seen to display its sequential character as a fourth part of the sequence.

We note also that Claire's question not only selects John as its recipient, but also that she refers to him as 'baby'. This category might be hearable in a number of different ways, for example, as referring to an infant or more pejoratively, perhaps, to an adult 'acting like' an infant. 'Infants' comprise a membership category within the 'stage of life' device. This has three interchangeable varieties of categories. One variety contains the membership categories 'baby', 'toddler', 'child', 'adolescent', 'teenager', 'young woman', 'middle-aged man', 'old woman'. A second variety contains the numerical 'age terms' such as '1-year-old', '6-year-old', '40-year-old', for example. A third variety contains the 'age classes' such as 'young', 'old', 'oldest', and so on. The stage-of-life device is an example of a 'positioned-category device'. As such, it comprises membership categories that occupy, or are arranged in, different positions, higher and lower, relative to one another. One feature of such an arrangement of categories is that it affords both praise and derogation. The basic formula here is as follows: if a person is an X, but behaves like a Y, where X and Y are positioned higher and lower relative to each other as members of a positioned category device, then that person is due either praise or complaint.

As we indicated in Chapter 2, the selection of descriptions of persons is not shaped in terms of correctness criteria so much as considerations of situational relevance and appropriateness. With respect to stage-of-life categories, Sacks (1992a) has shown how their selection varies according to such things as the conversational topic at hand and the relationship in which the speaker stands to the person described. For example, Sacks discusses the case of a woman in her fifties. When it is reported that she has recently died, she is described as 'quite young'. On the other hand, when it is revealed that she has recently married for the first time, she is categorized as 'quite old'.

As Sacks' example illustrates, stage-of-life categories are used frequently to make assessments and express normative judgements. They may be used as 'deliberate mis-descriptions' in order to make an evaluative negative point about another's conduct (cf. Atkinson, 1984). In contrast, in our second breakfast exchange we take it that the term 'baby' can be heard as expressing endearment from one partner to another rather than being either praise or derogation. In this sense, Claire's reference to John as 'baby' is a way of expressing the intimate relationship between them. Here, as elsewhere, the manner in which one speaker addresses another both marks and embodies the nature of the relationship in which they stand. Speaking in this way is a category-bound activity of intimates; it is a way of 'doing intimacy'. Furthermore, the intimacy between them can be heard in the way that Claire elaborates her question. In saying 'Fifty per cent less fat', she displays her sensitivity to issues of health and diet, and thus her concern for her partner. We take it that the absent response to the initial question/ offer of a croissant, which prompts the elaboration, is analysable as indicating John's awareness of the potential unhealthiness of croissants. Therefore Claire's elaboration invokes a categorial distinction between types of croissants in terms of their fat content. In this way, then, Claire's utterance is 'recipient designed'; it takes into account the relevant identity of the other person and Claire's knowledge of his interests and concerns.

Additionally, it would appear to us that Claire's offer of the croissant is produced under the auspices of another category membership. Thus, she is already eating a croissant herself and her question can be heard as occasioned by her incumbency of that category. In asking if her partner wants to join her in this activity (having a croissant with morning coffee), she can be heard to propose an interest in them doing something together. We can also imagine that some sociologists might want to propose a gender analysis of this piece of interaction. They might see it as manifesting patriarchal features. In such an analysis, Claire is seen as offering John a croissant because she takes it as her responsibility as a female to prepare and offer the food to the male in the household. However, since we can find no evidence for this analysis in the orientations of the participants in the data itself we will not consider it further.

A homecoming

So far we have presented some brief snippets from family life to show how the connections between utterances are sequentially organized and how they may be also categorially understood. We now turn our attention to a more extended extract from a family conversation. This more extended stretch of data will enable us to examine some organizational features that are not apparent by looking at the kind of brief and short exchanges that we have considered so far. The reader will notice that a number of transcription conventions are used in the data below. Let us briefly explain these. The first is that some attempt is made to reproduce the actual ways in which words or sounds have been produced by the speakers. To this end, many spellings are not 'correct' and words are sometimes run together. Also, where a speaker has raised his or her voice above a normal conversational level, volume is indicated by the use of capital letters. Audible outbreaths or sighs are indicated by 'hhhh'. Second, contextual information is marked by the use of double brackets. Third, measurable silences within or between utterances are indicated by time in seconds. Finally, talk that is untranscribable is indicated by single brackets.[3]

In the following transcript, then, the speakers are Susan (S), her husband Hugh (H) and their teenage daughter Lydia (L). Lydia has just arrived home from school.

((*L enters house, closes front door*))
```
 1  S:  Y'right?
 2  L:  (I've got) pains.
 3  H:  ((faintly from distance)) did you say you'd put
 4      my socks in the basket, darling?
 5  S:  PARDON?
 6  H:  ((faintly from distance)) did you say you'd put
 7      my socks in the basket?
 8  S:  I DID, SORRY.
 9  S:  What happened?
10  L:  I've got a pain here hhh. On my leg there hh
11      hhh. 'An' I'va pain (…) here on my leg, there.
12      hh.hh.
13  S:  What's it from?
14  L:  'An' I'va pain here on my leg, here.
15  S:  What's it from?
16  L:  From running.
17  S:  Why've you been running, heh heh running?
18  L:  Round the corner.
19  S:  Who've you been running away from?
20  L:  Not running away from (1.0) running away (0.5)
21      running to for –
22  S:  Running to?
23  L:  To catch Liam (0.5) the freak (…)
24      ((H enters))
25  H:  How, how are you?
26  L:  I'm in pain.
27  H:  You're in pain, what have you been doing?
28  L:  Running (1.0) too fast.
29      (2.5)
30  S:  (…)
31      (3.5)
32  S:  Have you had a nice day?
```

```
33       (1.0)
34  L:   Yeah.
35       (1.5)
36  L:   I said -
37       (1.0)
38  S:   Sorry?
39  L:   We were playing football an' they'd all crammed
40       on top of Liam an' he was lying on the floor
41       like that (…) Somebody stood on his fingers an'
42       he was limping along an' I go 'You okay' an' he
43       goes 'No, I'm just limping for the sake of it'
44       an' I go 'Oh yeah, an' I've hurt my leg as well
45       an' I might not be going to swimming tomorrow'
46       for a joke, yeah, an' he goes 'Oh, why not, I'm
47       gonna miss you'.
48  S:   (…) he's in Carnarvon.
49  L:   What?
50  S:   Carnarvon, yeah?
51  L:   (…) Yeah.
52  S:   Yeah.
53  L:   An' I go 'I might nor be there tomorrow because
54       (…) I might have hurt my leg (…)' an' he goes
55       'Oh, it will be really bad without you there',
56       I go like 'OK, fine' hahah.
57  S:   Mmm.
58       (3.5)
59  ?    (…)
60       (4.5)
61  S:   Can I get you a drink?
62  L:   Yeeess.
```

In a lengthy conversational extract such as this there will be many organizational features to which one can attend. We only have space sufficient to discuss a limited number of these. The two features that we will concentrate on are the parents' greeting of the homecoming child and the story that the child tells about her day.

At the beginning of this sequence the daughter, L, is greeted by her mother, S, with 'Y'right?'. It is noticeable that while this utterance could be taken as simply a greeting, and as the first part of a greetings pair, thus requiring only something like a return greeting in response, L does not treat it in this way. Instead she replies that she has 'pains', thus treating S's query as more than just a greeting. She takes it as an invitation to report on her state as someone just returned home from school. As we shall see, this invitation to report on her day shapes the talk until the end of transcript.

Conversation analysts have referred to the kind of structure that is observable here as an 'invited story'. They note that stories in conversation do not simply 'happen', but exhibit distinctive sequential properties. These properties relate to the organization of turn-taking in conversation. The key point is that telling a story requires that the speaker retain the conversational floor for an extended – sometimes a very extended – utterance. Given that one method of speaker turn transition involves 'next speaker selecting himself', and that a current non-speaker can monitor the current speaker's talk for possible 'turn transition places', the problem can be posed of how a speaker is able to retain the conversational 'floor' for long enough to produce a story. We noted earlier that turn transition takes place at specific points in talk and that prospective next speakers have the task of identifying possible turn transition points in a current speaker's talk. Given that the completion of a sentence is one such point, a story composed of a number of such sentences might be prone to an interruption after the completion of each sentence. How, then, does a speaker wishing to tell a story produce his or her talk in such a way as to indicate to others that his sentences are not to be treated as turn transition relevance points until further notice? The distinctive sequential features of conversational storytelling comprise structural solutions to this problem.

For example, it is common for someone who has a story to tell to initiate that story not by simply launching into it, but by 'prefacing' their story with an utterance that has the character of a story announcement. Thus a speaker might say something like 'I've had a terrible time', to which the recipient might then respond 'Oh, what's the matter?'. The announcement utterance has the effect of inviting the other to 'give permission' for the telling of a story. Taken together, the story announcement and the positive response comprise a 'story preface'. Such prefaces are integral to the overall structure of the telling of stories in conversation. They provide a means by which story tellers and the co-conversationalists manage the sequential environment for the story to be told. In the case at hand we do not have a story announcement, but something structurally equivalent, that is, a story invitation (see Cuff and Francis, 1978). Thus, at line 1, S's 'Y'right?' has the same effect as a story announcement and acceptance, namely to provide the conversational conditions for an extended turn at talk in which a story can be told.

L's talk about having pains is briefly interrupted by a call from upstairs by S's partner, H, asking about his socks. Once the socks problem is dealt with, the conversational topic returns to L's pains. S asks 'What happened?' (line 9). This question functions as a 'news receipt' and returns the conversational floor to L who responds by specifying two of the locations of the pains in her legs ('I've got a pain here hhh. On my leg there hh hhh. 'An' I'va pain (…) here on my leg, there. hh.hh.'). S tries to get an explanation of the origins of the pains (line 13) but receives a description of the location of one of L's pains. What is interesting here is the 'failure' of S's question at line 13 (it has to be repeated at line 15). One possibility is that the list of L's pains is incomplete and even though S appears to want to seek answers as to their origin, L is not ready to provide them until the current activity she is engaged in, namely 'listing', is over. When we say the list is incomplete, we wish to draw attention to a phenomenon discussed by Jefferson (1990) and explored elsewhere by Atkinson (1984), namely the 'orientation to three-partedness' in the construction of lists. It appears from analysis of listing in conversation and other contexts, notably political speech-making, that lists are preferably constructed with three items such that where only two may be mentioned the lister provides a third with a 'generalized list-completer'. These include phrases such as 'things like that', 'and stuff' and 'and so forth'. For L, on this occasion, she had managed to mention only two of her pains before S asks about their causes. Accordingly, in terms of an orientation to three-partedness, L can be heard to complete her list.

So, L completes the list of her pains whereupon S repeats her question, 'What's it from?'. This then receives an answer from L to the effect that they are 'From running'. S treats this explanation as incomplete; she questions L further to discover more (lines 17 and 19). To each query L produces only short, 'minimal' responses. However, eventually she explains that the pains in her legs are due to her chasing a boy called Liam (line 23). Whether L would have continued at this point to tell her story is difficult to say. However, we note that having described Liam as a 'freak' H enters and asks, 'How are you?'. In a sense, we find ourselves back with the original greeting from S that invited L to report on how her day had been. Again, as with the response to S's initial 'Y'right?', L replies by informing H about her pains. This can be heard to initiate a second question–answer sequence (lines 25 to 28), this time between H and L, on the topic of the pains.

At line 32, S then asks 'Have you had a nice day?'. This follows L's answer at line 28, a two and a half second pause at line 29, an indecipherable utterance from S at line 30 and another pause, this time of three and a half seconds. We take it, then, that S's question at line 32 marks S's analysis that the story about the pains initiated by the original 'Y'right?' is now concluded. L replies 'Yeah' then, after a pause, she begins to tell a story about events at school that form the background to her leg pains. We take it that her continuation of the story about the pains and their causes is in response to L's analysis that she still has the conversational floor to complete and that the topic initiation at 32 is not something she wishes to take up. Indeed, her 'Yeah' at 34, followed by the pause at 35 would seem to indicate this, and this is confirmed by her hearable continuation of her story, beginning with 'I said –' at 36.

L's story hearably finishes at line 56 when she says 'I go like "OK, fine" hahah.'. That it is completed at this point is acknowledged by S at line 57, with 'Mmm.'. We note that minimal utterances such as 'Uh huh' and 'Mmm' may be interjected and understood as 'continuers', whereupon those who produce them indicate to the storyteller their continued attention to the story and their disinterest in taking over the conversational floor themselves. In this case, the acknowledgement at line 57 is followed not by a continuation on L's part, but by a three and a half second pause. We suggest therefore that the 'Mmm' at line 57 marks recognition of the end of the story. This recognition is further consolidated by the initiation by S of a new topic at line 61, 'Can I get you a drink?'.

This 'homecoming' data is also interesting with reference to its categorial features. The making of an inquiry about the events of the day is a standard feature of homecoming situations. Members of a domestic unit conventionally greet their returning co-members with such a query, be these children returning to the family home or partners returning at the end of the working day. Such a query, then, is both category bound and context embedded. In other words, the activity is bound to the categories operative in domestic life, such as the standardized relational pairs, partner–partner and parent–child, but is also made relevant by the occasion of the homecoming. Such an inquiry is expectable and appropriate, such that its absence might be taken as indicative of a lack of interest in or care about a family member. Not only is it expectable in general, but this kind of query has a proper interaction location. It is something that should be done upon or soon after the persons arrival home. Standardly, inquiries about 'your day' to a homecoming family member are positioned immediately after greetings.

As argued earlier, our methodological strategy is to take note of observable features and then to ask how such features will have been produced. The production will involve the use of methodical procedures. In the data to hand, we note that S's inquiry about L leads on to a series of questions and answers in which L is repeatedly asked for further details about her pains and their origin. We take it that such questioning appears normal and natural; readers of the transcript will be unsurprised by S's recognizable concern for L's welfare/health. Why is it that such expressions of concern appear so normal and natural? In other words, this very familiarity of S's concern raises then the question of how it has been produced. We suggest that it has been produced under the auspices of her category membership as a parent. Just as in the previous chapter the mother in the story 'The baby cried …' unsurprisingly picked up her baby in response to its crying, so in our data it is a predicate of the category 'parent' to care for and to be concerned about the welfare of one's offspring. In announcing that she has a pain, L can be heard as providing a problem for her parent. As is exhibited in this data, it is predicate of a parent to take up and deal with such a problem.

To come at this slightly differently, if this homecoming were to have been told as a story it might anticipatedly consist of: a report that a daughter comes home and complains that she has pains; and the mother expresses concern and seeks to get to the bottom of the matter. In the same way as Sacks has noted in a story about a speeding motorist being arrested (Sacks, 1992a: 254), and in the news story that we analysed in Chapter 3 about the mugging, police and witnesses, so in this data we have the utter unremarkability of the mother's concern appearing on cue upon notification that her daughter is in pain.

In terms of the use of viewers' maxims for understanding, which we introduced in Chapter 3, the care and concern that S exhibits in relation to L permits the inference that she is L's parent. Furthermore, the persistent questioning of L by S is not heard as an interrogation, and thus as intrusive or oppressive, but rather as exhibiting parental care and concern to get to the bottom of the trouble. That it is heard in this benign fashion derives from the operation of the category pair 'parent–child' in the context of the reporting of a trouble by the child. Here, then S can be understood to be operating with reference to a norm of parent–child relations, that is, parents should care for their children and take on their troubles. Such care and concern can be seen as emerging naturally from the category relationship in which the parties stand.

Conclusion

In this chapter we have applied our three-step method for doing ethnomethodology to the phenomenon of ordinary conversation. Thus, we have first taken what is observably the case about the sequences of talk we have analysed. Second, we have asked how these observable features have been produced by the participants. Third, we have sought to describe some methods used by the participants in their production. What we have found in employing this approach is not simply that ordinary conversation is socially structured, but that it is methodically produced and managed in its course by conversational participants. In other words, sequential structures like those discussed above, for example adjacency pairs and expanded three- and four-part structures display participants' ongoing analysis of the talk as it unfolds. Such analysis is 'structural' analysis in the sense that it deals with what conversationists orient to with respect to the positioning of one conversational item relative to another. It is clear that such positioning is a normatively organized matter for conversationists. This does not mean that the norms govern mechanically what conversationists may do. Rather, it means that conversationists orient to the ordered relations between one conversational action and another. In producing their talk, then, they display their analysis of prior talk in terms of those orderly relations.

We should also point out that our materials not only exhibit members' orientations to the sequential organization of talk, they also reveal the close connection between the sequential and categorial organization of talk. Participants' turns at talk thus not only display their analyses of the form and content of prior turns, but they also exhibit speakers' orientations to the category membership of their co-conversationists. As we have seen, the distribution of conversational actions amongst speakers may reflect categorial relations in which they relevantly stand. In other words, talk may be both recipient designed and grounded in locally relevant categorial entitlements.

The sequences of talk that we have analysed in this chapter have all been taken from family life settings with which we confidently assume readers will have some degree of familiarity. The point is that one does not have to travel beyond the familiar and ordinary in order to conduct rigorous ethnomethodological sociology. One does not have to seek out special kinds of talk in order to appreciate the local production of social life. This has the advantage, from the point of view of the reader as a prospective ethnomethodological sociologist, that data can be collected relatively easily from everyday situations to which he or she has access. Aside from a good quality tape recorder, all that is required is that the data then be approached with the appropriate analytic sensibility that we have outlined.

Student activity

1   Record a few minutes of naturally occurring conversation in your own or someone else's home, for example, over the dinner table.
2   Identify some sequential structures used by the participants in the production of the conversation.
3   Consider whether there is a relationship between the conversational actions performed and the categorial identities of the speakers and how such a relationship is visible in the talk.

Further reading

J. Heritage (1984) *Garfinkel and Ethnomethodology*. Cambridge: Polity Press. Ch. 8.
G. Jefferson (1990) 'List Construction as a Task and Resource', in G. Psathas (ed.), *Interaction Competence*. Lanham, MD: University Press of America and International Institute for Ethnomethodology and Conversation Analysis.
M. Speier (1973) *How to Observe Face-to-Face Communication: A Sociological Introduction*. Pacific Palisades, CA: Goodyear.

Notes

1   For an introduction to conversation analysis, see Hutchby and Wooffitt (1998), Sharrock and Anderson (1986), Silverman (1998) and Ten Have (1999).
2   There are, of course, exceptions to this that we cannot explicate here. Thus, Sacks draws attention to 'interruptives' that may be legitimately done and to the

fact that laughter in conversation requires for its intelligibility that it be tied closely to laughable matter to which it is a response. The consequence is that 'overlap' is, in a sense, a normative requirement of laughter.

3   The transcription symbols used in the following transcript were developed by Gail Jefferson. For explication of the full range of such symbols, see Atkinson and Heritage (1984), Hutchby and Wooffitt (1998), Schenkein (1978) and Ten Have (1999).

5

Going Public

So far we have suggested that it can be fruitful to engage in armchair research by examining how one makes sense of newspaper headlines and the production of our reactions to television news stories. We then moved from our armchair and considered some instances of talk in everyday conversation within family settings. In both chapters we have followed the method set out in Chapter 2 to begin with what is ordinarily observable and recognizable and then to reflect upon the accomplishment involved in these observable and recognizable phenomena. We will now leave the home setting and venture forth into the street. As in Chapters 3 and 4, our procedure in this chapter is to start out with what is observably the case and then to ask how this is being produced.

Our purpose in focusing on activities observable in public settings such as the street is not to try to construct some overall account of such activities in general; rather, it is to look at specific instances of what may be observed in public settings and then to seek to account for how these particular occurrences are produced by the parties to them. There is little point in trying to account for activities in general if, in the process, one loses sight of the detail of activities and fails to account for the particular. It may well be the case that as a result of analysing single episodes we can build up generalized claims, but these have to be capable of being shown to be demonstrably operative at the level of local specifics to be considered adequate in terms of the principles of ethnomethodology.

Public settings are a useful location for doing ethnomethodology. The openness and accessibility of public settings means that they constitute a readily available research site – no special access or permission is required for one to study them. You can mingle with other members of society on the street and observe their activities. In what follows, then, we will consider a range of such activities and investigate the structures of interaction and the methods of production they involve. However, given our preference of working from data pertaining to specific instances of social activities, we are inevitably faced with the problem of obtaining usable data. In the previous chapters where we have been examining talk-in-interaction, usable data was relatively easily obtained in the form of transcriptions of recorded talk. Talk has the dual advantage of being easily recordable and also reproduceable on the printed page. As we turn to activities in public settings, we face the difficulty that many such activities are predominantly or even wholly non-verbal. How, then, are we to solve this problem with regard to social activities in the public domain?

Perhaps the ideal solution is to station oneself in a suitable location and use a video camera to capture public interaction on tape. However, we assume that access to expensive audio-visual equipment is likely to be beyond the reach of most beginning students in ethnomethodology. Furthermore, the student may well find that they run into ethical and practical difficulties in any attempt to covertly video-tape the activities of people whom they do not know in the public domain. Accordingly, we have chosen to begin with a much simpler method. This consists of an adaptation of our first method of analysis, that is, self-reflection which we used in Chapter 3. We have already made the point that every member of society is necessarily an observer of social life. Therefore the ethnomethodologist can legitimately employ his or her own observations of public activities as a form of usable data. Accordingly, we have chosen to tape-record our own participation in public life as our source of data. To generate such data this is what we did. One of the authors used a small audio tape-recorder with a microphone clipped to his shirt and recorded a running commentary on an ordinary activity that involved interaction in public settings. The activity in question consisted of a walk to his local supermarket to do some shopping. The rubric under which this commentary was conducted was to describe in detail what he observed and experienced as he walked along the street and shopped in the supermarket. The commentary, as reproduced below, is not continuous. We have marked the silent passages with dots; clearly there are things going on during these times (such as cars passing) but as there is no record of these they do not figure in the analysis. The commentary follows.

A walk to the supermarket

I'm going out the front door, putting my keys in the lock, shutting the front door, walking out the front door at the moment, hello hello hello hello, you're still with me ... So, here we go I'm walking down the path, the mic is in place, walking down the drive, cars are passing, and I'm walking along the path, there's Love Lane on my left, I'm going to the supermarket to buy some bananas ... I'm walking along this bit of the street, and just up here there's a junction and it's a bit of a, bit of a dodgy junction, there are cars coming towards me, and straight ahead, and sometimes coming around the corner to my right which makes it a slightly problematic crossing point so I normally cross the road here, look to my left there's nothing coming, nothing coming ahead so I cross over to the other side of the road so I avoid having to cross at the, the three-way junction really ... So, I've crossed over and I'm walking along this path, it's about three or four feet wide, cars are passing by ... Oh, there's the first pedestrian, I notice somebody walking on the opposite path, at the junction, a young woman in a denim jacket, actually I thought she might be one of Japanese students who seem to be around at the present time, visitors, but any way I'm walking along on the left and she's walking around thirty feet in front of me, in the same direction as me on the opposite side ... There's nobody else around. There's a car coming towards me on the other side of the road. It goes by, and a 'A' reg. Volvo is just coming out of one of the university car parks ... Just walking along, another car goes by, had a family in it ... Still walking and there's a couple of joggers just joined the path ahead of me, and the woman who was on my right and ahead of me is now some twenty, thirty feet behind me ... And now I've reached the main university buildings ... There's a couple there saying goodbye to one another, an older guy and a young student ... A couple of guys are walking towards me ... Just as they approach me they step off the pavement and into the car park and head across the car park, so I am able to continue as it were uninterrupted in my walk ... There's a couple of people off to my left in the car park walking towards the library, a young woman has just crossed over the road and joined my side of the path, and I glance up and she is just looking straight ahead, and now I have reached the one-way part of the street, and I am kind of looking down at the pavement, you get some dog shit here on the road here, on the pavement and I'm just looking at the pavement as I go, walking on the right side of the road now, I'm walking quite close to the wall ... up ahead of me [sounds of people talking] ... Well, up ahead of me just then there was a car parked on the pavement where it got wider and there was a couple of people, a man and woman, speaking to the driver, apparently saying goodbye. They didn't move out of my way, they didn't have to, the pavement is wide enough at that point for me to just walk past on the inside, closer to the wall and there's a good three foot gap for me to walk through so once again no collision, no interactional difficulties ... I continue walking down College Road which is deserted and up in front of me is the T-junction with Holyhead Road and that's likely to have rather more traffic, pedestrians and cars ... I can see a young man with shopping bag, he's probably been to the supermarket, he has just walked past the fish and chip shop which is open ... Now, as I come up to the newsagents on my right, telephone boxes just in front of me, I normally cross over at this point, I look, there's nothing coming, so I cross over the road by the Bellevue pub which is on my left, and it says 'Open at 7 p.m.' ... So, I'm now on Holyhead Road, there's cars, I can see a few pedestrians in the distance, there's a young woman, now, where's she going, OK, she didn't glance up at me, as she came towards me she looked up and kept to her left side of pavement and I kept to my left of the pavement and we walked by with no problem ... I just saw someone that I know, Harry, I thought I might say, have to say hello to him but in fact he's gone in the shop and there he is buying something, and I've just passed another young woman, again she passed on the left to her and I passed on the left to me, she looked as she passed me, I looked up and she was looking over at the newsagents on the opposite side of the road, where the owner was standing outside talking to somebody ... Now, I'm coming down the hill, there's three women on the other side of road, walking in the opposite direction to me, they appear to looking for something, as if they may be new to the area, this is, after all, the university term is about to begin, so there's a lot of new people in town and they have that sort of checking things out kind of look ... Up ahead of me, just coming out of the supermarket are two guys ... They take up a position on the right side of the pavement so I move over to the right, my right side of the pavement, in order to avoid any confusion there, so ... Now I am going down the stairs into the supermarket ... There's the café, people are sitting around and I'm walking along the side of the store here, the parking lot is on my right, couple of people are at the cash machines, there's a young woman striding ahead of me coming from the car park, going into the store I would say, other people are loading their shopping into their cars, there's a couple of assistants ... Anyway now I am going into the store ... There's a couple of people with shopping bags coming out ... Now I've got my shopping basket and I'm going to look for bananas, oh, there's somebody else at the banana counter, oh they have just gone away, now somebody else has just come ... What we need is a nice bunch of bananas, when you're looking for bananas you want something reasonably firm ... We know that this supermarket is not always that reliable, but they look OK so we'll get those, we'll get five, and we'll walk through the store, avoiding the old lady with the shopping trolley, to my left and walk through the aisles here, I'm going to go down past the milk along to bread and the thought occurs to me maybe I'll just ... ah, as I turned the corner there some guy was coming towards me with a basket and we more or less, we could have collided, and he stepped to his left and said 'Sorry' to me in a very quiet voice and then once again I met another person coming towards me but he likewise indicated where he was going to walk, that is to say he stepped to his left whilst I kept walking straight ahead ... Now I'm walking down this aisle and it's, I am going to have to step in between a woman with a basket and some people looking at lager ... As I approach, the person seems to be attentive to me and steps forward so I walk by unheeded ... So check-out time ... That one is pretty full, I only have two items so I could go probably, if I go up the end here, there doesn't seem to be anybody queuing, so with a bit of luck even though this is the re-scan point, it's the shortest queue ...

Me: Hi.
Cash: Four eighty five, please.
Me: One, two, three, four, five.
Cash: That's fifteen change.
Me: Thank you.

... So that little transaction's completed unproblematically, and I'm going out the store, there's an old guy with a cart in front of me, so it's going to be a bit difficult to get by him, so I'm going to slow my pace here and wait for him to go through the doors, which he does, turning right ... [recording interrupted for several seconds due to microphone falling off] ... I had to slow my pace for a bit until the pavement got wider and the old guy got out of my way and I was able to resume normal pace ... Now, as I come up the steps there is a guy about to come down the steps and he looks at me, I think, at what I am doing, as I come up the right side of the steps he instead of cutting into the steps by the shortest route goes over to right side of steps coming down in order not to collide with me, so I am now on my way back ... There's traffic, cars up ahead, somebody up ahead, with a shopping bag, they've been to the supermarket too, there's a rather smart looking black guy coming down the road, with a very vivid blue shirt and a big black briefcase, and as he goes past me, I stay on the right and he stays on what is right for him, by the kerb and we walk past, he's looking in the shops, past the Indian takeway ... There's a young woman with a child just in front of me ... I think she, as she comes past the tobacconist she just pulls him slightly to her right and there is plenty space for us to pass ... Up ahead there's a guy hanging around outside the barber shop next the pub, he looks like a worker, paint on his trousers, waiting, doing waiting, people are at the cash machine over the other side of the street, lots of people parked on the pavement around here, outside the shop people are parked I guess you could say illegally, there's a double yellow line there, but at the same time there's a kind of layby, so it's a bit of an ambiguous situation ... Now along the road in front of me the path is quite narrow, about two and a half feet and there is an old lady standing behind her front gate and there's a lady standing on the pavement speaking to her, so I'm going to approach but there's not really enough room ... Well, that was OK, the lady who was on the pavement standing, she didn't move at all as I approached and in fact I didn't have to step into the road in order to pass, there was probably about eighteen inches, I just I was able to walking on the kerb itself in order to get by ... Now the pavement comes to an end here so I have to cross over ... I look around to make sure there is nothing coming up behind me, cross of the road in a diagonal fashion and I'm back on the other side ... I look down Princes Road just to see if a friend of mine's car is there, to see if he's around ... Now, that was interesting because I got to a slightly narrower bit of the pavement, it's widened out again now, but probably a good six foot wide, and I was walking maybe a foot or two from the wall, a guy came along and as he passed me he gave me a wide berth as it were, he actually stepped into the road as he came towards me in order to walk past ... And now the pavement completely is empty ... On the other side of the road there's a man with his dog ... Now, somebody is walking up behind me, and probably has a bit of difficulty getting by on the inside, I'm aware of him coming up behind me so I just move to my right a little and he is in fact there ... but rather than come round me on the right side where there is plenty of room, he stays to my left and cuts through and goes up the path to a house ... Now, this is a road, College Road, with traffic calming ... Up ahead there's a car trying to get into the university car park by the exit route, the barrier is down, the barrier won't go up, so he has to reverse, he's in a Y-reg. Mercedes, he's going to try again, no the barrier won't rise for you, you clearly do not know the system here, I turn around and speak:

Me: You have to go in just down there.
Man: You do?
Me: Yeh.
Man: Down the end?
Me: Yeh, just past the telephone boxes.
Man: Thank you.
Me: This is the coming-out barrier.
Man: Right, thanks.

So, here we are walking down College Road ... Couple of guys on the right side strolling ... Well, I continue walking ... Oh well, over the road there looks what you'd probably say is a mother and a father and a young woman but could even be grandmother and grandfather and a young woman, somebody checking out the place, I don't look up as I walked by ... I think he looks over towards me as but he doesn't stare or anything, has a little look, a casual look, monitors that someone is coming along and then carries on talking to what could be his daughter or even his granddaughter ... So now I'm at that junction I mentioned at the beginning ... Now here because you can see clearly to left, the junction is not so tricky at all, and actually I don't look behind me, there could be something coming up behind me, but I just look to my left and I look straight ahead and there is nothing coming, and I don't hear anything, so I just carry on across the road and I get across the road ... And as I am walking along the last bit of pavement ... I hear somebody's footsteps and I look around and without taking them in fully I can see that there is somebody behind me and given the pace of their approach and the sound of their feet on the pavement, louder than would be the case with walking, I am able to see that it is in fact a jogger and as they come past it is indeed a guy with a black T-shirt on and shorts and jogging with a plastic bottle in his left hand and he comes past me on my right ... I in fact move as I know he is coming, I move over to the left in order to give him space to pass, he could have actually stayed on the pavement, there would have been room enough but he stepped into the road, to my right as he came past and once he got past me he got back onto the pavement and is now running into the distance and I can't see him anymore as I go into the driveway up to my house, my shopping trip concluded.

Even a casual reading of this commentary shows a number of things. First, there is a wide range of activities to be observed in the street and in the supermarket. Thus, drawing only on those reported in the above commentary, people can be observed walking, moving aside to allow others to pass by, crossing the road, running, talking to one another, saying goodbye, apologizing for getting in someone's way, looking in shop windows, using a cash machine, queuing, carrying their shopping home, waiting, driving cars and parking up. Given the extent of this collection of activities observed and observable, we clearly cannot focus on them all. Therefore in what follows we will pay particular attention to four topics. The first is walking, the second is the categorization of the people encountered, the third is forms of talk in public settings and the fourth is the activity of queuing.

Walking

As is clear from the commentary, one form of behaviour you are certain to witness in the street is walking. Walking is a routine and usually unproblematic activity that almost everyone engages in. What is more, it is something that we do without thinking about it, we simply take for granted the skills and competencies involved. One might think that such skills and competencies were simply physical ones, ones that we acquire in early childhood. However, as our commentary shows, walking is a socially organized activity, and as such it involves social skills and competencies as well as physical ones. As with talking, the methods used in accomplishing such an apparently mundane social activity as walking are taken for granted. One such basic skill is navigation: walking trajectories were selected, taking into account the presence and position of others in the street, pace was varied according to the pace of others in the vicinity and engagement in the activity was adjusted with reference to scenic details such as the conduct of other persons. Therefore even though persons do not speak to one another as they walk in the street, none the less they co-ordinate their activities in quite precise and methodical ways.

As our commentary shows, persons walking along the street have to navigate their way around others, both persons walking in the same direction as themselves and those who are coming in the opposite direction or at right angles. As users of the street, we know how to walk without colliding into other people. This is evident in several passages in the commentary. For example:

> Well, up ahead of me just then there was a car parked on the pavement where it got wider and there was a couple of people, a man and woman, speaking to the driver, apparently saying goodbye. They didn't move out of my way, they didn't have to, the pavement is wide enough at that point for me to just walk past on the inside, closer to the wall and there's a good three foot gap for me to walk through so once again no collision, no interactional difficulties …

> So, I'm now on Holyhead Road, there's cars, I can see a few pedestrians in the distance, there's a young woman, now, where's she going, OK, she didn't glance up at me, as she came towards me she looked up and kept to her left

side of pavement and I kept to my left of the pavement and we walked by with no problem …

As ethnomethodologists, we need to explicate the social competences involved in these successful navigations. For example, how do persons do 'looking where they are going'? That this is a learned ability is indicated by the fact that children cannot be relied upon to accomplish it successfully (how often do parents find the need to remind their children to 'mind where you are going'?). It is clear from the commentary that walking is a social skill that involves, among other things, monitoring other walkers to see how their walking trajectory compares with one's own, anticipating the possibility of collision and, if necessary, changing course to avoid this.

The commentary further suggests that persons walking toward one another do this navigating in a concerted way – each takes account of the other's path and that they mutually adjust their direction to ensure that they pass one another successfully. This kind of co-ordination typically is done without great difficulty – so long as one person indicates through the movement and alignment of their body that they are intending to pass on a particular side. The second walker will then re-align their movement to co-ordinate with the first, and passing is successfully achieved. But sometimes there is a problem, typically because both parties take up the 'first' slot simultaneously and both move in the same direction, thus creating a mutual collision path. When this occurs, remedial action has to be taken – one walker has to shift to the opposite trajectory. There are two instances of this in the commentary:

> I'm going to go down past the milk along to bread and the thought occurs to me maybe I'll just … Ah, as I turned the corner there some guy was coming towards me with a basket and we more or less, we could have collided, and he stepped to his left and said 'Sorry' to me in a very quiet voice and then once again I met another person coming towards me but he likewise indicated where he was going to walk, that is to say he stepped to his left whilst I kept walking straight ahead …

Although we do not have data to present on this, we assume that our readers are well aware that it can sometimes happen that walkers recognize the problem of possible collision and yet select trajectories that reproduce it! That is to say, they respond to it in the same instant, with the result that their remedial actions simply reproduce the problem. At this point, such persons may mark the mutually recognized problem with a nod or a smile with one perhaps indicating to the other to 'go first' in selecting their trajectory.

Another aspect of navigation concerns pace management. Our commentary contains materials relevant to this phenomenon. For example:

> … I'm going out the store, there's an old guy with a cart in front of me, so it's going to be a bit difficult to get by him, so I'm going to slow my pace here and

wait for him to go through the doors, which he does, turning right [recording interrupted for several seconds due to microphone falling off] … I had to slow my pace for a bit until the pavement got wider and the old guy got out of my way and I was able to resume normal pace …

As this extract suggests, persons adjust or manage their pace by taking into account the pace of others. This is not to say that just because others are walking fast or slow then we match their pace. Rather, we mean that routinely persons maintain a regular walking pace and that this is broadly similar to that of others'. However, occasionally the local circumstances are such that one's pace cannot be sustained. In the case at hand, the observer's pace could and would have been maintained even though the old man was walking noticeably slowly were it not for the fact that there was insufficient room for him to pass by without collision. Although much of the time persons walk at what is recognizably normal walking pace, some users of the street may move at a pace that is noticeably slow or fast relative to this. In such circumstances particular navigational problems may be created. We have seen above how the case of the slow old man occasioned a moderation of the commentator's pace. In the example that follows it is the commentator's normal pace that apparently creates a navigational problem for someone who is proceeding quickly. For example:

And as I am walking along the last bit of pavement … I hear somebody's footsteps and I look around and without taking them in fully I can see that there is somebody behind me and given the pace of their approach and the sound of their feet on the pavement, louder than would be the case with walking, I am able to see that it is in fact a jogger and as they come past it is indeed a guy with a black T-shirt on and shorts and jogging with a plastic bottle in his left hand and he comes past me on my right … I in fact move as I know he is coming, I move over to the left in order to give him space to pass, he could have actually stayed on the pavement, there would have been room enough but he stepped into the road, to my right as he came past and once he got past me he got back onto the pavement and is now running into the distance and I can't see him anymore …

One further aspect of navigation relates to the activity of walking together. There are two instances of this phenomenon in the commentary:

… A couple of guys are walking towards me … Just as they approach me they step off the pavement and into the car park and head across the car park, so I am able to continue as it were uninterrupted in my walk …

… Up ahead of me, just coming out of the supermarket are two guys … They take up a position on the right side of the pavement so I move over to the right, my right side of the pavement, in order to avoid any confusion there …

On the street one frequently sees people walking side-by-side and can recognize them as a unit. From the point of view of the members of the walking unit, walking like this involves concerted work; it requires the management of pace and interpersonal distance. As persons walk together they have to continually adjust their speed and direction of their walking so as to maintain the unit that they constitute. Though we can present no data on this, we suggest that it is easily observable that adults accomplish this work unprompted, but children walking with adults are often less collaborative and have to be reminded about what is required in walking together. In the manner in which they accomplish the concerted activity of walking together, multiples of persons make it available to others to see them as the social unit they comprise, such things as a couple, a parent with children, or a group of friends.

In constituting such a unit, persons still have to do the sorts of navigating work that was described above, but do this in a way that sustains the shared definition of themselves and others as a walking unit. In both of the instances from our commentary reproduced above, it was observed that the 'two guys' did not separate, rather they maintained their togetherness and stepped to their right 'as a unit'.

From the point of view of the walker approaching a walking unit, particular navigational problems may arise. Faced with such a unit of persons walking abreast, those approaching from the opposite direction have a choice of either walking through the group, thus splitting its unity, or diverting their path so as to walk around them. Sometimes, it may be the case that in order to avoid difficulties of mutual free passage, the group may divide into separate side-by-side walkers or indeed sub-units of the group if the group is larger than two persons. The arrangement of persons may shift to a line or file of persons, one behind the other, thereby freeing up more passing space. Occasionally, of course, on the other hand, if a group wishes to mark its occupancy of the pavement it may do so by noticeably refusing to walk in a file but arrange themselves side-by-side in such a way that it is difficult for oncomers to get around them without a very marked diversion. Since the alternative to this extreme diversion is to 'push through' the group, the interpersonal challenge that such an arrangement comprises is obvious to both parties. As Ryave and Schenkein (1974: 268) note:

> It is well known that maintaining a large group walking-together (and thereby forcing other walkers either to step aside or break the ranks of the approaching ensemble) is a classic street challenge.

It is notable that, faced with such an oncoming prospect, persons may choose to cross to the opposite pavement well before the approaching group comes into close range. That they do this is further evidence that persons monitor the street as an environment of walking trajectories, and do so not just in the short range, that is, the distance immediately in front of them, but also over a longer range. Persons can and do look ahead to see how the pavement is unfolding before them as a walking environment and can anticipate possible problems many yards ahead.

Returning to the extracts from our commentary, no such confrontational issues arose. Instead, the two-party walking unit in each case shifted its trajectory just as an individual walker typically does. Furthermore, in the encounter described in the second extract, there occurred a mutual shifting of trajectory between the observer and the two guys.

Categorization and co-presence

A further phenomenon that is made available by our commentary concerns the ways in which we make sense of the identities of those we encounter in public places. It is a readily observable feature of the street that persons, unless they are observably together, do not interact but go about their business in apparent isolation from one another. People walking in the street pass each other by with only the barest of glances necessary to avoid collision, and usually without even eye contact, and talk rarely occurs between persons who are not together. Our commentary confirms this at several points. For example:

> A young woman has just crossed over the road and joined my side of the path, and I glance up and she is just looking straight ahead, and now I have reached the one-way part of the street, and I am kind of looking down at the pavement, you get some dog shit here on the road here, on the pavement and I'm just looking at the pavement as I go, walking on the right side of the road now, I'm walking quite close to the wall …

> So, I'm now on Holyhead Road, there's cars, I can see a few pedestrians in the distance, there's a young woman, now, where's she going, OK, she didn't glance up at me, as she came towards me she looked up and kept to her left side of pavement and I kept to my left of the pavement and we walked by with no problem …

Goffman has drawn attention to the phenomenon of mutual non-engagement in public places with his concept 'civil inattention'. He notes that users of the street do not normally have the right to initiate interaction with 'just anyone'. Civil inattention, Goffman (1963: 84) says, occurs when:

> One gives to another enough visual notice to demonstrate that one appreciates that the other is present (and that one openly admits to having seen him), while at the next moment withdrawing one's attention from him so as to express that he does not constitute a target of special curiosity or design.

Put very simply, then, 'civil inattention' means that members of society are required to respect the privacy of others, even when they are co-present in a public place. Thus, for example, it is not acceptable to pay to others more than 'passing' attention; it is acceptable to glance at someone who passes you in the street but it is not acceptable to stare at them. A glance is different to a stare in that it does not carry the same interactional implications; by glancing at someone one is able to take in who they are and what they are doing while minimizing the risk that looking at someone carries of bringing about eye contact and the possibility of interaction. To further avoid this possibility, persons may be careful to time their glance at another, doing it while the other's gaze is not in their direction. This phenomenon was experienced by our observer in so far as he accomplished his glances so as not to establish eye contact with the approaching walkers whilst monitoring what they were doing.

Thus, one must not be misled by the term 'civil inattention' into thinking that persons are not doing anything when they disattend one another in public places. The concept is intended to draw attention to the fact that the avoidance of interactional contact is an accomplishment. Of course, in some circumstances avoiding what Goffman calls 'face engagement' is not easy. Such face engagement entails the risk of being understood as an invitation or a preliminary to social interaction with them.

Although we do not have data to present on this, avoidance of interactional contact is readily observable and clearly influences spatial arrangements in such settings as public transport vehicles, cafeteria, lifts and, as the following personal anecdote suggests, public beaches:

> One of the authors, on a recent family holiday, noted the orderly manner in which groups of persons assembled and arranged themselves on a large sandy beach. First, it was noticeable that the full depth of the beach was not used. Groups congregated in the third of the beach closest to the water's edge. Second, and more significantly in terms of our current theme, there appeared to be almost a geometric pattern to how groups located themselves *vis-à-vis* one another. The early groups to arrive located themselves at distance of roughly twenty metres apart. Each new group to arrive seemed to recognize the normative distance currently in operation. However, once all the twenty-meter spaces in the first third of the beach were occupied, people began to place themselves at points equidistant from existing groups, thereby establishing a new normative distance of approximately half the preceding one. As further groups arrived, they could be seen to orient to this new spatial norm.

A comparable phenomenon has been described with respect to observations made elsewhere, namely seating arrangements on public transport vehicles. Levine, Vinson and Wood (1973) observe that persons entering the vehicle will avoid sitting next to another passenger if at all possible. They describe (1973: 209–210) the ways in which persons locate a seat when entering a crowded subway train:

> … we were able to form some general conclusions about who sits next to whom. Newcomers usually look for seated people who appear self-contained, that is, who are sitting squarely in their seats and either directing their attention to newspapers or books or concealing any interest in their surroundings with blank faces. When choosing among different but equally uninvolved

riders, people tend to sit down next to others of the same sex. The least desirable people chosen as 'seatmates' seem to be older, shabbily dressed people and people apparently lacking in self-control, sprawled in their seats and looking as if they are not going anywhere.

Given the ubiquity of the norm of civil inattention one might imagine that persons in public places take no notice at all of others around them, but of course this is not the case. As we have just suggested, maintaining civil inattention requires a certain kind of awareness of and orientation to others. It means that persons have to be able to take in their immediate environment at a glance, without the need to study what is happening. Consider the fact that persons, as they go about their business in the street and other settings, do manage pretty well to see what is going on around them despite constraints of civil inattention. It is apparent that members of society can go about their business successfully using the street as a social environment. In other words, they can understand what is going on around them, who is in the street, what they are doing, why they are there and so on, without having to stare at or otherwise study other people.

Goffman's concept of civil inattention and the analyses that it affords illuminate some of the features of interaction in public places. However, Goffman's analysis goes no further than offering general characterizations of the interactional work involved. Furthermore, by accounting for non-engagement in terms of normative rule-following, his analysis displays the difficulties generally exhibited by accounts of this kind. Specifically, normative explanations fail to elucidate the methods by which persons recognize the situated relevance of such rules or norms. Thus, given that there are occasions when strangers can and do talk to one another in public places, how do members of society analyse their circumstances so as to find that disattention is the appropriate course of action here and now? Also, given ethnomethodology's interest in normative rules as 'members phenomena', one must be cautious about attributing such rules without clear evidence that they are demonstrably relevant for participants to a given situation. The difficulty lies in simply assuming that some observed pattern of conduct is the product of motivated compliance with a rule. For a rule to account for such a pattern it needs to be shown that the persons involved are actually oriented to it in producing their conduct. As we pointed out in Chapter 2, when discussing the methodological principle of demonstrable relevance, members' orientations must be visible in talk and action for them to be admissible as an ethnomethodological account. Unfortunately, Goffman's writings seldom provide the kind of detailed naturalistic data that would satisfy this requirement.

A further reservation we have about Goffman's concept of 'civil inattention' is that it presumes a simple categorial dichotomy as the prevailing relationship in public settings. In other words, persons are assumed to perceive others as either known (friends, acquaintances and so on) or unknown (strangers). This dichotomy fails to take account of the analytic work that persons do as users of the street and other public settings. The concept suggests that persons operate in a blanket fashion, governed by a rule that requires them to avoid and ignore everyone who could be defined as a stranger. This analysis does not take account of the detailed ways in which persons analyse the street and the multiplicity of categorial identifications of its occupants. We suggest that the street is better understood as a categorially organized environment, where the categories involved are far more numerous and complex than simply 'myself' and 'strangers'. Furthermore, the category 'stranger' is itself best understood as an occasioned category rather than a universal perception. The categorial identification of persons encountered in public settings is clear from several extracts in our commentary:

> Oh, there's the first pedestrian, I notice somebody walking on the opposite path, at the junction, a young woman in a denim jacket, actually I thought she might be one of Japanese students who seem to be around at the present time, visitors, but any way I'm walking along on the left and she's walking around thirty feet in front of me, in the same direction as me on the opposite side …

> … Still walking and there's a couple of joggers just joined the path ahead of me, and the woman who was on my right and ahead of me is now some twenty, thirty feet behind me … And now I've reached the main university buildings … There's a couple there saying goodbye to one another, an older guy and a young student … A couple of guys are walking towards me …

> … Now, I'm coming down the hill, there's three women on the other side of road, walking in the opposite direction to me, they appear to looking for something, as if they may be new to the area, this is, after all, the university term is about to begin, so there's a lot of new people in town and they have that sort of checking things out kind of look …

> Up ahead there's a guy hanging around outside the barber shop next the pub, he looks like a worker, paint on his trousers, waiting, doing waiting, people are at the cash machine over the other side of the street, lots of people parked on the pavement around here, outside the shop people are parked I guess you could say illegally, there's a double yellow line there, but at the same time there's a kind of layby, so it's a bit of an ambiguous situation …

Others are perceivable in a variety of ways, depending upon the circumstances at hand, such that they provide for occasions in which shared relevancies may provide occasions and be expressed through talk. It is to this topic that we turn to in the next section.

Talking with strangers

Despite the prevalence of civil inattention, it is observable that occasionally persons who are 'not together' do in fact speak to each other. In our commentary there is one instance of this:

... Now, this is a road, College Road, with traffic calming ... Up ahead there's a car trying to get into the university car park by the exit route, the barrier is down, the barrier won't go up, so he has to reverse, he's in a Y-reg. Mercedes, he's going to try again, no the barrier won't rise for you, you clearly do not know the system here, I turn around and speak:

Me: You have to go in just down there.
Man: You do?
Me: Yeh.
Man: Down the end?
Me: Yeh, just past the telephone boxes.
Man: Thank you.
Me: This is the coming-out barrier.
Man: Right, thanks.

In this case the talk was initiated by the observer because he could see that the driver of the car was unfamiliar with the car parking arrangement at the university and was attempting to enter the car park via the exit barrier. In other words, the driver was categorized by the observer as a person in need of help. It was this categorization that provided for the observer initiating interaction by offering advice.

In a discussion of talk between unacquainted persons, Sacks (1992b) notes that talk between strangers displays distinctive conversational features from talk between the acquainted. One notable difference is that talk between the unacquainted typically does not begin with an exchange of greetings. This can be seen in the above extract from our commentary. Whereas acquainted persons initiate conversation through a greetings exchange, such as 'Hi' – "Hi" or 'How are you?' – 'Fine, how are you?', persons who are unacquainted initiate talk in ways that have different implications for the projected course of the talk. As Sacks (1992b: 195) puts it:

A feature of 'stranger–stranger' interaction in the city apparently serves as a way to show that the initiator is specifically, while talking to the person he's talking to, not 'beginning a conversation' with him. And that is that techniques other than greetings are used to begin the thing. Those techniques consist of such a first utterance as solves the question of how come I'm talking to you; things like 'Excuse me, could you tell me where the subway entrance is?', 'Pardon me but do you have the time?' etc. Such a 'ticketed' first utterance is plainly a 'beginning', but is such a thing as when it has been returned to, the interaction will be, if not complete, completable with a 'thank you – you're welcome' exchange.

In contrast to talk that is initiated with a prospective greeting exchange, such as 'Hello ...', Sacks (1992b: 195–6) comments:

... these sorts, when they are done as a beginning, announce also what it will take to bring that interaction to a close. So that people who, if you say 'Hello' to them will ignore you, will answer, I take it, if you say 'Pardon me, could you tell me where the subway is?'.

Sacks' point here, then, is that the initiation of talk between unacquainted persons tends to begin in ways that make it possible for the parties to anticipate the projected termination of the conversation. The sequential implications of greetings exchanges are open-ended; they do not enable the participants to project the end of the talk. Once the greetings exchange is completed and a first topic introduced, the talk can potentially ramify into other topics and the conversation continue in non-anticipatable ways. In contrast, what Sacks calls 'ticketed' openings (and the exchange in our extract above contains such an opening) between the unacquainted involve a projectable completion to the conversation: the conversational 'ticket' only entitles the ticket holder to talk on the topic provided for by the ticket.

This analysis would seem to account for the brief and limited nature of the exchange, such as that contained in the commentary and others which we imagine the reader may easily observe, such as those involved in asking strangers for directions and asking for the time. Such interaction is done in ways which make it clear that the interaction has a specific boundary. For example, consider the format that is typically employed when someone seeks information or directions to a particular place or asks for the time. The format involves typically a direct question on the topic of interest, perhaps sometimes prefaced by an 'Excuse me'. Such a format is evident in the following examples. In the first a man is walking down the street and two young boys come towards him. As they approach, the following exchange occurs:

Boy: Have you got the time, please?
Man: Sure, ahh [looks at watch] it's twenty to five.
Boy: A'right.

In the second example, a man and woman are walking along the street, obviously together, when a car pulls up alongside them. The driver winds down his window and the following exchange takes place:

Driver: Excuse me, can you tell me how I can get to
             Smith Street?
Walker: Er, yeah, you got to turn round and go back down
             the way you came. Then it's the, er, third on
             the right.
Driver: OK, thanks.

In both cases, then, the initiator of the interaction does so by means of a question that states what it is they want to know, thereby displaying their reason for talking. At the same time their initiation projects the termination of the sequence.

Persons who are unacquainted with each each other have occasions to talk to each other besides seeking information. An additional take on talking to strangers is afforded by Sacks (1992b: 194), who says:

It is otherwise routinely nobody's business on the one hand and perhaps unsolvable on the other, what's on the mind of the person who's passing you. Furthermore, it's your business to not make it their business as to what's on your mind, e.g., by crying in the streets. Crying in the streets is not a thing that somebody's encountering somebody doing it can solve – except classificatorily, e.g., they can say it's some private problem – and it's something you shouldn't cause them to try to solve.

However, there are events that have a public character such that, within a given temporal frame, it is legitimate to assume that it will be on others' minds just as it is on one's own. Such mutually oriented public happenings provide legitimate grounds of conversational openings in which one may refer to the publicly available matter. Examples of such public events might be major sporting achievements or political events or major tragedies and disasters. Conversational openings exhibit in the way they are constructed, a trust that their recipient will know what one is talking about. Such openings also have a 'ticketed' character: by inquiring, for example, about the outcome of a public event or the fate of a public figure who has been the object of an assassination attempt, one projects the completion of the conversational exchange. Considerations such as these may help us to understand how it is that apparent strangers are willing to talk to one another in times of public tragedy or disaster. For example, one of the authors was returning from holiday abroad and on boarding a cross-channel ferry was approached by a woman he did not know. The following exchange took place:

Woman: Isn't is awful!
Man: What?
Woman: Haven't you heard the news?
Man: No, what's happened?
Woman: Princess Di's been in a car crash and she's been killed.
Man: Oh, that's terrible.

It is notable that this exchange does not begin with a greeting and is therefore not an 'open-ended' beginning. Rather, in describing something as 'awful' the initiator indicates to the recipient the projected shape of the interaction. The point of the interaction is to note and share a response to the awful event that has occurred. Sacks (1992b: 197) notes that such exchanges provide a means by which camaraderie can be expressed in relation to public tragedies and disasters. As he puts it:

> In any event, my main point is that the reported type of beginning, such as 'How is he?' with its structural character of requiring some other, in particular a stranger, to know what in the hell you are talking about, and with its feature of not making them have to figure out what kind of interaction they're getting into – as with the 'Hello' beginning – is not an incidental sort of way to begin

such conversations, and that how these conversations begin is part of the solution to the problem of how it is that camaraderie develops in the cities during disasters. So the lesson is, if we want an answer to the question 'How does camaraderie develop in the cities during times of disaster?' then the organisation of conversation is relevant to an answer.

Thus, like asking for directions or finding out the time, a public disaster provides a topic for conversation with an understood boundary. Talking to strangers, then, is an occasioned matter which is both categorially organized and displays an orientation to sequential organization of talk.

Queuing

We conclude this chapter with a consideration of one activity commonly observable in public settings; queuing. In the commentary there is an example of this phenomenon:

> So check-out time … That one is pretty full, I only have two items so I could go probably, if I go up the end here, there doesn't seem to be anybody queuing, so with a bit of luck even though this is the re-scan point, it's the shortest queue …

Me:	Hi.
Cash:	Four eighty five, please.
Me:	One, two, three, four, five.
Cash:	That's fifteen change.
Me:	Thank you.

In this extract the observer has completed his shopping and approaches the supermarket check-outs. He scans the row of check-out counters and sees that some have several people with loaded trolleys. He moves along the row seeking the check-out with fewest people at it. He selects a particular check-out queue because it appears to be the one with the shortest queue. Although our observer does not comment in detail upon his queuing experience, as ethnomethodological sociologists we can pose the question 'What interactional competencies are involved in the activity of queuing?' For one thing, the physical arrangement of persons in the queue makes the orderly character of the queue visible, both to those in it and to others. Thus persons in the queue, and others not in it (but perhaps intending to join it), can see the length of the queue by looking at the number of persons arranged in it. They can also see where in the order-that-is-the-queue any given individual is located, simply by looking at the position of that person *vis-à-vis* others. In other words, the queue has – or, better, is – a social organization. This organization is based on the 'first come, first served' rule, but also on the rule of 'one at a time'. This latter rule gives the queue an 'ordinal' organization; each place in the queue can be occupied by only one person (or party). However, the queue as a social organization is not constituted simply by these rules operating 'automatically'. There is more to a queue than simply these rules in themselves, since persons create the queue by the situated ways in which they operate the rules.

To consider the methods involved in the accomplishment of queuing we will draw upon two ethnomethodological studies of this phenomenon, Livingston (1987) and Lee and Watson (1988). Livingston considers how a queue is produced and sustained by those within it. In other words, to describe how a queue is accomplished, we need to consider how persons 'make the queue happen' by using the rules. One way in which the rules are used is to notice and respond to 'deviant' queue behaviour. One form this can take is where a 'gap' is created by someone not moving forward appropriately. Livingston (1987: 13) describes what can happen in such a case:

> At one time or another we have all been in a queue where the person in front of us did not move up properly, but maintained too large a distance between herself and the person in front of her. ... All of our gestures and movements – our shuffling in place, impatient gestures, our peering around her – while performing the queue-relevant task of exhibiting the queue specific disorderly behaviour of the person in front (and, therein, the queue's proper orderlinesses) are generally useless in bringing about compliance.

The first thing to notice here is that the rules of queuing provide not just for certain kinds of deviant behaviour, but also establish who has the right (indeed, the responsibility) to undertake remedial action to restore proper order. Not only is it clear who has behaved in a deviant fashion to create the 'disorderliness' of the gap in the queue, it is also clear who should take 'sanctioning' action to prompt the deviant to comply. The orderliness of the queue itself allocates the role of 'control agent' to a specific person (in the first instance). This person, of course, is the one who is standing immediately behind the person who has not moved up. She has the right (duty) to take action if the deviant does not do so herself.

This raises a second point, however. Why, in a case like this, are we (the person behind the 'gap creator') reluctant to ask the person to move up – preferring to use indirect means (shuffling, grimacing, peering and so on) to remedy the situation and only resorting to an explicit request when these methods fail? Indeed, our first strategy often is to do nothing, hoping that the gap creator will recognize and spontaneously remedy the situation by moving forward of their own accord. If queuing rules give us the 'sanctioning' role, why are we so tardy about exercising it? The answer lies in the fact that the queue is a self-managed organization. We take it that the persons making up the queue are competent queue members: they know how to queue just as we do ourselves. Thus we can take it that the person in front is capable of recognizing that a gap has appeared, and that the reason for this gap is their own failure to move forward. That they have not moved forward appropriately could simply be due to the fact that they have not noticed the movement of the queue in front of them. After all, standing in a queue is pretty boring and it is expectable that someone's attention might have wandered momentarily – we know this is possible because it happens to us. So we give the deviant the benefit of the doubt – rather than rushing into sanctioning behaviour we allow her some time to put things right.

But how much time should we give her? How do we know when sufficient time for spontaneous remedial action has been granted, so that we now are entitled to initiate some sanctioning behaviour? Also, what sorts of sanctioning behaviour should we produce? Should we try indirect methods like those described by Livingston, or should we move straight to an explicit request? Clearly, the rules of queuing are of little use to us here – they tell us broadly what to do, but they do not tell us how or when to do it. We have to solve these matters for ourselves, and we do so by orienting to the particular circumstances of the occasion. For example, much may depend on what we can see as the cause of the person in front's failure to move up. If the person has been distracted then we may see that it is proper to wait for the distraction to cease. But, even here, there are different kinds of distractions with different moral import – the issue is whether the persons has the *right* to be distracted by what they are doing. Thus, if the distraction is a mobile phone call and the person is too busy talking on the phone to notice that the queue has moved up, we would perhaps treat this differently than, say, if the person has dropped something on the ground and is collecting it up, or is a parent dealing with a fractious child.

The key point here is that persons in a queue are required to attend to the orderly character of the queue, and to do what is required to maintain that orderliness. Another way of putting this is to say that the queue is a social object that is 'participant produced' and that persons are required to orient to its participant produced order as indicating and displaying what they should do as a member of the queue. In an earlier chapter we introduced the notion of membership categorization devices as collections of identities which go together in occasioned ways to constitute a social scene or event. The queue can be seen as just such a device consisting, at the minimum, of at least two membership categories: 'head of the queue' (or 'first in line') and 'tail of the queue' (or 'last in line'). Like 'family' and 'sports team', the queue is a 'duplicatively organized' device: there is a minimally adequate set of categories with differing rights and identities. Thus the person who occupies the category 'head of the queue' has different obligations as a member of the queue than the person who is last in line. The former, but not the latter, has to attend to the state of the service transaction, so as to recognize when it is complete and she can vacate the category 'first in line' and move to occupying the category of 'currently served'.

So far we have been discussing formal or 'line' queues, such as are typically generated in organizational settings by a set of established arrangements to manage the provision of a service to members of the public. However, there are other situations in which queuing is less formalized than in service organization settings. In these situations the order that is the queue is more occasioned and spontaneous, and it is not always easy to see a one-by-one line. It looks as though persons are simply a milling crowd, yet when the time comes for these persons to do what they are waiting to do, they then transform themselves spontaneously into a definite order. We cannot use our commentary to consider this topic but we can turn to a study by Lee and Watson (1988) of passenger behaviour on a railway station platform that addresses this form of queuing.

Lee and Watson, using video-tape of a Paris Metro station platform, observed that persons standing on the platform do not form themselves into a queue in advance of the train's arrival in the station; they simply disperse themselves fairly randomly along the platform. Sometimes, such as when the platform is particularly crowded, early-comers will establish themselves nearer the platform edge with late-comers further back. As the train comes to a halt, the dispersed crowd forms into 'clumps' at the points at which the train doors stop. These clumps have the character of spontaneously formed queues; persons who get nearest to the doors as the train comes to a halt are thereby at the 'front' of the queue, while those behind them are at the 'back'. But there is no clearly discernable one-by-one order; 'front of the queue' is a category occupied by several or many persons at this point. Also, allocation of persons to first or second positions (or, better, 'ranks') is largely contingent, determined by the physical fact of where the doors happen to stop. It is also noticeable that the persons at the front of the queue do not move to stand directly in front of the doors. The position they take shows their orientation to the rule that alighting from the train takes precedence over boarding; they stand a little distance back from the doors so that persons leaving the train are not confronted with a 'wall of humanity' as the doors open.

Let us now return to our question. If there is no formal line on the platform, how is the actual order of boarding determined? For it is an observable fact that persons do board the train in an order – the doors are only wide enough to allow one or, at the most, two persons to board at a time. How, then, does the milling crowd on the platform become a one-(or two)-at-a-time line through the doors? As the above has already implied, this transformation does not happen all at once, but in stages. First, as the train draws in and comes to a stop, the crowd becomes a set of strategically placed clumps, each of which consist in discernable ranks of persons. Second, when the doors open and the alighting passengers have got off, the boarders move forward and their ranks are transformed into a one-at-a-time boarding order. But how, specifically, does this happen?

Lee and Watson emphasize that it is important to keep two points in mind. The first is that the boarding order is an 'in-situ accomplishment'; whatever the actual order is by which the crowd of would-be passengers board the train, that order is accomplished there and then in the action of boarding itself. That is to say, persons (somehow) manage to bring off the activity of boarding as an orderly collective activity in the course of doing it. They do not, for example, engage in any prior collective action of planning or agreement – they do not decide on the boarding order and then enact it. They simply perform the activity in such way that a definite boarding order is achieved. The second point in accomplishing this order (typically) is unproblematic and untroublesome; it usually happens in a quite smooth and co-operative way.

So what are the means by which this activity is done? Lee and Watson propose that the key to describing the methodical accomplishment of boarding order and other kinds of spontaneous queuing is what they call the 'queue constructional unit'. The minimal form of this unit consists in two persons, one of whom occupies the queue identity of 'first person' *vis-à-vis* the other (who thus, conversely, occupies the position 'second'). Thus the minimal queue constructional unit is a two-person unit, made up of a first person and a second person. The boarding order is accomplished through the 'chaining' of such minimal units; that is to say, at any given point in the process of boarding, someone who is 'second person' to the person in front of her is at the same time 'first person' to the person behind her. Therefore, accounting for the overall process of boarding order means accounting for how chained two-person units are constructed. Any two persons achieve a minimal unit in and through the ways in which they negotiate the taking and/or offering of first person position. By the way in which he or she physically positions him- or herself in relation to another or others immediately around him or her, a person makes it clear to those others which person they are 'going second' to and also to which person they are 'being first'. This process of negotiation is largely non-verbal; the communication of position is not done in words but by specific body movements and gestures (though, exceptionally, verbal expressions may also be used, for example 'After you').

Conclusion

In this chapter we have considered a variety of activities that are observable in public settings. We have noted the methodological difficulties that are involved in doing ethnomethodological sociology of such settings. We suggested that one solution to such problems is to make use of the method of self-monitoring and self-description. This method has the advantages both of being readily usable and non-intrusive and providing access to subjective experience of activities in public settings. Of course, it has the disadvantage of not being capable of capturing the kind of behavioural detail possible through the use of video-tape. The methodological difficulties of investigating non-verbal conduct in public settings may account for the relative underdevelopment of this field of inquiry in ethnomethodological sociology. However, we have tried to show that such inquiry is possible without sophisticated technology, and can produce interested and valuable findings.

Student activity

1 Locate a public setting in which queuing is being done. Observe the queue from the 'outside' and write a detailed description of the queue and its members.
2 Become a member of the queue and through observation and self-reflection identify the orientations of the queue members through which the queue is realized and managed.

Further reading

E. Livingston (1987) *Making Sense of Ethnomethodology*. London: Routledge and Kegan Paul. Chs. 4, 6 and 7.

G. Psathas (1991) 'The structure of direction-giving in interaction', in D. Boden and D. Zimmerman (eds), *Talk and Social Structure*. Cambridge: Polity Press.

A. R. Ryave and J. Schenkein (1974) 'Notes on the art of walking', in R. Turner (ed.), *Ethnomethodology*. Harmondsworth: Penguin.

D. Sudnow (1972) 'Temporal parameters of interpersonal observation', in D. Sudnow (ed.), *Studies in Social Interaction*. New York, NY: The Free Press.

6

Using Talk to Get Help

In Chapter 4 we discussed conversation, and in particular how conversationists produce and manage the sequential, turn-by-turn character of conversation in methodical ways. We showed that the turn-taking organization of conversation is a product of the situated work of conversational participants. We now turn to consider some of the things that people do through conversation; broadly, the issue to be raised is how social tasks are accomplished in and through talk. Ordinary conversation – that is, conversation that is purely sociable – can be contrasted with talk in which persons are engaged in the performance of a social task. In Chapter 1 we noted how different ordinary conversation is from forms of 'ritual' talk, such as a wedding service or a university graduation ceremony. Whereas the latter occasions involve preset utterances in a fixed order and a predetermined order of speakers, ordinary conversation is notable for the fact that neither the length and content of utterances nor the order of speakers is fixed in advance. We have seen that this does not mean that such things as turn type, turn size and turn order in ordinary conversation are random and disorganized. Rather, the orderliness of these features is methodically produced 'from within' by conversationalists, in and as the ongoing course of their conversation. The overall shape of an ordinary conversation, therefore, is an emergent and unpredictable product of its utterance-by-utterance production. While conversational talk displays structural order at the utterance-by-utterance level, some aspects of which we have discussed in Chapter 4, there is no common pattern to the overall character of ordinary conversations in terms of such things as the number of utterances, the distribution of utterance types and the order of speakers.

When we turn to 'task talk' of various kinds, however, we can notice that such talk appears to display a greater degree of predictability in these respects. This is especially so where persons are talking together not simply as conversationists, but as occupants of specific institutional identities. Conversation analysts have coined the term 'institutional talk' to refer to such talk. Examples of such talk include news interviews, job interviews, police interrogations, doctor–patient consultations and teacher–pupil interaction in classrooms. Conversation analysts note that in such settings as these many of the conversational features that are open to emergent utterance-by-utterance ordering in ordinary conversation are more pre-structured.

In this chapter we consider the social activity of 'getting help'. We will not be concerned primarily with how persons obtain help or advice from friends or family, though this is a quite legitimate topic of inquiry for ethnomethodology. Rather, we will focus upon what is involved in obtaining help from persons who have some institutional role or responsibility for providing help of some kind. Since the main means by which persons in our society can seek help from official agencies is via the telephone, the data we will be discussing consists in telephone conversations concerned with getting help. It is an increasingly common feature of our society that members of the public can seek help and advice over the telephone from help-lines and other agencies. Conventional sociologists have noted how technologically mediated communication has not only supplemented but, in many cases, replaced face-to-face social interaction. As ethnomethodologists we have no interest in theorizing this transformation in terms of generalizations about the nature of modern society. What we are interested in, as the reader will by now be aware, is the question how such interactions are accomplished. Furthermore, whatever the significance of this social change, the important point for us is that it provides an increasing range of opportunities for the investigation of the interactional organization of seeking help and advice. We are confident that the student of ethnomethodology will already have some familiarity with such an activity, whether it involves calling a child or student help-line, transport timetable inquiries, citizen's advice bureau, a high street bank call centre, an emergency service or other such agencies.

In contrast to previous chapters, our discussion in this chapter does not draw upon data that we have gathered ourselves. Rather, we will discuss some classic ethnomethodological studies relating to, first, calls to a suicide prevention centre, and second, calls to emergency services such as the police. With respect to the first of these, our discussion will primarily be concerned with categorical issues pertaining to the accountability of the call and the need for help. With respect to the second set of studies, the focus will be upon the sequential organization of the calls.

Suicide: no one to turn to

Getting help is a socially organized activity in several respects. One of these concerns the fact that persons who feel themselves to be in need of help may be aware that not just anyone can be approached. Though they might not put it in these terms, such persons know that there is a normative relationship between the nature of their problem and the sorts of persons who can properly be consulted. Therefore an issue for such a person can be that not simply do they have a problem requiring help, but whether there is any-one available to them who fits the moral requirements of a person from whom help can legitimately be sought. We can think of this decision prob-lem as involving a kind of 'search'. The search for help, as it was labelled by Harvey Sacks in a classic study (Sacks, 1967), is membership category orga-nized. We outlined the concept of membership categorization devices in Chapter 3 and explained their used in common-sense understanding. In the present context, to say that the 'search for help' is categorially organized is to say that it consists in a search of the membership categories that com-prise proper persons to ask for help, to see whether these categories are occupied by persons who are available to be approached. If the person finds that the set of categories that comprise 'proper persons from whom to seek help' is unoccupied, she may conclude, and may *properly* conclude, that she has 'no-one to turn to'.

Sacks' study concerned telephone calls to a suicide prevention centre. A consistent feature of the calls was the way that callers would explain their suicidal feelings. Central to these feelings was the fact that they felt alone, with no-one they could approach about their troubled state of mind. Callers frequently would say that calling the suicide prevention centre was a last resort, something they had been driven to do because they had no-one else to turn to. The counsellor typically would question the caller on this, getting her to explain why and how she had come to this perception. In so doing the counsellor would inquire about specific membership categories (for example, 'Are you married?' 'Have you spoken to your parents?', 'Do you have any close friends you could talk to?') or about the state of the individual's set of 'persons to turn to'. In reply, callers would explain how the set of categories were effectively 'empty', that is, how it was that the persons in them were unavailable to be approached for help.

Example 1
Counsellor: You don't have anyone to turn to?
Caller: No.
Counsellor: No relatives, friends?
Caller: No.

Example 2
Counsellor: Uh, tell me. Is there, uh, is there any-one close to you, friend or family and so forth, that you could, uh, kind of be in contact with over this evening to kind of help you over the hump?
Caller: If I had someone like that I'd probably never b— never got to this point.

Example 3

Counsellor:	What about your parents?
Caller:	I can't tell them. I'd rather kill myself than tell them.
Counsellor:	You can't tell them what?
Caller:	Anything.
Counsellor:	Not even that you're suffering and need to be in a hospital?
Caller:	No.

Thus both the counsellor and the caller recognized the incumbents of these categories as members of the set of persons to whom, in principle, it would be proper to turn to for help. In justifying their claim that they had no-one to turn to, callers would explain how it was that persons in these member-ship categories could not be approached. It is notable that in some instances the counselor would not simply accept these explanations as facts, but would quiz the caller about them and often suggest a different interpreta-tion of the caller's situation *vis-à-vis* others. In other words, the counsellor would question whether 'no-one to turn to' was a correct version of the caller's situation. Although the counsellor has no personal knowledge of the individuals concerned and no other information about them than what the caller has provided, she is able to assess the caller's account and come up with a candidate alternative versions of the caller's relationship with specific category incumbents. In proffering such versions, the counsellor invokes common-sense knowledge of category relations, what 'anyone knows' about how given categories of persons may act or feel towards specific others.

Example 4

Counsellor:	Now, you have your boyfriend. I think he is entitled to be let in on what's going on.
Caller:	Well, he's never had a problem himself in his life. I don't know. I just don't want to tell him about it. I know he's real kind, but I haven't gone with him that long. I've just been going with him for two months. Before that I went with someone for two years.
Counsellor:	What happened to him?
Caller:	He was afraid of problems.
Counsellor:	I see. So you're afraid you'll scare this fellow away?
Caller:	Yes.
Counsellor:	But if he does care about you at all, I think he would want to share your trou-bles, you know at least be a listener, because you – let me tell you something about what I think is going on with you …

A further thing that is apparent in the talk between callers and suicide counsellors was that there was an issue about 'embarrassment' on the part of the caller. This sense of embarrassment manifested itself in various ways, one being a quite frequent reluctance on the part of callers to give their name and/or address, and another being a felt need to justify why they should be calling up the suicide prevention centre about their troubles. When quizzed by the counsellor about why she was embarrassed and concerned to justify making the call, a caller would explain by saying that she did not feel comfortable about seeking help from strangers. In other words, the suicide centre counsellor was perceived as outside the set of 'persons to turn to', and the fact that the caller had resorted to contacting someone outside the set was a matter of embarrassment.

Example 5

Caller: Maybe it was a mistake to call. I don't know. But I mean …

Counsellor: Why do you think it might be?

Caller: Well, you know, it seems to reach out for help to strangers is, I don't know. It seems to be very – like I shouldn't do it. Like my family and friends don't help me, I mean why should I go to a stranger for help, you know?

Counsellor: Sometimes you need professional help.

Example 6

Counsellor: Let me ask you another thing. We're very interested here. We get calls from people who are often very reluctant to give their names or just don't. Why is that? What problems prevent you or what makes you hesitate?

Caller: Well. One feels like such a goddam fool you know?

Counsellor: Why?

Caller: I'm well over 21, and I should – you know – if I had a sister or a brother or a husband or somebody to talk to, I'd talk to that person. But I feel like such an idiot when you have to call up a stranger and say 'will you please let me talk to you'.

We have so far summarized the data on which Sacks based his study of 'the search for help', but what of his analysis of these data? As noted above, Sacks proposes that the search for help is a category-organized search; it is a search of certain categories in a collection. The general collection that is relevant to the search for help he calls 'Collection R'. R is the collection of membership category devices whose structure Sacks describes as 'standardized relational pairs'. We outlined the features of these category devices in Chapter 3, so will not detail them in full again here. Suffice to say that with reference to suicidalness a standardized relational pair device is one in which the two categories making up the device are mutually defining and linked in a way that involves mutual rights and obligations concerning the activity of giving help. Thus such devices comprise a structure of common-sense knowledge that members of society routinely employ in making decisions concerning help with personal problems such as suicidalness. In this regard, the collection R can be sub-divided into Rp – those pair relations in terms of which the seeking and giving of help are known to be appropriate – and Ri – those for which the seeking and giving of help is known to be inappropriate. Examples of Rp pairs are: husband–wife, partner–partner, brother–sister, parent–child, friend–friend, neighbour–neighbour and colleague–colleague. The collection Ri has one principal member: the category pair stranger–stranger.

In the telephone calls to the suicide prevention centre, Sacks noted that workers receiving the calls, presented with the 'I have no-one to turn to' account for the call, invariably would make reference to person categories drawn from Rp to see whether the caller was indeed correct in their judgement of their interpersonal condition. Correspondingly, callers would respond to, or even anticipate, such queries by providing details of the non-availability of persons in the requisite categories, thus confirming to themselves and the suicide prevention centre worker that they indeed had no-one to turn to. Furthermore, Sacks notes that it is not just the case that a person experiencing suicidal or deeply troubled feelings *can* engage in a search for help by reviewing their Rp set of relationships, but that such a person *should* do so. In making this search the person is required to attend to the rights he has towards others by virtue of standing in an Rp relationship with them. Thus, as we have seen, much of the talk between caller and counsellor involved discussion of whether the caller had adequate grounds for her conclusion that she had no-one to turn to, that is, whether the circumstances justified treating the occupants of a given Rp pair as 'unavailable'.

The sense of embarrassment manifested by callers to the suicide prevention centre is a product of the fact that they find themselves in the position of approaching a perceived member of their Ri set. In so far as they categorize the counsellor as a stranger, this categorization makes the counsellor someone they do not have the right to consult about their suicidal feelings. Faced with this interactional difficulty, counsellors respond by attempting to get the caller to accept a different category relationship as the relevantly applicable one, one which makes the call a correct and appropriate action. As can be seen in Example 5, this relationship is professional–client, a key member of the set that Sacks calls 'Collection K'. This collection consists of relationships involving a distribution of knowledge (hence 'K'), and includes such pairs as expert–novice and qualified practitioner–unqualified practitioner.

From the standpoint of this collection, then, rather than being reluctant and embarrassed about calling, the caller should recognize that she has done the right thing, since by calling the suicide prevention centre she has placed her problem at the feet of professionals who possess expert knowledge of such problems. If the counsellor can get the caller to accept this re-categorization, then interactional difficulties such as reluctance to give a name will be eased. Moreover, as professional to client, the counsellor can legitimately advise the caller and expect that her suggestions may be acted upon.

Calling the police

As calls to suicide counselling lines illustrate, a general feature of 'getting help' interaction is that it involves not simply a request for help by the person calling, but also an assessment of the 'trouble' by the party who is called. Inviting the caller to describe her search for help is one way in which the suicide counsellor can come to an assessment of the nature and depth of the callers' problems. For example, the account the caller provides of her search for help can provide the counsellor with materials for deciding whether the caller is at risk of suicide or not. Such 'requestee–assessment' is a ubiquitous feature of requests for help. The mere fact that a party is approached for help does not mean that they will give it; how such a party responds to a request for help will depend on several issues. These include the nature and seriousness of the trouble, the ability of the caller to specify what kind of help is required, and the relevance of the called party as a source of help or remedy.

In this section we consider these issues with reference to calls for assistance to the police and other emergency services. In developed societies, citizens have the right to call for official assistance for a wide variety of urgent problems and troubles. Also, in such societies there are services dedicated to providing such assistance rapidly and effectively. Mobilizing such assistance is usually done by telephoning a dedicated emergency number (999 in the UK, 911 in the US), which is manned on a 24-hour basis. Let us begin by considering an example of such a call (data taken from Whalen and Zimmerman, 1987: 173).

Example 7
```
D = Dispatcher, C = Caller
D:  Mid-City Emergency.
C:  Um, yeah, somebody jus' vandalized my car.
D:  What's your address?
C:  Thirty-three twenty-two: Elm.
D:  Is this uh house or an apartment?
C:  Ih tst uh house.
D:  Uh - your las' name?
```

```
C: Minsky.
D: How you spell it?
C: M-I-N-S-K-Y.
D: Wull sen' someone out to see you.
C: Than' you.
D: Umhm, 'bye.
C: 'Bye.
```

We noted at the beginning of this chapter that task talk tends to display a more predictable sequential character than ordinary conversation, in terms of such things as the number of turns, turn types and turn distribution. In the example presented, one can note not simply that the call is relatively brief, amounting to just 14 utterances, but that all the necessary information required to enable emergency assistance to be dispatched is conveyed. Furthermore, the manner in which this interactional task is accomplished seems to comprise a definite interactional structure. Indeed, according to Whalen and Zimmerman (1990), such a structure is a widely prevalent feature of the organization of emergency calls. They propose that the structure is comprised of five components: an opening/identification/acknowledgement; a request; an interrogative series; a response; and a closing. Thus the call presented above begins with an identification ('Mid-City Emergency') and acknowledgement sequence ('Um, yeah'), followed by what can be heard as a request for assistance, taking the form of a report of a trouble ('Somebody jus' vandalized my car'). There then follows an interrogative series, in which the dispatcher asks the caller for his address and name, after which the official response is given and a closing sequence terminates the call.

If we compare emergency calls with ordinary telephone calls, then, it is clear that emergency calls have some characteristically distinctive features. It is not simply the fact that emergency calls are on the whole both more brief and more mono-topical and businesslike than ordinary calls. Rather, the point that Whalen and Zimmerman are making is that they display quite different structural properties. This can be demonstrated by considering the opening of emergency calls. Such openings tend to be more sequentially compact than openings of ordinary telephone calls. Thus ordinary telephone calls involve opening sequences which are made up of certain standardized interactional components: an identification/recognition exchange, a greeting exchange and a 'how are you' exchange. Thus opening sequences in ordinary calls can be quite extended, typically stretching over six, eight or even more utterances. They normally lead into, and conclude with, the introduction of, the reason for the call. At this point the participants move out of the opening sequence and into the body of the call. By contrast, opening sequences in emergency calls are typically very brief, often amounting to just two utterances. As we have already indicated, the 'prototypical' pattern consists of an official identification by the 'dispatcher' (the official who mans the emergency line) followed by a statement of the request for assistance by the caller. Consequently, by the third utterance slot, the 'business' of the call is established as the topic of the talk. This pattern can be illustrated as follows (data taken from Sharrock and Turner, 1978: 176):

Example 8
```
D: Newton Police.
C: Yes, I'd like to repar- report a car stolen.
```

In other words, emergency calls differ from ordinary calls in that the business of the call tends to be reached much more rapidly. This is hardly surprising, you might think, given that the emergency number is a dedicated line for persons in need of emergency assistance. Assuming that both caller and called know this to be the case, it might be expected that any and all 'unnecessary' elements will be dispensed with.

This 'truncated opening sequence' that is characteristic of emergency calls is indicative of an orientation to the need for such calls to be interactionally economical. It seems reasonable to suppose that both parties – the person calling and the call receiver – have an interest in getting done the necessary business of the call in as swift and efficient a way as possible. Thus it might be anticipated that whereas ordinary telephone conversations can be lengthy and rambling, the talk shifting from one topic to another in the course of the call, the conversations that comprise emergency calls would be succinct and to the point. The reasons for assuming this are obvious; apart from the fact that the rationale of the emergency line is to deal promptly with emergencies, there is the further consideration that for an emergency line to be effective it must be available at all times. Thus unlike suicide counsellors, who may endeavour to keep the caller talking, emergency dispatchers may be assumed to orient to the need to respond to the caller's request for assistance in as speedy a way as possible. On this basis, one might presume that the caller's request for assistance, as the first part of a request–response pair, would be followed in the next utterance by the dispatcher's response to the request. However, as Whalen and Zimmerman emphasize, the response is always delayed until further information has been obtained from the caller. The 'interrogative series' that is inserted between caller's request and dispatcher's response typically is concerned with establishing information deemed necessary as a precondition of response. Thus in the example above, the dispatcher asks the caller to supply his address and his name. That such information is a precondition of giving the caller a response to his request is indicated by cases where the callers query the need for the information requested by the dispatcher. In such cases, the dispatcher does not simply move on to the response phase, but rather recycles the information request until it is met. For example:

Example 9
```
D: Could I have the address please?
C: Uh: do I have to give that?
```

D: We need a complainant, ma'am.
C: Uhh, sixty: nineteen.

Thus providing a response to an emergency call would seem to involve certain essential items of information. These include the nature of the problem for which assistance is required, the name and address of the caller, and the location of the trouble. Only when these have been elicited will the dispatcher inform the caller that assistance is on the way. In Example 7, these essential items would seem to be obtained in an interactionally efficient way; each request for information by the dispatcher is followed by an utterance that supplies that information requested. In this call, then, the trouble for which assistance is requested is identified in the second utterance; the dispatcher then gets a location by asking for the caller's address and elicits the caller's name. The business of the call is managed with efficiency and is recognizably completed with the dispatcher informing the caller that assistance will be sent, thus leading to a closing exchange.

In other words, some emergency calls display what can be called a 'minimal sequential form', in the sense that the required elements involved in requesting assistance and responding to such a request get done in a minimal number of (or relatively few) utterances. However, not all emergency calls display such an efficient character. In order to begin to consider the kinds of interactional complications that can occur in emergency calls, and which lead them to deviate from the 'minimal' call, let us consider in some detail what is 'unproblematic' in Example 7. There are several features of this example that are worth noting in terms of the notion of a minimally adequate call. The first is 'seriousness of the trouble'. The caller describes an event that is of a sufficiently serious (criminal) character as to clearly justify police action. It is notable that the dispatcher does not request any further descriptive details about the event itself – his subsequent questions concern the caller's name and location. How is it that the dispatcher is able to treat the caller's description of the trouble as *prima facie* grounds for official action? After all, the dispatcher only has what the caller says has happened to go on. In deciding whether emergency assistance is appropriate, the dispatcher does not have access to what has really happened, but only to the caller's account of this.

The trouble that the caller reports in this call is an instance of what (following Sharrock and Turner, 1978) we will describe as a 'Class 1 Trouble Report'. By this phrase we refer to reports of events that anyone can recognize as legitimate grounds for calling for the assistance of the police or other emergency services. The characteristic feature of such events is that the caller need provide no justification or explanation for having made the call, beyond the reported event itself. Indeed, the seriousness of the event is such that the caller might have been found negligent or irresponsible had she not made the call. In making the call, then, callers can be expected to orient to the need to describe the event that has motivated the call in such a way as to make it evident to the dispatcher that it is indeed a 'Class 1' trouble.

In Example 7, the establishing of a Class 1 trouble is accomplished economically by the caller in her first utterance: 'Somebody jus' vandalized my car.' By producing a report of a recognizable Class 1 trouble, the caller provides the dispatcher with adequate grounds for moving on to other informational requirements This order is a normative one – dispatcher's treat the specification of the nature of the trouble as a 'first item of business', and will only move on to other matters when this has been provided. Thus a key aspect of a dispatcher's competence is to be able to recognize a Class 1 trouble when a description of one is produced (data taken from Eglin and Wideman, 1986: 349):

Example 10

D: Emergency Centre.
   (1.0)
C: [*softly*] Please, can I have help (0.5) the Prince Edward.
D: What, where to?
C: Mennoland. Now, I'm hiding in the closet I can't get out.
D: What's the problem? How come you're hiding in the closet?
C: I'm in a mess. Look, if I come out he's going to shoot me.
D: OK, what's the address there?

We note that in this call the caller's first description of her situation ('I'm hiding in the closet I can't get out') is not treated by the dispatcher as grounds for moving on in the call; he asks for further specification of the problem. However, this request for more details produces something that the dispatcher immediately recognizes as a Class 1 trouble ('If I come out he's going to shoot me'). No further information about the nature of the trouble is sought, the dispatcher moves immediately on to location.

Returning to the call in Example 7, if it had been the case that the caller's description of the trouble did not straightforwardly convey that a Class 1 trouble had occurred, then it is likely that the dispatcher would have sought further details before moving on to these other matters. The key point is that not any description that the caller produces will do as an adequate account on which the dispatcher can act. Emergency assistance is not mobilized simply because a member of the public requests it; the request has to be accompanied by an account of the problem that the dispatcher can recognize as a bona fide trouble justifying police or other emergency intervention. Unless and until such an account is provided, no assistance will be granted. A critical feature of such accounts, therefore, is what Sacks has called the 'co-selection of descriptors'. This phrase refers to ways in which the descriptive terms employed in an account 'hang together' to convey a sense of the being described.

A further noticeable feature in the formulation of the trouble provided as the reason for the request for assistance is the caller's relation to it. A general issue in emergency calls is how the caller stands in relation to the matter that has prompted the call. Whether and how a request for assistance will be responded to depends upon not simply the described event that constitutes the trouble, but also whether the caller is the proper person to report this event and request assistance from the police. Many Class 1 troubles are 'public troubles/emergencies' – that is, events of such seriousness and import that any citizen encountering one has both the right and the duty to bring it to the notice of the authorities without delay (for example, 'There's a fire in the building across the street'). For other Class 1 troubles, however, there is a specific party who is the proper party to make the call – such as the person who is the 'victim' of someone else's actions. Being the victim of a criminal act conveys specific rights – the right to sympathy and assistance being foremost. It also carries with it what might be called 'epistemological rights' (that is, rights concerning states of knowledge). Thus, in normal circumstances, a victim has the right to be believed when she reports to others what has happened. As the victim, she can and should be presumed to know better than anyone else what has befallen her. In this respect, we note in relation to Example 7 what the dispatcher does *not* ask: for example, he does not ask 'How do you know (that your car has been vandalized)?' We can take it that the dispatcher assumes that the caller can simply 'see' the vandalization of his car (it was fine when he left it but on returning he found it had been broken into and damaged).

A third feature to note is temporality – more specifically, the temporal relationship between the event called about and the call itself. Making a call to the emergency line is properly done, not simply for troubles, but for troubles that are current – that are happening now or have just happened. Both callers and dispatchers orient to the immediacy of the event as a significant feature in establishing the appropriateness of emergency response. Thus in Example 7 the caller conveys immediacy by saying that 'Someone jus' vandalized my car'. This can be heard as establishing a relation of immediacy between the call and the event that has prompted it: the vandalizing of the car has just happened, it has just been discovered, and the car owner has called the emergency line as soon as he could after the discovery.

Problem calls

'Minimally adequate' calls like Example 1, in which the sequential components of the emergency call are 'got through' in an interactionally efficient way, are the exception rather than the rule. Studies of emergency calls by ethnomethodologists have shown that the co-ordination and alignment between caller and dispatcher that makes for a minimally adequate call, though it may look straightforward enough in the case cited above, is in reality usually much more problematic. Brevity and efficiency may be the ideal to which the participants orient, but it can be difficult to achieve. In many calls, establishing what the trouble is for which assistance is sought turns out to be anything but straightforward and, unlike the above case, is rarely achieved in a single utterance exchange. Thus, for example, it is common for a caller to use her first turn simply to state that she needs emergency assistance, without stating what kind of assistance or giving any account of what the trouble is for which it is sought. For a dispatcher to mobilize police or emergency assistance it is not enough for something to be a trouble from the point of view of the caller. The fact that a caller may perceive something that is happening as warranting official intervention does not guarantee that such intervention will be forthcoming. Since dispatchers do not activate emergency response on demand, but only when they recognize that there is a situation warranting police or other emergency intervention, the absence of an account of the trouble has to be remedied. Such an opening invariably is followed by a request by the dispatcher for the caller to specify the trouble. This request may produce a 'useable' account of the nature of the trouble – that is, an account upon which the dispatcher can act – but in some cases it does not. In such cases the dispatcher's need for an account of the trouble on the basis of which he can decide what sort of assistance is appropriate can lead to an extended sequence, in which the dispatcher repeatedly seeks to get the caller to clarify just what the nature of the problem is.

Example 11

```
D:  911. What's your
C:  YES. I NEEED AN AMBULANCE!
D:  What is the problem, ma'am?
C:  I DON'T KNOW - MY SISTER - I DON'T KNOW WHAT'S WRONG
    WITH HER. hhh I'M AT THE HORSESHOE INN
    hhh
    OH MY GOOOOD hhh hhh PLEEEASE HURRY!
```

As this example indicates, a caller's main concern can be the urgency of the need for assistance, and communicating this urgency can, for her, take precedence over other matters. Here, the caller uses her first utterance turn to appeal for assistance, rather than to specify the problem for which it is sought. In addition, the emotional consequences of the caller's direct involvement in the emergency situation can serve to obstruct efficient communication with the emergency dispatcher. However, the mere fact that the caller is convinced that the situation is an emergency is not sufficient, on its own, for the dispatcher to mobilize assistance. As we have seen, the dispatcher requires a range of information, including the nature of the trouble, the location and the caller's name or identity. Furthermore, since the dispatcher has no access, beyond what the caller herself says, to the situation that has led the caller to call, it is on the basis of the caller's talk that the dispatcher has to decide whether the dispatching of assistance is appropriate. If the caller's talk does not provide the dispatcher with adequate materials for understanding the kind of trouble involved it will be treated as incomplete, since it does not enable him to make this decision. (Increasingly in contemporary computerized emergency systems there is a division of labour between call-takers and dispatchers. Whereas in older systems the person taking the call is also the one who is responsible for dispatching the appropriate emergency units to the scene of the emergency, in these systems the call-taker is required to complete a computerized dispatch notice which is then sent electronically to the dispatcher. Among other things – for example, location reference – this notice requires the call-taker to code both the nature and the degree of urgency of the emergency in accord with a predefined coding system.)

It would appear, then, that the onus is on the caller to produce an account of the trouble that enables the dispatcher to recognize it as a police or emergency service matter. We saw above that in some calls a description is produced that is immediately recognizable as a Class 1 trouble, a matter which is unequivocally police or emergency service relevant. In such cases the talk can move swiftly to locational and other information necessary for the dispatch of help. However, in other calls the question of whether the trouble that has motivated the call is a police matter is more problematic. Class 2 troubles are those states of affairs which do not immediately and obviously present themselves as police or emergency service relevant matters. In such cases, a description may have to be quite extensive before the grounds for police intervention become apparent. In these calls, the caller's initial description of the trouble may leave open whether this is a proper police matter or not, requiring the dispatcher to seek further details in order to establish this (data taken from Sharrock and Turner, 1978: 190–191, amended):

Example 12
D: Newton Police.
C: Hello …?
D: Yes?
C: I have a complaint, um, my neighbor is (0.5) le-subl- well, renting her garage out, and, ah, there are these young boys, now they seem awfully nice an' everything but I don't know they're missing an awful lot of school, they're fifteen-year-old types (0.5) an, they've got, apparently they've got seven old cars, I guess they buy these old cars, but about a month ago they went to town *smashing* one of them with a pick-axe just absolutely annoying, you know, pounding all day, –
D: (Mm)
C: – and I have a dog that barks a lot an' I guess he's not taking too kindly to these kids.

D: (Mm)

C: [caller goes on to further describe the behaviour
of the boys, that 'they are spending most of the
day there' and that she is 'getting a little
annoyed about it.']

D: Do these cars all got license on them, lady?

In this call to her local police department the caller is reporting the behaviour of a group of boys in her neighbourhood. The call illustrates some features of 'Class 2 Trouble Reports'. Notice that the call is announced as a 'complaint'; the caller makes no claim that this is an emergency, nor does she assert that what the boys are doing is seriously illegal or dangerous. As a police relevant matter, the trouble she is reporting might be seen to fall into the category of a 'public nuisance'. This class of trouble is more problematic from the point of view of mobilizing police action than Class 1 troubles. For example, while a public nuisance can warrant police intervention, the police tend to regard such matters as things that citizens should first attempt to resolve among themselves, only calling the police when their attempts to deal with the situation are unsuccessful. It is often apparent that callers know this in so far as it is typical, in calls like the above, for them to provide some account of their attempts to remove the nuisance and how these have failed. Conseqently, complaint calls about public nuisance often display a 'story' character. In constructing her story, the caller demonstrates the seriousness of the trouble – what might at first seem to be a rather minor thing turns out, with the provision of more details, to be more serious. Such a story may also provide for how it is that the caller is only now informing the authorities about the problem. Unlike Class 1 troubles, where the duty of the citizen is to call the police immediately upon coming across the trouble, the right time to inform them about a Class 2 trouble is more tricky. For example, the events that can come to justify a finding of public nuisance have a developmental character; they unfold over time. Therefore a prospective caller may be aware that, if the complaint is made too soon, she may open herself to being seen as 'stirring up trouble' rather than simply responding to it.

In these ways, then, callers like the one in Example 12 can be seen as engaged in 'making a case' for police action, in a way that it is not necessary in calls concerning Class 1 troubles. It is to be expected, then, that a caller who is calling about a Class 2 trouble may be attentive in a rather different way to the response of the dispatcher to the trouble she describes. The caller may monitor the dispatcher's response, not so much for confirmation that the requested assistance is on its way as for evidence that the claimed status of the trouble is accepted and thus that the caller was justified in making the call. In other words, the caller may listen to hear whether the reason for the call is viewed positively or negatively. With this in mind it is worth noticing the dispatcher's question 'Do these cars all got license on them, lady?'. We take it that this question can be heard as an attempt by the police officer to establish whether or not there is anything illegal going on in the situation the caller has described. As such, it suggests that the dispatcher has been unable to find recognizable illegality in what the caller has described so far. But, more than this, the fact that the question is placed immediately after the caller has produced her account of the matter she is complaining about means that it can convey something about the dispatcher's assessment of the call. By immediately asking whether there is anything illegal going on, the dispatcher can be heard as responding negatively to the caller's account, questioning – by implication rather than overtly – whether there are any grounds for police action in the caller's complaint, and thereby implying that the 'nuisance' she has described is not in itself sufficiently serious to justify police intervention. In this respect, it is notable that the closing sequence of this same call (many utterances later) consists of the following:

Example 13

```
C:  I had (a) friend in one day an' an' I know it was
    just - in fact they suggested then to phone an'
    complain 'n' I think I (0.5) checked at the depart-
    ment but I didn'teh (0.5) say (I said) they were
    making -
D:  You
C:  - a big
D:  No, well, I'll fill in a report, Miss's Thompson,
    and e-thank you so much for phoning.
C:  OK, thanks
D:  'Bye, now.
C:  'Bye 'bye.
```

We suggest that two things are interesting here. The first is the way in which the caller explains her decision to call the police as motivated by a suggestion by a friend. By invoking a third party in this way, the caller can be heard as implicitly recognizing that a possible hearing of the complaint she has made is one that finds it to display personal animus. The reference to the friend, as one who (independently) concurs with and confirms her own assessment of the problem, can be taken as a defense against such a possible hearing.

The second interesting point concerns the dispatcher's response. The police dispatcher has available to him a variety of possible ways of dealing with a call, according to the nature of the trouble reported. Reports of Class 1 troubles, as we have already suggested, should normally be responded to by the immediate dispatch of the relevant emergency service. However, there are alternative ways of disposing with other kinds of calls that report matters of lesser urgency and seriousness. Of course, one possibility is that a dispatcher can inform a caller that nothing will be done about the matter. However, this kind of response, amounting as it does to a total rejection of the caller's request for assistance, might be something that dispatchers (especially in local police departments) would seek to avoid if at all possible, unless the call is perceived as a hoax or the reported matter is seen as transparently irrelevant to the police (in which case the dispatcher will most likely inform the caller that 'This is not a police matter' and hang up). We take it that police and emergency service dispatchers are likely to be attentive to the need to reassure callers wherever possible that something will be done. Without such reassurance there is the possibility that the lack of police/emergency response can itself become the subject of a further citizen complaint. One response available in cases where the dispatcher is unconvinced that police intervention is warranted is to assure the caller that a report will be filed. This response has the advantage of establishing that official notice has been taken of the complaint, without specifying any particular course of action on the police's part. In the call above, it is perhaps significant that – despite the negative assessment implied in the dispatchers first utterance – this closing response is not produced until the conversation between the caller and the dispatcher has been going on for several minutes, during which the caller has been given ample opportunity to elaborate her complaint.

Conclusion

In this chapter we have considered some of the interactional properties of telephone calls that involve 'calling for help'. The emphasis in Sacks' study of calls to a suicide prevention centre was upon the categorical organization of callers' self-report that they had no-one to turn to. The studies of emergency calls by Whalen and Zimmerman, among others, focus instead on the sequential organization of such calls. However, as our discussion has shown, categorical issues concerning the nature of the trouble for which emergency help is sought have implications for, indeed may shape the development of, the trouble reporting and help seeking sequence. The categorical distinction between Class 1 and Class 2 troubles serves to influence the nature and extensiveness of the interrogative sequence as well as the official response for which it provides. In this respect, then, the analytical distinction between categorical and sequential order should not be thought of as marking a clear and rigid demarcation between different levels of order. In terms of members' orientations, category and sequence are clearly and intimately connected. The character of the connection between categorical and sequential aspects of interactional order is further elaborated in the next chapter, when we turn to the investigation of interaction in educational settings.

Student activity

1   Using a tape recorder, record a call to a help-line or customer service centre. If you cannot record both ends of the conversation, record your own end and use this to reconstruct the talk of the other party.
2   Consider the overall sequential organization of the call. What activities were performed and in what order?
3   What categories and membership categorization devices are displayed in the talk?

Further Reading

R. Hopper (1992) *Telephone Conversation*. Bloomington, IL: Indiana University Press.

G. Jefferson and J.R.E. Lee (1981) 'The rejection of advice: Managing the problematic convergence of a "troubles-telling" and a "service encounter"', *Journal of Pragmatics*, 5 (5): 399–422 (also in P. Drew and J. Heritage (eds) (1992) *Talk at Work*. Cambridge: Cambridge University Press).

H. Sacks (1967) 'The search for help: No-one to turn to', in E. Schneidman (ed.), *Essays in Self Destruction*. New York, NY: Science House.

E. Schegloff (1968) 'Sequencing in conversational openings', *American Anthropologist*, 70 (6): 1075–95 (also in P.P. Giglioli (ed.) (1972) *Language and Social Context*. Harmonsworth: Penguin).

D. Zimmerman (1992) 'The interactional organization of calls for emergency assistance', in P. Drew and J. Heritage (eds), *Talk at Work: Interaction in Institutional Settings*. Cambridge: Cambridge University Press.

7

Observing Education

Everyone has some familiarity with the social world of education and the social activities that are to be found there. As a student, you will have daily access to the world of higher education, spending much of your time in lectures, seminars, discussion groups and other activities of university life. Furthermore, most of you will have recently emerged from the world of the school. There you will have encountered such things as lessons, assembly and examinations. In line with our general approach, our question is: how are the familiar scenes and activities of educational life – what is observably the case – accomplished by the parties to them and what do persons use in accomplishing those events and activities? We begin with some observable features of university lectures. We assume that our readers will be well acquainted with this educational activity. Furthermore, it is one that may be readily observed in the course of any student's university life. We then turn to an educational setting from which our readers will be slightly more removed. We thereby consider some ethnomethodological studies of the organization of classroom interaction, and power and authority in the classroom.

Some organizational features of university lectures

In line with our methodological preference for beginning with concrete observational data, let us start by considering the opening part of an actual university lecture in sociology. The setting is a lecture theatre in a university. The students are assembled, around fifty or so. They are seated, some chatting to their neighbours, some sitting in silence apparently waiting for the lecturer to arrive. The next thing that happens is that someone enters the lecture room and goes to the front, standing behind the podium and placing some papers upon it. Having arranged her papers, the lecturer looks up at the assembled student cohort and the following interaction takes place:

Example 1

L: Good afternoon.
(34.5) [Lecturer passes piles of handouts to students sitting in the front row, students stop talking amongst themselves and look towards the
lecturer]

L: There should be two handouts ( ) one with a (.)
two pages with a staple through them and ( ) one
page on its own.
[background general laughter]
Three pages in all.
(2.5) [quiet background laughter]
So, (3.0) are you all right now?

S: [faintly] Yeh.
(2.5)

L: Are you OK?
( )

L: … paper …
( )

L: between two ( ) notions ( ) reality (.) work
( ) and they are ( ) on this sheet here ( ) reality work in everyday life ( ) in other words what
ordinary people like ( ) you and me ( ) do with
notions of reality (.) in the course of their (.)
activities ( ) y'know sometimes we speak of what's
real and what's not real and what's imaginary and
so forth ( ) so that's what I mean by reality work
in – in (.) everyday life ( ) and then there's
something else that we might call reality work (.)
in sociology (.) what things – er ( ) the kind of
work that sociologists do ( ) when they (.) pose
these stranger questions (.) like 'How is social
reality constructed?' ( ) OK (.) now, I want to
keep that distinction (.) in mind (.) it's gonna
( ) come up time and time again.

We note first that when the lecturer says 'Good afternoon' that, judging
from the students' response, it is not understood just as a greeting (that the
students do not return), but rather as an announcement, even an instruction, that the lecture is about to begin.[1] The lecturer is not merely greeting
the students as she might outside the lecture theatre, rather she can be
heard to be announcing that the lecture is about to begin and instructing
them to get ready for what she has to say. The announcement/instruction
just happens to take the form of a greeting in this instance. Now, if the
'Good afternoon' is hearable as an announcement or an instruction, the
question is, how? Our answer to this question recalls a piece of classic

ethnomethodological analysis by Payne (1976). This concerned the opening of a history lesson in a secondary school, which he observed, tape-recorded, transcribed and analysed using the same method of analysis that we have adopted in this book. We therefore observe how this talk is readily understandable as the beginning of a lecture, and then ask how it is produced in such a way that it is understandable in just that way.

As Payne suggests, for talk to be understandable as the start of an educational event such as a lecture, then it has to display certain features that constitute it as the start of a lecture and it has to be recognized as such by the participants in it. As with lessons, the two features that have to be present are: co-presence of lecturer and student(s) (teacher and pupils in the case of lessons in school); and talk that can be recognized as, in our case, lecture talk. So, for the greeting to be understood as the start of a lecture, there must be persons present who are identifiable as lecturer and students. However, the mere co-presence of these two membership categories does not constitute the lecture in itself; in addition, the incumbents of these categories have to produce talk and actions that are recognizable as a lecture. As we shall see, the recognizable co-presence of these category incumbents and the sense of their talk are inextricably linked.

For 'Good afternoon' to be understood as the start of lecture it must be understandable as having been spoken by someone identifiable as a lecturer to people recognizable as students. We have spoken of someone entering the room, going to the podium, arranging papers. If this someone had entered the room and started fiddling with the screws on the overhead projector, or if she had started cleaning the windows instead of the blackboard, then the students might have thought 'Who is she?' and 'What's she doing?'. But she didn't, rather she recognizably did the kinds of things that lecturers do – stood around, shuffled about a bit, looked out the window, and then, looking at all the students rather than at any one person in particular, she said 'Good afternoon'. How is it, then, that this person is recognizable as a lecturer?

Our answer to this question is that she can be so recognized because she can be seen to be doing activities bound to the category 'lecturer'. Walking to the front, standing at the podium, looking at the assembled students, cleaning the blackboard and so on are examples of category-bound activities in terms of which we may see at a glance that this person is a lecturer. However, perhaps most importantly, it is the talk – the 'Good afternoon' – that comprises the evidence that this person is a lecturer. For one thing, it is routinely the case that it is lecturers and not students who say such things to all and sundry, whereas students if they say it at all are likely to say it only to a select few in this context. More importantly, however, giving instructions and making announcements are examples of activities bound to the category 'lecturer'. Accordingly, we assume that this person is a lecturer because she is doing something that is predicated of the category 'lecturer'. Our assumption, furthermore, entails the use of the viewer's maxim that we introduced at the end of Chapter 4, namely if an activity can be seen as being done by an incumbent of a category to which it is bound, then: see it that way. Furthermore, in addition to being visible as a lecturer because of category-bound activities such as these, speaking in this way can be understood to 'constitute' the person present as a lecturer. Had the person not done the kinds of things we have mentioned, then it would have been difficult for us to see her as a lecturer on this occasion.

We can now return to our original question, namely how is 'Good afternoon' understandable as the opening remarks of a lecture? We have established that the lecturer's category membership as such is accomplished by category-bound activities of this sort. This locally constituted identity of 'lecturer' can now be appreciated as providing a resource or method used to make the utterance intelligible. It is not just the words themselves that make 'Good afternoon' the opening remarks of a lecture. After all, such a greeting may be spoken in a wide variety of contexts. As with any spoken words, their meaning depends on the context of their utterance and, we suggest, a crucial feature of any context that is to be taken into account is the relevant categorial identity of the speaker. Garfinkel (1967) points out that words such as those contained in the lecturer's greeting are 'indexical expressions'. They do not have a stable or objective meaning for all times and places in which they may be used. Thus, if one wants to find out more about a word listed in the index of a book, one has to turn to the page or pages indicated in order to read the word in its context. Only then can its sense or meaning be appreciated. In the same way, then, the meanings of words are inseparable from the contexts of their expression. So, taking into account the contextual feature of the social identity of the speaker is a method for arriving at the sense of the indexical expression 'Good afternoon'. Furthermore, as the above analysis has shown, there is a two-way reflexive process going on here. It is not just that the identity is used to clarify the meaning of the words, it is also the case that the sense of the words helps to constitute the sense of the identity of the speaker. Both words and identity mutually inform one another.

A further feature of the context is the apparent social identity of the recipients. Accordingly, we can see that the instruction/announcement embodied in 'Good afternoon' also imputes a category to the recipients. To whom might someone recognizable as a lecturer issue such an instruction? Our suggestion is that the lecturer's instruction allocates and presumes a particular category of recipient. The students to whom the utterance is addressed are proper recipients and in turn are constituted as such by the utterance; it is a category-bound responsibility of the membership category 'student' (at least when they attend lectures) to be attentive to those who lecture them. The students' response, furthermore, exhibits their analysis of the lecturer's utterance and can be seen to constitute their category membership as students. Thus, they responded by ceasing to talk amongst themselves and evidently prepared to listen to the lecturer. By being constituted as students through the instruction and by constituting themselves as such via their response, further resources (the identity of the recipients) are provided for understanding the lecturer's utterance as the start of the lecture.

Viewed in terms of its sequential organization, the students' response can be seen as a collective second part to the lecturer's first part, and it was via this particular method that conditions for the lecture to be delivered were established. Taken together, the instruction and the response comprise an 'instruction-compliance' adjacency pair that serves as a 'pre-sequence' to the main business of the occasion. Indeed, we trust that our readers will be familiar with what typically happens when the second part of such a pair is not forthcoming. The lecturer waits (as she did on this occasion for 4.5 seconds) for compliance to take place and sometimes may have to re-issue the instruction/announcement that lecture is about to begin.

The selection of methods to achieve the conditions for lecture-delivery is also categorially organized. It is perfectly possible for student attentiveness and readiness for a lecture to be achieved with a more direct injunction such as 'Be quiet please, I want to begin' and it is not difficult to imagine some educational circumstances wherein such direct injunctions might be made. However, we suggest that such direct injunctions are quite exceptional in the context of university lectures. This is because the particular form that is used to convey the instruction to come to attention may be understood as recipient-designed. That is, indirect instruction could be heard as reflecting the maturity of its recipients in this instance in that they do not need to be told directly to come to attention in the way that might be required, for example, when teachers have to deal with younger students.

Lectures such as this one, then, are educational events that have recognizable beginnings, and such beginnings are practical accomplishments. They are accomplished both categorially and sequentially. They involve the use of members' methods of membership categorization and the sequential organization of talk. In the case at hand, the lecturer's greeting/instruction and the students' response comprise a two-part sequence for beginning lectures. The achieved sense of the lecturer's greeting/instruction and the response to it constitute the lecturer's *and* the students' method for establishing an appropriate state of readiness for the lecture. All of these activities, we suggest, were taken into account by the students in understanding what was happening, and by the lecturer in designing her behaviour. In short, these various organized activities were used as methods for starting the lecture. The parties to the occasion – the lecturer and the students – accomplished the start of the lecture together and they did so in detail. Furthermore, we would suggest that it is a feature of all educational events that they have beginnings and endings. It is also the case, therefore, that there have to be ways of accomplishing transition from a previous state of affairs to the educational activity in question. Given that educational events standardly involve two parties, namely the lecturer or teacher on the one hand and a group of students on the other hand, then the transition into the educational activity, be it classroom lesson or university lecture, involves the accomplishment of a focusing of attention. In other words, as in the case of the lecture, this transition can involve a shift from generalized unfocused activity amongst the group of students to a collective focusing on the lecturer or teacher. It is this transition that is typically described as 'getting ready' to begin the lecture, the lesson, the seminar and so forth.

One might anticipate that having announced that the lecture is about to begin via the greeting 'Good afternoon', and thereby having obtained an appropriate state of readiness on the part of the students, that the lecturer's next action would be the lecture's delivery. As we can see in our data, however, the lecture itself is preceded by the preliminary activity of distributing handouts to the students. We note that the lecturer describes what is being distributed as 'two handouts' and elaborates this description with a rather pedantic and humorous explanation. The laughter that follows, while we cannot be definitive about its source, is possibly a response to the parody in the lecturer's explanation, mimicking as it hear-ably does in its 'two pages plus one page equals three pages' a school teacher talking to young children. Although the lecturer does not explicitly state that the handouts relate to the topic of the lecture, we take it that the reader, along with the students involved, will treat them in this way. It is also clear from the lecturer's subsequent remarks, 'So, are you all right now?' and 'Are you OK?' and from the fact that the lecturer observably waits for the handouts to find themselves in the possession of all the students in the room, that the successful distribution of the handouts is treated by the lecturer as a precondition of the start of lecture delivery.

We do not have available a video recording of this lecture's beginning and we are not therefore in a position to describe more of its detail. Specifically, we can neither analyse precisely how the lecturer monitored the distribution of the handouts to find that this had been successfully accomplished and that delivery of the lecture could now begin, nor can we say anything about how the lecturer marked in non-verbal ways her satisfaction with the distributive process and her intention to start the lecture. We take it that the students could see that the handouts had been distributed and could anticipate that the lecturer's next utterance would comprise the opening of the lecture itself. That they are able to do so indicates their understanding of the social activity of lecturing. Thus, when the lecturer says '... between two notions of reality work and they are on the sheet here' we take it that the students would have no difficulty in hearing this as the start of the lecture.

Whilst we cannot reproduce here the entirety of the lecture, we note that once the lecturer commences to speak on the lecture topic, she continues to do so without interruption until the closing of the lecture. In other words, the lecturer talked for forty minutes or so and the students listened and took notes. That this is standard practice will be no surprise to our readers. However, as ethnomethodological sociologists we want to ask how it is that this state of affairs has been produced by the parties to the lecture? Furthermore, it is not that the students do not speak at any point. As the transcript above shows, they laugh and they speak when addressed by the lecturer during the preliminary activity of distributing the handouts. It is clear, therefore, that the delivery of the lecture as an activity has its own particular interactional order, one that has to be accomplished in its course by the participants. Fundamental to this order, it would seem, is an asymmetrical distribution of rights to speak. The lecturer appears to have the right to speak continuously from the beginning of the lecture to its end, whilst the students do not have any such right. Of course, the lecturer does not speak continuously. There are frequent and sometimes quite lengthy pauses (for example, several seconds) in the lecturer's delivery. What is notable about them, however, is that they appear to be 'owned' by the lecturer; the students do not speak at these junctures in the lecture. In other words, the students do not treat these stoppages as possible completion points of the lecturer's turn at talk. Rather, then, pausing appears to be treated as an integral feature of lecture delivery.

There appears, then, to be a particular 'speech exchange system' in operation in the activity of lecturing. It may be thought of as involving a modification of the turn-taking organization for ordinary conversation. In ordinary conversation, as we pointed out in Chapter 4, persons may select themselves to speak at any turn transition relevance point in a current speaker's talk provided that current speaker has not selected a particular next speaker. In lecturing, however, it is the entirety of the lecture that constitutes the lecturer's turn at talk, even though it may consist of several hundred complete sentences or other utterances. In terms of our earlier example of how talk can be understood categorially as 'lecturer' talk and 'student' talk, this pattern of a lengthy lecturer turn and the absence of student talk can be said to be a pre-allocated arrangement of speaking rights and types of turns that is category bound. Indeed, without such a pattern it seems to us that it would be difficult to see an event as a lecture in the first place. Such pre-allocated features and modifications of conversational organization would appear to be constitutive of the phenomenon of the lecture.

Identity and interaction in a reception class

Educational events, of course, are not confined to the university lecture theatre. Furthermore, all educational events have recognizable beginnings and endings. We turn now to a different educational setting. This allows us to observe some additional features of educational interaction. In this section we will turn our attention to educational activities to be found in the first year of schooling. A regular feature of the classroom day in this particular reception class (and probably many others) was the occasional assembly of the children in a part of the room set aside for whole-group activities such as storytelling, question and answer sessions and singing together. This session was known as 'carpet-time'. We consider some data drawn from two carpet-time sessions in the first weeks of a primary school reception class. Our materials permit us to examine some aspects of the organization of turn-taking in classroom interaction.

At one afternoon carpet-time the children were instructed to assemble on the carpet as follows:

Example 2
```
 1  T:   Come and sit on the carpet.
 2       [general noise as they assemble on the carpet]
 3  T:   We're nearly ready.
 4       [general noise as children get into sitting
 5       positions on the carpet]
 6  T:   Right, let's see who's ready. Tony's ready and
 7       Wendy's ready and Kevin's
 8       ready and Bobby, oh. Now, there's lots of people
 9       ready.
10  P1:  We can't play out coz it's raining.
11  P2:  We can't go out? Can't we not?
12  T:   Well, we'll talk about that in a minute. First
13       of all (0.5) when Tracy's found
14       her bottom (1.0) have you found your bottom
15       Tracy? (0.5) and when Lee's
16       sitting still (0.5) Neil, just go back to where
17       you were because there's no
18       more room just there (0.5) get on the carpet
19       Lee (0.5) are you on the carpet?
20       (0.5) have you found a space? (1.0) Zoe, go and
21       put that pink toy animal in
22       your drawer before we start, please (1.5)
23       Right, good morning boys and girls.
24  Ps:  Good morning teachers, good morning friends.
```

In relation to this data we will consider the speech exchange system for classroom interaction. With respect to the first we begin by observing that it is readily apparent that the teacher's utterance 'Come and sit on the carpet' has a similar function to that of the university lecturer's 'Good afternoon'. That is, it can be understood as being directed towards the group as a whole (in so far as no one in particular is selected to speak) and towards establishing the conditions for the educational activity due to follow. Thus, the teacher's instruction at line 1 can be heard as the first part of an adjacency pair of actions (Sacks, Schegloff and Jefferson, 1974), namely 'instruction-compliance'. As a first-pair part and in its specifics as an instruction, it implicates compliance as its second-pair part. Since these pupils are in the first weeks of their schooling, in her use of this first-pair part the teacher might also be understood to instruct the children in the sequential ordering or structures of classroom life.

As is often the case, there is some delay in the achievement of this compliance and it is here that we find a major difference between university lectures and classroom interaction in school. Thus, in order to establish the children's (eventual) compliance, the teacher makes use of a series of follow-ups to her original instruction. These follow-ups can be heard to monitor and evaluate the children's behaviour. Some of these evaluations are positive: the teacher can be heard first to acknowledge the compliance of some of the pupils; she evaluates positively their actions. Other evaluations have negative implications: the particular named acknowledgements serve also to remind those who have yet to comply that they too should be in a state of readiness. By implication these children who are not yet ready are evaluated negatively. Thus, lines 3–9 of the above transcript contain several references to 'readiness'. The first of these, occurring at line 3, is the teacher's description that 'We're nearly ready'. It can be heard first to identify a population, namely a 'we' that is apparently nearly ready. The 'we' of 'we're nearly ready' can be heard to include both teacher and the pupils since the next activity cannot begin until everyone is ready. That is to say, they – both teacher and pupils – cannot move onto the next activity until the present one is completed. However, whilst this 'we' can be heard to include both teacher and the pupils – since until they are *all* ready then the session cannot begin – it is the pupils' readiness that is problematic. Consequently, the evaluation does not include the teacher's readiness as a matter of self-report. The readiness in question projects and anticipates a state of affairs yet to be achieved by all the pupils. Furthermore, the teacher's utterance can be seen to be a reflexive or constitutive feature of the scene it describes. It not only describes the scene, but also hearably directs the children towards a future state of affairs comprising particular scenic details of appropriate sitting and attentiveness.

If the first evaluation of partial or near-readiness is applied to an undifferentiated 'we', and thereby names the class as a cohort (Payne and Hustler, 1980), lines 6–9 contain some more specific references. At line 6 the teacher says 'let's see who's ready'. This, again, is an instruction to those who are not yet ready; it is also an announcement that she is about to do the 'seeing' in some way. The children's unreadiness is being monitored, as it were, as is their progress towards readiness. The teacher then announces a list of who is ready. This listing can be heard in several, interrelated ways. First, it can be heard to positively evaluate – that is, approve and reward – those who are now describable as ready. Second, it can be heard to remind, encourage and show the others who remain unready what the teacher is waiting for. Thus, some children have already accomplished readiness whilst others have yet to achieve it. It is in this sense that the teacher's utterances are directed to two categories: the ready and the unready. For the latter, the description consists of instruction, for the former acknowledgement. Two tasks, as it were, are here accomplished simultaneously.

In instructing children in their responses and in the teacher's evaluations of their responses we can see a familiar structure of classroom interaction. Mehan (1979) has referred to this as the Initiation-Response-Evaluation sequence, or 'IRE' for short. This sequential structure or sequence is a pervasive one in classrooms, especially in relation to formal instruction. Indeed, following further explication by McHoul (1978), this sequence has been understood as a key feature of the speech exchange system for classroom interaction. In terms of this sequence, pupils can only speak when invited to do so by the production of an 'initiation' utterance (for example, a question) on the part of the teacher, and their responses are routinely subjected to an evaluation ('That's right,' 'Yes,' and so on). A key point here is that the conversational floor does not, on completion of the evaluation, then pass to the pupil. Rather, it remains with the teacher, who may (or may not) then produce a further initiation.

In this way, studies of the IRE sequence in operation are consistent with those studies (cf. Speier, 1973; 1976) that have documented the restricted rights of children to speak in the school. This is expressed in the pre-allocation and restriction of certain types of turns at talk to particular membership categories, specifically those of teacher and pupil. There can be little doubt that this arrangement frequently prevails. However, the notion that there is a stable speech exchange system for classroom interaction is in some respects misleading. In our view, it over-simplifies and over-generalizes particular observable features of teacher–pupil interaction. It is, of course, clear that the IRE sequence is used frequently. It is used, for example, in the extract above, where the pupils were instructed to sit on the carpet and where they then comply and are evaluated for having done so. However, this particular sequential structure for classroom interaction is by no means the whole story in the first year of primary school. In addition to the occurrence of these forms of talk there are numerous exceptions to and differences from the basic IRE format. Such exceptions have been observed before, by Heap (1979).

In the carpet-time data, for example, there are many instances or places where pupils initiate and are not censured for doing so. Therefore, it may be that greater analytic scope and a more thorough appreciation of teacher–pupil interaction is afforded by abandoning the notion of a speech exchange system for all classroom interaction on the grounds of its over-simplicity and over-generality. In its place, we would suggest an alternative avenue of inquiry. This retains the notion of a speech exchange system but localizes it to particular classroom activities. Just as there is not a single category relationship between teacher and pupils, we suggest that there is not a single speech exchange system for classroom interaction but several, often within a single classroom session or lesson. These systems are locally produced and manage orders of classroom talk that operate 'until further notice'. That is to say, one thing that is observable is that sometimes pupils speak to the teacher without having been selected to do so. We will consider some data that exhibits this feature and then offer an account of it via the notion of 'local speech exchange systems'.

To consider the 'local' and 'situated' character of speech exchange systems, we examine first the following extract:

Example 3

```
 1  T:   I have to put a number on here. We've got lots
 2       of things to send along to Mrs C today.
 3  P1:  Mrs A?
 4  T:   Yes?
 5  P1:  I've got some medicine in the house.
 6  T:   You've got some medicine as well? What's the
 7       matter with you?
 8  P1:  I've got bad cough.
 9  T:   Oh.
10  P2:  And I've got some medicine in the house an'all
11       coz I've got a bad cough an'll.
12  P3:  So've I.
13  T:   Now, let's see who's here for their dinner coz
14       I have to do the dinners first, don't we.
```

In this extract, three different children speak on the topic of their coughs and medicine. The topic would appear to be one that had already been addressed prior to the commencement of tape-recording, that is, earlier in the session. However, it is significant that the topic is now re-introduced or re-engaged with a summons–answer sequence. In other words, a child initiates (to use Mehan's concept) the topic first of all by summoning the teacher (P: Mrs A?) who then answers (T: Yes?). The child who summons the teacher and reports that he has medicine in the house and has a bad cough is followed by a second and a third child on the same topic. The key point about this is that it would seem that, as far as the children are concerned, the 'speech exchange system' that is now in operation is that each child can take a self-selected turn to inform the teacher of their own particular status and circumstances relative to this topic. Each child takes it that if a first child can speak then so can he or she, at least until further notice. Those children who follow the first do not wait for the teacher to invite them to speak. For them, it is another one of those occasions when if a first child takes a turn then this provides for subsequent turns of the same type by other children. For the children, it would seem, repetition rules. A similar arrangement is visible in the following extract:

Example 4

```
194  T/Ps:  [song: 'I hear thunder']
195  T:     Shall we do that one again?
196  P's:   Yeaaas!
197  T/Ps:  [song: 'I hear thunder']
198  T:     Right.
199  Pa:    I know that one.
```

```
200  Pb:    So do I.
201  T:     Do you?
202  Pc:    So do I.
203  Pd:    So do I.
204  Pe:    I know that one an'all.
205  Pf:    My sister knows it.
207  Pg:    So did us at Nursery, didn't we?
208  Ph:    Aha.
209  T:     Now then, there's another funny one. Would
210         you like to hear the funny one?
211  P's:   Yeaaaas!
212  T:     It's like that one, but it's funny. It's
213         about dinner.
214  T:     [sings]
215  T:     Do you know what stew is?
216  Pa:    What?
217  Pb:    Yes.
218  T:     What's stew?
219  Pa:    What?
220  Pb:    It's meat.
221  T:     It's meat, yes, it's a kind of meat.
222  Pc:    If I tasted it I would have yacked it out.
223  T:     [sings]
224  T:     That's a funny one. Right (0.5) now then,
225         what colour is the sky on a rainy day?
226  Pa:    (grey)
227  Pb:    (blue)
228  T:     Shhh …
229  Pc:    (grey)
230  Pd:    (blue)
231  T:     Oh, I can't hear if you all shout out! Let's
232         do it the proper way. When you come to school
233         you put your hand up. Now, you look out of
234         the windows (0.5) David as well.
```

Here, then, a similar speech exchange system can be said to be operative in lines 199–208. After the teacher's 'Right' at line 198, a child volunteers the information that he knows the song in question. This touches off a series of self-selections from a number of children. The teacher does not inhibit this flow of information. Each child can be said to be oriented to prevailing conditions under which turns are currently being produced; each self-selected turn not only provides an environment for a next one but is also cumulative. It is a reflexive feature of the setting. It is this accumulated context of self-selected turns that can be understood as providing for the self-selections that then occur after the teacher's question at line 225. The teacher does not select any child in particular to speak but directs her question to the class as a whole. Accordingly, in the absence of any instructions about who may speak several do so at once. In contrast to lines 199–208, however, the teacher now censures the children with 'Shh ...' (at line 228). Two more pupils self-select at lines 226 and 227, again in overlap. The result is some explicit instruction from the teacher on 'proper way', namely 'When you come to school you put your hand up'. The transcript continues:

Example 5

```
231  T:   Oh, I can't hear if you all shout out! Let's
232       do it the proper way. When you came to school
233       you put your hand up. Now, you
234       look out of the windows (0.5) David as well.
235  Pe:  (blue)
236  Pf:  (grey)
237  Pg:  (blue)
238  Ph:  (blue)
239  T:   And (0.5) shhh, I didn't ask you to shout out.
240       I shall choose somebody. I shall choooose (1.5)
241       Michelle, what colour is the sky today?
242  Pm:  Brown.
```

Despite the teacher's instruction in the 'proper way' the children again (lines 235–238) self-select in overlap. Accordingly, the teacher censures them a second time (line 239) and states that she will 'choose somebody' to speak. She chooses (note the pause in so doing – waiting for the children to demonstrate proper candidacy) Michelle. Michelle's answer, however, is incorrect:

Example 6

```
239  T:   And (0.5) shhh, I didn't ask you to shout out.
240       I shall choose somebody. I shall choooose
241       (1.5) Michelle, what colour is the sky today?
242  Pm:  Brown.
243  T:   Do you think it's brown? I don't know about
244       brown.
245  Pn:  (no)
246  Po:  (blue)
247  T:   Oh no! I didn't say shout out. Put your hands
248       up and I'll ask somebody else what they think.
249       I shall ask (0.5) David?
```

```
250 Pd: Err, err (1.0) it's grey.
251 T:  Right …
```

Again, after the teacher's evaluation turn at line 243, the pupils self-select in overlap. As a result, the teacher restates the rule about 'shouting out' (at line 247).

On the basis of the data considered so far it might appear that the difference between censured and uncensured self-selections lies in the fact that those that are censured are produced 'in overlap'. It seems that the teacher invokes the one-at-a-time rule and the speak-only-when-selected rule when more than one pupil talks at a time. However, on closer inspection it is evident that it is not overlap *per se* that matters, rather it is the character of the overlap that is crucial. This can be appreciated via a consideration of the following two extracts:

Example 7
```
195 T:   Shall we do that one again?
196 P's: Yeaaas!
```

Example 8
```
209 T:   Now then, there's another funny one. Would
210      you like to hear the funny one?
211 P's: Yeaaaas!
```

In both of these cases, then, the children speak in overlap (lines 196 and 211), but they are not censured for doing so. The key difference between these cases and the censured overlaps considered above is that these overlapping pupil turns are done in unison. As such, the children can be heard to speak 'with one voice'. Speaking with one, unitary voice can be treated as the equivalent of a single answer and therefore as less troublesome for the teacher. Some overlaps, then, consist of children speaking in unison, with one voice, whilst other overlaps consist of a disunity of voice, with different children offering different answers. It is this difference that appears to make a difference for the teacher in this case.

So, speech exchange systems in our view are not so much generalized systems, they are locally produced, operative for now, contingent, until further notice, situated arrangements that are oriented to and that provide the grounds for pupil talk. One such system consists of the children self-selecting, one-at-a-time, in response to a teacher's question addressed to the entire class. However, when this method for organizing interaction runs into trouble in the sense that the children speak in overlap, then the pupil self-selection system is suspended and substituted by the 'proper way'. In this sense, the proper way is one way of organizing turn-taking that finds its place only under certain circumstances.

Power and authority in the classroom

It might be thought that the asymmetries of turn-taking noted in the previous section constitute evidence of the prevalence of teacher power and authority in the classroom. This is a tricky issue for ethnomethodological sociology because of its methodological commitment to describing the methods used by participants to accomplish social activities. Such a commitment is undermined in much sociological work by the presumption that power and authority are explanatory concepts and that all the analyst is required to do is locate differences between persons' behaviour and the rights and expectations associated with it, and then attribute the reasons for those differences to a distribution of power and authority amongst the participants in some field of social interaction. Unfortunately sociological assertions of power and authority are rarely coupled with demonstrations that participants in some setting are actually oriented to a distribution of power and authority. Two ethnomethodological studies in the field of education that have attempted to do so are those of Payne and Hustler (1980) and Macbeth (1991). We will, in this final section of this chapter, discuss some of their findings and then consider how far they can be considered to be rigorous and adequate analyses of these phenomena.

Power in the classroom

Hustler and Payne begin by reminding us that in a sense 'everyone knows' that society delegates power and authority to teachers, and in a classroom it is the teacher who has the power and the pupils who are the subordinated parties in the teacher–pupil relationship. However, even if 'power' is so obvious, the question remains for ethnomethodological sociology: how does a teacher and a class of pupils provide for this commonly known feature of the world? According to Hustler and Payne, power is manifested situationally and, for the most part, unnoticeably. One particular observable feature of classroom life, and one which is exhibited in the data they present, is that teachers make use of a variety of features of the occasion of the lesson in their accomplishment of a power relationship. The particular feature they look at is the 'timed' nature of a lesson.

Time and its passing is a continuously relevant feature of lessons. In their analysis Hustler and Payne focus on the 'periodicity' of lessons, that is, the fact that they take place at particular times. The periodicity of lessons is available to the teacher as a resource to be used in various ways. Their focus is on how the timed or periodicized character of the lesson can be used to constitute a power relationship. To show this they use five extracts. In each of the five extracts the teacher can be understood to be making available his orientation to the time of the lesson as his time, and can be understood as claiming as basic to the category 'teacher' an entitlement to lesson time as 'teacher's time'. In so doing, he accomplishes a power relationship *via-à-vis* the pupils. This is taken for granted as common sense in the everyday life of schools. The data are as follows:

Example 9

```
1  P:  Sir (can you write about -
   T:  (- these people
   P:  - his eer - his mo - his eer wife an is eer
       daughter?

   T:  No - just - you've onl - you haven't got time to
       write about th - jus - it's Alfred we're inter-
       ested in. … If you're interested in this - you
       can - read about it yourself - an' ya can - if ya'
       want t'make some - extra notes yourself - in your
       own time from the book - then you can by all means.

2  T:  Yes, you can do that if you like ( ) - LISTEN
       - when you've packed up - and you sat quietly …
       (think about) letting you go for break.

3  P:  Sir, ma bag's broke - ink (went) all over me
       books so I (had) to dry them all out).
   T:  Oh - an' did have to be in my lesson … uhm.

4  P:  Sir - sir, can you take it home?
   T:  Can you take it home? - No, you can look at it
       in your spare time at school.

5  T:  Yeah, we're coming on to that later y - you're
       rushing ahead a bit we haven't got to that yet - he
       hasn't fought the important battles yet - you're
       right though 'ee does - have - escape - an' he
       has to start all over again.
```

As Hustler and Payne point out, one of the central methodical ways in which the teacher makes use of the timed nature of the lesson is to claim that time as his time. In extract 1, they note that in telling the pupils that they can do the other writing up in 'their own time', the teacher is implying to them that this (that is, lesson time) is not their own time; this is not time in which they can do what they want. Rather, this is time when the teacher has control over what they may and may not do; lesson time is teacher's time, when he has control. Similarly, in extract 2, the teacher is telling the pupils that when they have done what he wants them to do just now – that is, pack up and be sitting quietly – he will think about letting them go for break. The break is a time when they are free, but to say that he will let them go to break clearly implies that they are not free to do as they please now.

In extract 3, the teacher describes the lesson as *his* lesson. He is describing the organization of the day and pointing out to the pupil that at this particular moment in the day the pupil is involved in this teacher's time. If the breaking of the bag had happened during some other lesson, it would have been in some other teacher's time. In extract 4, in talking of 'spare time' the teacher is again indicating that the lesson is his teacher's time. Finally, in extract 5, the teacher is again indicating to the pupil that he is not to go on to the things he might like to. He speaks of the pupil as 'rushing ahead'. He is reminding the pupil that the time available is only enough for the pupils to do what he has already decided; whatever else they may be interested in, it is not permissible just now. By the teacher's disqualification of the pupil's suggestion as 'rushing ahead', the class might hear that the teacher has the power to do that: it is he who decides what can and cannot be covered in the time available.

Hustler and Payne's point, then, is that through continually making it known that as far as he is concerned lesson time is his time, the teacher is providing himself with a resource for controlling the activities of the pupils. He is able to say what can or cannot happen in his time. Hustler and Payne's conclusion is that it is through the orientations displayed in these extracts that the teacher observably accomplishes a measure of his power relationship over the pupils. Through references to time and its ownership, the teacher demonstrates his control over what the pupils can and cannot do, over the speed with which they are to pursue his directives and over the manner in which they are to conduct themselves.

Teacher authority as practical action

Our second ethnomethodological study is by Macbeth (1991), in an article on 'Teacher Authority as Practical Action'. The data for his study consisted of video recordings of nine classrooms involving tenth graders (15-year-olds) over four to six consecutive days. Where Hustler and Payne produce a membership categorization analysis of power, focusing on how a power relationship is exhibited in teachers' talk with pupils, Macbeth engages in a sequential analysis of authority.

We are precluded by length considerations from giving a full exposition of Macbeth's work and so we will focus on one particular aspect of this sequential investigation. The particular structure of teacher authority we wish to highlight involves something that is seemingly very mundane indeed, so mundane that unless one pays particularly close attention to its sequential placement and to the consequences that are associated with it, then one would tend to overlook it. This is the humble pause. Pauses are not simply periods of silence. Pauses can be seen to constitute a turn, or at least a part of a turn, in talk-in-interaction. Pauses, at least in Macbeth's data, occupy distinctive positions within talk; they are linked systematically with what preceded and with what follows. They have local 'practical significance'. Furthermore, 'the practical significance of silence on its every occasion is a locally produced significance, produced by the parties from within their local affairs' (Macbeth, 1991: 289).

What, then, do teachers and pupils 'do' with pauses? It appears that one thing they do is exercise authority. They do so by combining pauses with 'addresses' to produce an 'address-pause' and it is this combination that comprises a method through which authority can be achieved. The 'address' part of this structure consists of the teacher speaking to a particular students or students and addressing them by their name(s), as Joe, Jack or Jim. The pause then follows before the teacher speaks again. In order to appreciate this sequential structure and its use in the classroom we will consider the following extracts from the corpus of Macbeth's data:

Example 10
```
[Following an unannounced quiz.]
55      (2.0) [several lines of chatter; teacher speaks
56      over it]
57  T:  So I'm goin' to uhm
58      (3.0) [chatter continues unabated]
59  T:  Now, let's come together again. (.) [whistles]
60      Tim (0.5) Juanita.
61      (2.0) [chatters dips]
62      Kevin.
63      (2.0)
64      Wan' chu ta' come tagether 'n tha class ...
```

In this data extract we can see two instances of the address-pause. At line 60 the teacher uses the address part to get the attention of Tim and Juanita. Before this, the children had been chatting, as the transcript shows, but now (see line 59) it is time to 'come together'. Likewise, at line 62 Kevin is addressed, and there then occurs a two-second pause before the teacher continues to talk to the class. The addressing of Tim and Juanita and Kevin is designed to remind them that they should also cease chatting, along with the rest of the class. The pause that follows is a 'space' during which the pupils then have the opportunity to show that they have understood what the teacher means by addressing them. By ceasing to speak they will have not only shown that they have both 'found themselves' in the teacher's address but will also have understood what it was about their behaviour that motivated the address in the first place. By pausing after the address the teacher can be understood to be waiting for the students' compliance with the instruction embodied in the address. In the absence of further addressing we can infer that the children have indeed stopped chatting and that the teacher's authority has been successfully exercised. There is an address-pause in the following extract that works slightly differently.

Example 11
```
[While checking individual progress and fielding ques-
tions, the teacher speaks to everyone, and calls for
order.]
```

```
26  S:  Miss Cone, this pencil too sma(l)(l)
27  T:  - shh -
28  S2: That's whut happen' ta mine (0.5).
29  T:  Hey you guys!
30      (1.0) [T turns away from twosome, out to class]
31      I doen' get whut's up, bu' I' doen like whut's
32      up
33      (2.0)
34      Kim
35      (0.7)
36      turn' around(d) ...
```

In this extract it can be seen that the next position to the address-pause is a turn taken by the teacher, who continues her line of address to the targeted student(s) and seems to speak of the affairs that prompted it at the outset. That is to say, as in the previous extract, the teacher first addresses the student and then pauses, during which time the student is supposed to cease whatever it was the teacher found unacceptable. Indeed, Kim was turned around in her seat and now, in the space provided by the pause, she corrects herself and ceases to turn round. It is noticeable that in the space of the pause Kim has turned around, so that 'turn round' is in the third position of the sequence. According to Macbeth, it is at first sight a redundant address. However, as he shows, the pause is in fact used to accomplish interactional work. Kim's turning toward the teacher shows that she has found her address. The teacher saying 'turn round' after she has done so shows to Kim and to everyone else the sense of the address for what it was (a call to pay attention).

Finally, let us consider the following extract:

Example 12
```
[T class is about to begin a writing task.]
1  T:  OK before you get started, (.) let' me answer any
2      questions that you have (0.5)
3      Caroline Dawn Julie
4      (0.7)
5      Julie. Keep' it down.
6      (hhh) Ah, (0.7) you may pick (.) anyone (.) you
7      like, but make sure you know the person (.)
8      well. An' jis start writing.
```

Here, Caroline, Dawn and Julie have been talking together. The teacher addresses them and then pauses, and as in the previous extracts it is in the duration of this pause that the targeted students are supposed to demonstrate their compliance with the teacher's instruction contained in the address. As we can see, however, the follow-up address of Julie and the teacher's statement of the reasons for the address in the first place appears also to be motivated by Julie's failure to demonstrate compliance in the space of the pause. This second address serves to restate what it is that Julie is now expected to do. We take it from the absence of any further attention from the teacher that she will have complied with the teacher's wishes.

In the light of our earlier argument that the participants have to demonstrably orient to power as a condition for it to be an adequate description of what is involved in what they are doing, how are we to assess the studies by Hustler and Payne and Macbeth? Exerting control, restricting freedoms and telling people what to do all appear to be examples of power, and more specifically a power relationship between teachers and pupils. The studies we have considered describe how the relationship between teachers and pupils in the classroom is interactionally organized. In particular, they show how the students and pupils analyse and understand the teacher's talk as such things as instructions, calls to attention, reproaches and reprimands. The pupils' response reveals what the teacher's talk meant to them. In the data we have discussed, the pupils did not challenge the teacher's talk and only in the last extract was the teacher required to repeat her instruction. In so far as pupils responses exhibit their analysis of teacher's power and authority, their compliance does indeed show that this was a real phenomenon for them.

Conclusion

In this chapter we have considered some observational data relating to educational settings of various kinds. We began with some data on the beginning of a university lecture. Our concern was to analyse the intelligibility of the lecture's beginning. We drew attention to the relationship between membership categories and category-bound activities, as exhibited in talk, in this regard. We also examined briefly the speech exchange system for university lectures, and this provided the touchstone for a comparative analysis of speech exchange between teacher and pupils in a reception class. In the final section of the chapter, we examined two ethnomethodological studies relating to the phenomena of power and authority in school.

We could have discussed many other ethnomethodological studies in the field of education since this area has been one of the most popular and productive for ethnomethodological sociology. We have not mentioned, for example, studies of the accomplishment of educational assessment (Mehan, 1976; Heap, 1980; 1982), of the practicalities of educational decision making (for example, Cicourel et al., 1974; Mehan, 1991) and the interactional use of technology in the classroom (for example, Heap, 1989). The exception to this plethora of investigations is the field of higher education, where despite our analysis of the lecture relatively little work has yet been done (but see Garfinkel, 2002 for a suggestive study). Given the access that our readers have to the world of higher education, this would seem to provide a good opportunity, not only to engage in some ethnomethodological sociological work, but also to add to the ethnomethodological tradition in the field of education.

Student activity

1 Using a tape recorder, record the opening few minutes of one or more lectures.
2 Consider the phase before the lecture delivery begins. How are the participants observably doing 'the lecture has not yet begun'?
3 By what means is the transition into the delivery of the lecture accomplished?

Further reading

H. Garfinkel (2002) *Ethnomethodology's Program: Working Out Durkheim's Aphorism.* Lanham, MD: Rowman and Littlefield. Ch.7.
S. Hester and D. Francis (eds) (2000) *Local Educational Order: Ethnomethodological Studies of Knowledge in Action.* Amsterdam: John Benjamins.
D. Macbeth (1990) 'Classroom order as practical action: the making and un-making of a quiet reproach', *British Journal of Sociology of Education,* 11(2): 189–214.
G. Payne and T. Cuff (1982) *Doing Teaching.* London: Batsford.
G. Payne and D. Hustler (1980) 'Teaching the class: the practical management of a cohort', *British Journal of Sociology of Education,* 1 (1): 49–66.

Note

1 The non-return of a greeting is normally a noticeably absent phenomenon. In ordinary conversation, the production of a greeting provides for the immediate production of a greeting return. Should such a greeting return not be produced in the next conversational slot, further talk may be occasioned to deal with the problem. If a person says 'Hello', then the assumption is the recipient of the greeting will say 'Hello' too (or words to that effect). Such greetings, in other words, come in pairs, the one makes relevant the next. As we have seen, such adjacency pairs are connected in a particular way such that the absence of the second pair part is both noticeable and accountable matter. In other words, the sequence is organized normatively: it is normative that the second part of the sequence here is produced in the next slot after the production of the first-pair part. For example:

A: Hello
   (Pause 1.5)
A: You OK?
B: Sorry, I was miles away.

One can imagine that A and B could have been any one of the students encountering the lecturer in the street. However, in this case the 'Hello' would not have been understood as a pre-lecture greeting. Likewise, if one student said to the student next to her 'Good afternoon', then this would not have been heard as the start of the lecture.

8

Going to the Doctor

So far in this book we have discussed how ethnomethodology can be applied to activities and situations with which just about anyone in our society can be assumed to have some familiarity. In this chapter we also look at a situation that pretty much everyone has experienced: going to the doctor. However, although we have all taken part in interaction with doctors and other medical professionals and thereby are familiar with some aspects of medical practice, there are, of course, many aspects of modern medicine that are strange and unfamiliar to the lay person. While we may have picked up some medical knowledge through our dealings with doctors, and possibly from other sources such as medical programmes on television, we cannot as lay persons claim to understand medical knowledge in the way that medical professionals do. The very fact that we go to the doctor when feeling unwell marks our recognition of his or her superior knowledge of medical matters.

This knowledge imbalance between the lay person and the medical professional is just one instance of a basic feature of modern social life. After all, we live in what sociologists have called a 'knowledge society'. By this term they point to the fact that our everyday lives are shaped in many and varied ways by the application of technical knowledge. This is knowledge that we ourselves, as ordinary lay persons, do not have mastery of, and we therefore rely on experts to supply and apply such knowledge for us. So pervasive is this reliance on professional expertise that some sociologists have suggested, tongue in cheek, that the instruction found on the back of electronic devices – 'No user serviceable parts inside' – could serve as a motto for the relationship between professionals and lay persons in modern society.

To consider what is involved in managing the relationship between ordinary persons and professionals in daily life, this chapter will examine what is involved in 'going to the doctor'. Dealing with illness was once a far more non-specialist matter than it is today. In pre-industrial times, especially among the lower orders in society, the treatment of ailments was managed within one's immediate family or community and medical knowledge, such as it was, was passed down from one generation to the next. Nowadays, however, being ill quickly brings one into contact with medical professionals. As sociologists have long emphasized, being ill is much more than just a physical condition. It involves social relationships between, on the one hand, the patient (and members of the patient's family) and on the other hand, doctors, nurses and other medical personnel. What kinds of relationships are these and how are they interactionally managed? These are the key questions we will address in this chapter.

In line with our analytic practice already laid out in this book, we will begin with what is observably the case – things that anyone can observe – and ask how these observed features are interactionally accomplished. Our first topic is the decision to go to the doctor. We then consider the actual visit to the doctor.

The decision to visit the doctor

Let us begin with some self-reflection about what we know about the organization of medical services in the UK. Overwhelmingly, medical intervention in our lives begins with a decision to consult one's doctor or, in the case of medical emergencies, the casualty department of the nearest hospital offering such a service. We trust that this 'fact of life' is something that, with the exception of young children, is a matter of common-sense knowledge. Thus, everybody knows that the health system is organized on the basis that every person in the society has a doctor with whom they are registered – a 'general practitioner' (GP) in the UK – and who is available to be consulted about health problems. Equally, it is common knowledge that there are some acute medical conditions that warrant bypassing the GP and instead going straight to casualty. We may begin our analysis, then, by saying that for us, and we assume our readers, assistance with medical problems is organized in terms of a categorial distinction between two classes of such problems. On the one hand, there are those that are properly to be dealt with by one's GP and on the other hand, those of an emergency character for which a visit to a casualty department is the appropriate course of action. Our suggestion, then, is that such a distinction will be used in persons' decisions to visit their doctor or, perhaps, their local casualty department.

Self-reflection reveals other features of the social organization of medical provision. We know, for example, that persons who are incumbents of the membership category 'doctor' are medical experts; they engage in special activities and they have specialized knowledge and competencies that laypersons do not have. Furthermore, as ordinary citizens we have entitlements to be treated by them under appropriate circumstances (such as when we have a genuine illness). However, whilst it is easy to reflect upon and to recall such organizational features, we suggest that we need data from actual instances of the use of such knowledge if we are to produce more than reasonable and generalized conjectures about these matters. We need to ground our descriptions of the social organization of medical assistance in some real-life occurrences in which persons' knowledge of medical matters was used and thereby made available for analysis. Accordingly, we will consider the following data extracts, both of which involve persons in making decisions about visiting their doctor. The first consists of some field notes, the second a transcript of a conversation.

Field notes: going to the doctor

S received a telephone call at work one morning from his partner, W, who reported that she had received a call from the school secretary about L, their daughter. The school secretary had called to say that L was complaining of having earache. This was no surprise to W because L had already complained to her and S a couple of days before that she had an earache. At that point it was thought that she might have been suffering because she had been swimming, and nothing more was done about it. The secretary mentioned that her own children had recently had ear infections and that it would be sensible to have L's ear checked in case it had an infection and to therefore prevent it from getting any worse. Accordingly, W had made an appointment and said that she was picking L up from school and was taking her straight to the doctor.

In these notes, then, it is reported that S received a call from his partner, W, who had previously been called by the school secretary about their daughter's suffering with earache. We want first to focus on the word 'doctor' and ask, in line with our procedure for self-reflective analysis outlined in Chapter 3, how this word is understood in this context and what such understanding demonstrates analytically speaking.

We take it, and assume that our readers take it too, that the word means 'medical doctor', rather than, say, someone who has a doctorate in history, sociology or nuclear physics. Further, we take it that the category 'doctor' is understandable in this way because of its co-selection with other words in the field notes. In particular, the description of the daughter as having been complaining about an earache and the report that the school secretary's children had recently had ear infections are all somehow hearably consistent or congruent with the category (medical) 'doctor' but not, of course, with the other kinds of doctor mentioned above. In other words, then, the sense of the word 'doctor' is informed by these co-selected words just as the sense of earache and ear infection as physical ailments is afforded by our understanding of the meaning of 'doctor'. In the language of membership categorization analysis, then, we can say therefore dealing with physical ailments such as these is a category-bound activity of the membership category 'doctor' and, in terms of the viewer's maxim that we mentioned in Chapter 3, if an activity can be heard as being done by the incumbent of the category to which it is bound, then: see/hear it that way. For these reasons, then, we can understand the meaning of the word 'doctor'.

We also note that the doctor's appearance in the report is an utterly unsurprising one. Given the nature of the problems being reported, the doctor 'appears on cue'. We can speculate that had the problem reported been theft, then it would have been equally unsurprising if the police had so appeared. For us, and we assume for our readers too, it is, furthermore, a normative matter that the doctor should appear on cue. That is to say, the treatment of those who are ill is a moral and occupational predicate of the category 'doctor', just as it is a category-bound activity of parents to care for their children when they are ill and to take them for medical help when it is warranted.

The analytic significance of this, we suggest, is that W's report to S that she would be taking L to the doctor, the school secretary's advice that W should do so, and the unsurprising nature of the whole story demonstrates our and the characters' use of common-sense knowledge of the social organization of illness and medical help. Furthermore, such knowledge is organized, as we have indicated in the previous paragraph, 'categorially' in at least two senses. Thus, just as the school secretary offered her advice on the grounds that medical doctors are proper persons to seek help from when a child is suffering from an ear infection, then so also did W make her appointment with the doctor on the grounds that her daughter was suffering from one of the kinds of things with which persons categorizable as doctors are able to deal and for which she felt she should consult. We also note that W's understanding of the 'procedural' character of the social organization of medical help is indicated in her report that she had made an appointment to see the doctor. We shall return to the issue of appointments in a moment. We now turn to our second piece of data, a transcript of conversation about a child's injury.

Transcript: not going to the doctor
S = father, A = mother, D = daughter
[S has just returned home to find D in bed.]
S: Hi, how are you?
A: D's hurt her wrist.
S: Have you? Let's have a look.
D: It huuuurts!
S: Where does it hurt?
D: There, just there.
    [S gently touches wrist bone]
D: Not that bone.
S: No?
D: No, underneath, just there.
S: Can you move it?
D: I can move my fingers.
S: Can you move your wrist?
    [D moves wrist slightly]
S: Well, if you'd broken it, it would be really painful all over, and you wouldn't want to move it all. It's probably just a bruise. I know it's

```
     painful.
A:   No need for a trip to casualty then?
S:   No, I don't think so. Best wait and see how it is
     in the morning.
```

In the interaction captured in this transcript it is observably the case that A reports a trouble concerning her painful wrist, S assesses the extent of the injury and, together with W, decides not to take her to the doctor. How, then, are these observable features accomplished? Specifically, we want to ask: how is the injury assessed; and how is the decision *not* to go to the doctor made?

With respect to the first question, we note first that the kind of injury that A has is assessed interactionally via a series of question and answer pairs. The questions pertain first to the location of the injury and then to the issue of whether or not A can move her wrist. S appears to be interested in what category of injury it is: is the wrist actually broken or is it not? Second, in assessing what category of injury it is, S can be heard to deploy his lay knowledge of bone breakages. His question about wrist movement appears to based on his knowledge that moving a broken wrist is much more painful and difficult than moving one that is not broken. Third, in addition to S's orientation to a lay categorial orderliness of injuries, W can be heard to be attentive to the practical implications of these categorial assessments. Breakages imply visits to appropriate medical personnel, that is, the hospital casualty department, whilst non-breakages do not.

With respect to the second question, it is observable that after the series of questions and answers, W produces a query in the form of a 'formulation'. With respect to formulations, Garfinkel and Sacks (1986: 170) point out:

> A member may treat some part of the conversation as an occasion to describe that conversation, to explain it, or characterise it, or explicate, or translate, or summarise, or furnish the gist of it, or take note of its accordance with rules, or remark on its departure from rules. That is to say, a member may use some part of the conversation as an occasion to *formulate* the conversation ...

Furthermore, as they go on to say (1986: 171):

> Along with whatever else may be happening in conversation it may be a feature of the conversation for the conversationalists that they are doing something else, namely, what they are doing is saying-in-so-many-words-what-we-are-doing (or what we are talking about, or who is talking, or who we are, etc.).

The relevance of these remarks is this: W, in saying, 'No need for a trip to casualty then?' can be heard to be formulating the decision that the conversation is directed to making. It is this, the decision, that is the reason for the conversation; whatever else may be going in the conversation, its *raison d'être* is whether the injury warrants a visit to the doctor. Furthermore, in formulating the decision in this way, W can be heard to solicit a confirmation from S. As the data shows, such confirmation appears in the immediately following turn, 'No, I don't think so'. It is via this closing pair of utterances, then, that the decision afforded by the prior series of question and answer and the categorization of the injury they make possible, is made. The decision to visit the doctor (or not, as the case may be) is something that can be appreciated both sequentially and categorially.

Having considered the decision to go to the doctor, we now turn to some further aspects of the social organization of medical help. We will be concentrating on what occurs when doctor and patient encounter one another. However, before we do so we note two preliminary matters that we suggest are worthy of investigation. Both concern what happens between the decision to visit the doctor and the actual medical encounter in the surgery. The first concerns the activity of making an appointment, the second to what happens in the waiting room. We do not have data on either of these and so we cannot offer any observations or analysis for consideration. However, as our readers will know, one aspect of the procedural character of the social organization of medical help is that before the medical encounter can take place, an appointment will have to be made. As anyone who has made such an appointment knows, access to the doctor is organized in terms of a queuing system and as such may afford interesting ethnomethodological work, not least with respect to comparisons between such systems of queuing and those operative elsewhere (for example, in the settings we examined in Chapter 5). Second, even though an appointment may have been made for a specific time, on arrival at the surgery it is typically the case that one does not walk straight in to see the doctor. Rather, an announcement of one's arrival is routinely made to the receptionist and then some waiting is done in the waiting room. The organization of waiting may also provide interesting observations for analysis. These possibilities notwithstanding, we will now turn our attention to the medical encounter itself.

In the surgery

The method of ethnomethodological sociology tells one to begin to analyse a situation by noticing something that is recognizably going on. Only then can one begin to ask how what is going on is being produced. Following this method, perhaps the first thing to note about medical encounters is that they are overwhelmingly conducted through talk (though not entirely – we will return to this point later). It is in and through talk between patient and doctor that medical intervention is sought and given. What then can one say about such talk? The most obvious point is that it varies from ordinary conversation in two main ways. First, talk in the surgery largely consists in sequences of questions and answers, reflecting the fact that the main business of the occasion comprises the elicitation and communication of information. Second, the allocation of these speech actions is asymmetrically distributed between the participants. Studies of doctor–patient interaction show that, overwhelmingly, it is the doctor who asks questions and the patient who gives answers. In and through such question–answer sequences doctors seek from their patients information about why they are seeking medical help and patients explain the reason for their visit and may describe their symptoms: pains, aches, or other physical sufferings they are experiencing. The third point to note is that the consultation displays a typical overall processual structure: question–answer sequences in which an account of the patient's 'trouble' is given precede, and provide the basis for, statements in which the doctor may communicate advice, instructions or diagnostic judgements. We will look at this latter phase of the medical encounter presently, when we consider the work of Maynard (1991). To begin with, let us consider the 'elicitation' phase more closely.

If the medical consultation is essentially about the communication of information, ethnomethodological studies have shown that the exchange of information between doctor and patient is not equivalent, neither in the overall amount of information that is given by one party to the other, nor in the organization of the talk in and through which it is given. Put simply, patients tend to tell considerably more to the doctor than the doctor tells to them, and this distribution is reflective of the fact that it is doctors who ask most of the questions in medical encounters and patients who supply most of the answers. This is not simply a statistical phenomenon but an 'oriented-to' normative one. That is to say, there is a preference in the medical encounter for question–answer sequences to be doctor initiated.

One manifestation of this preference is the fact that the medical consultation typically begins, after an initial exchange of greetings, with a question by the doctor to the patient, inviting the patient to explain the reason for the visit: 'What seems to be the trouble?', 'What brings you to the clinic?', 'What can I do for you?' and so on. Questions such as these are designed to elicit what in medical terminology is known as the patient's 'presenting condition'. In other words, they invite the patient to provide an account of the trouble that he or she is experiencing. As such, they can be understood as legitimating an extended utterance, a 'story', in which the patient's symptoms are explained in the context of how these have arisen and developed to a point where they may justify medical action. That patients are invited to tell such stories accounts in large part for the quantitative imbalance in talk between the parties.

The patient's initial account typically is followed by further questions from the doctor, designed to elicit more details of the problem and information about the patient's relevant medical history. Thus, a typical consultation consists of a chain of question–answer pairs, with the doctor responding to each answer by the patient with a further question. For example:

```
Dr: Does anybody have tuberculosis?
Pt: No, not that I know of.
Dr: Heart disease?
Pt: No.
Dr: Diabetes?
Pt: No.
Dr: High blood pressure?
Pt: My father had that.
Dr: Did you ever have whooping cough?
Pt: Yes.
Dr: Scarlet fever?
Pt: No.
```
(Frankel, 1990: 238)

Notice the way in which this question–answer chain is built. The doctor's initial question has an 'interrogative' form. However, following the patient's answer, a further question is posed in the form of a single phrase: 'Heart disease?'. Subsequent questions also have a single phrase or single word form. These utterances do not have the standard grammatical form associated with questions, yet the patient has no difficulty in hearing them as such. Clearly, this is due to them being hearable as 'modified repetitions' of the initial question. Even though the doctor does not repeat the wording of the initial question 'Does anybody have …', he can be heard as asking this each time, such that, for example, the patient is able to reply to the utterance 'High blood pressure' with the answer 'My father had that'. Thus to describe this sequence of utterances as a 'question–answer chain' is to note that the participants treat it as such in the way they produce their utterances.

Question–answer chains like the one above are a common feature of doctor–patient consultations. They provide an interactionally efficient way in which a body of factual information can be transmitted from patient to doctor. The proliferation of this structure of talk is further evidence for an interactional preference for doctor-initiated questions. However, the clearest evidence of the preference for doctor-initiated questions is the fact that, when a patient does ask a question of the doctor, the utterance is produced in ways that mark its 'dispreferred' status. Typically this involves the production by the patient of a pre-question utterance – a question preface – that serves to provide for the upcoming question. Such question prefaces can take various forms; we will briefly mention two. One is the production of a pre-question question, for example:

```
Dr: Very good. (0.4) Let me see yer ankle.
    (2.2)
Dr: hhh. VERY GOOD.
Pt: I wanna ask yih som'n.
Dr: What's that?
    (0.6)
```

```
Pt:  hh.  (0.5)  I  have  (0.6)  (this)  second  toe  that  was
     broken.  (0.4)  but  I  went  to  the  p'diatrist  becuz
     I  couldn't  find  a  doctor  on  th'  weekend.  (0.4)  An
     he  said  it  wasn't  broken.  -  it  was.  So  it  wasn't
     taken  care  of  properly  'hh  An  when  I',m  on  my  feet,
     I  get  a  sensation  in  it.  -  I  mean  is  there  any-
     thing  (th't)  can  be  done?
Dr:  How  long  ago  d'you  break  it?
Pt:  Mmh,  two  years.
Dr:  Yih  c'd  put  a  matetarsal  pad  underneath  it  …
(Frankel, 1990: 241)
```

In this extract the patient announces that he wants to ask the doctor a question. This announcement comprises an adjacency pair 'first part', thus providing the doctor with a 'second part' slot which he uses to invite the patient to state his question. It is notable that the patient's question takes the form of a story (about a previous injury to one of his toes). The story provides the context for the actual question 'Is there anything that can be done?', which is placed at the end of the utterance.

A second question preface form that provides for an upcoming patient question is a 'noticing'. Here the patient marks some aspect of the ongoing scene as notable and then asks a question about it. For example:

```
Dr:  It's  OK  (1.3)  OK,  y'  can  grab  the  sides  again  if
     yih  want  to  (1.7)  Pull  against  the  sides  (0.5)
     That's  it,  fine.
     (3.2)
Pt:  That's  pretty  interesting.  -  How  come  you  do  that
     examination  sitting  up?  (0.5)  I  mean  hh.
Dr:  We're  gonna  do  it  lying  down  also.
Pt:  Oh  really.
Dr:  Yeh.
(Frankel, 1990: 241)
```

In this extract, the patient topicalizes the physical examination the doctor is engaged in by noting something interesting about it. This prefaces a question that asks the doctor to explain why the examination is done while he (the patient) is sitting up. As Frankel (1990) notes, the use of a question preface has the effect of reducing or delaying the impact of injecting a direct question into the interaction. Thus it is not that patients cannot ask questions of the doctor, but rather that they have restricted rights to do so, so that when they do it is in ways that avoid the production of an unadorned, interactionally stark question.

The pattern of asymmetrical alignment of questions and answers is a recurrent feature of medical consultations in which patients have referred themselves to their doctor. It is also apparent in other kinds of consultations, such as those concerned with the delivery of medical judgements or news following up on medical tests or examinations. Here, however, the question–answer sequence, while displaying the same categorical distribution between doctor and patient or patient's representative (for example, parent), has a distinctive structural character. Maynard (1991; 1992) refers to this structure as a 'perspective-display series'. Put simply, Maynard's studies show that when doctors have the task of delivering diagnostic bad news, they do so in a roundabout way that involves inviting the recipient to give his or her opinion about the problem. Only when this view is forthcoming does the doctor respond with a statement of the medical findings. Sequentially, then, the perspective-display series consists of at least three utterance turns:

1 Doctor's opinion-query/perspective-display invitation.
2 Recicipient's assessment.
3 Doctor's report of medical finding.

Maynard notes that this sequential structure is not unique to medical consultations. Something similar can be seen in ordinary conversation in circumstances where one participant has bad news to deliver. Frequently that participant will avoid direct delivery, instead prefacing it with utterances that invite the other to guess the bad news. Schegloff (1988: 443) provides an example of this from a telephone call between two women friends, Belle and Fanny:

```
Belle:  … I … I had something (.) terrible t'tell you.
        So uhh
Fanny:  How t' errible is it?
Belle:  hhhhh
        (.)
Belle:  Uhh ez worse it could be.
        (0.7)
Fanny:  W'y mean, Eva?
        (.)
Belle:  Uh uh hh
Fanny:  - Wud she do, die?
```

Here Belle announces that she has something terrible to tell, and when Fanny asks for a more specific clue, 'How terrible?', replies with a characterization, 'Ez worse it could be', that enables Fanny to guess both who the news concerns and what it is. This extract is not, strictly speaking, a perspective-display series, since Belle does not actually invite Fanny to give her opinion of the matter to be reported. It is better described as a 'clueing-guessing-confirming' sequence. Contrast this with the following, drawn from Maynard's (1992: 337) data:

```
 1 Doctor:  What do you see as his difficulty?
 2 Mother:  Mainly his uhm - the fact that he doesn't
 3          understand everything and also the fact
 4          that his speech is very hard to understand
 5          what he's saying a lot of the time.
 6 Doctor:  Right. (0.2) Do you have any ideas why it
 7          is? Are you, do you h? No. (2.0)
 8          h. OK, I (0.2) you know, I think that we
 9          basically in some ways agree with you, in
10          so far as we think that David's main problem,
11          you know, does involve, you know, language.
```

Here the doctor explicitly invites the patient's mother to express her opinion about her son's problem. In response to her view that this involves his inability to 'understand everything' and to produce speech that others can understand, the doctor then asks whether she has any view about the causes of this problem: 'Do you have any ideas *why* it is?' Only when the mother replies in the negative does the doctor provide a statement of medical opinion about David's problem. With reference to the three-part structure of the perspective display series outlined above, this data shows a slightly elaborated version, a five-utterance structure in which (1) the doctor's initial opinion-query (line 1) is followed (2) by the mother's perspective display (lines 2–5). This is then followed (3) by a further opinion-query, concerning the possible causes of the problem (line 6), (4) a negative response (line 7) and then (5) the doctor's report (lines 8–11).

Maynard reports that in every instance in his data corpus where doctors are reporting medical findings or opinions concerning a patient's problem, the interaction exhibited the sequential organization of the perspective-display series in either it's basic or, more often, an elaborated form. To understand why, it is important to consider the final turn in the sequence and how the doctor's speech action relates to the utterances that have preceded it. The distinctive feature of the perspective-display series is that it enables the doctor's medical report to be produced as a confirmation or elaboration of the opinion that the recipient has just expressed. In this way, the series operates to accomplish the 'co-implication' of the lay viewpoint with the medical one. This co-implication is most easily achieved where the lay opinion is perceivedly close to the medical one. In this case, the doctor's report typically takes the form of a reformulation – in more technical terms – of the recipient's proffered problem definition. In the extract above, for example, the doctor responds to the mothers view by confirming that the problem her son is experiencing 'involves language'.

Achieving co-implication is more problematic where the recipient's problem definition is at variance with the medical view, or where he or she takes issue with that view. In such cases the sequence tends to be longer and more complex, involving utterances in which the doctor upgrades and re-specifies the problem. Maynard (1992: 345) illustrates these complexities by means of several extracts from a lengthy interview between a pediatrician and the mother of a boy who is under treatment for severe behavioural problems. The first extract is as follows:

```
 1 Mother:  … from what I was told in the beginning and
 2          you told me too, he will outgrow this as
 3          he goes along.
 4 Doctor:  Well. Yeah. It's not exactly –
 5 Mother:  More or less, hhhh?
 6 Doctor:  … what I said.
 7 Mother:  Yeah.
 8 Doctor:  What – what do you think, I mean, do you
 9          think Barry will outgrow his problems?
10 Mother:  Well! I think so, in way – I hope so! In
11          ways. Because you know …
```

Here, the mother attributes to the doctor a statement that her son will 'out-grow' his problem (lines 1–3). The doctor replies by first producing an agreement token ('Yeah'), but then producing a qualified disagreement ('It's not exactly what I said'). In the course of his utterance, at a point at which its disagreement status, *vis-à-vis* his attribution, is apparent, the mother interrupts (line 5) to downgrade her previous attribution ('More or less'), and then agrees with the doctor's remark ('Yeah'). The doctor then produces an opinion-query, inviting the mother to give her view about the permanency or otherwise of her son's problems (lines 8–9). She replies by asserting her hope that these problems are temporary. In this extract, then, it is clear that the perspectives of the mother and the doctor are not in alignment. However, it is also clear that both parties orient to agreement on a shared perspective as the desirable outcome. This is indicated, on the one hand, by the qualified way in which the doctor expresses his disagreement with the mother's attribution, and on the other hand by the mother's retreat from her initial position to a downgraded one as soon as the doctor queries it.

This preference for agreement is evident at other points in the transcript. For example, at a later point in the discussion, (Maynard, 1992: 346) the following exchange takes place:

```
103 Mother:  (So that's) how I thought something was.
104 Doctor:  So that's why we –
105 Mother:  – Wrong there.
106 Doctor:  Right.
```

```
107  Doctor:  And (0.3) you know, we (.) agree with you,
108           you know, we-er-to the certain degree.
109           We feel that …
110  Mother:  Is he gonna be all right? Heh huh
111  Doctor:  We - we feel that (0.3) Billy is hyperactive.
112  Mother:  Yeah -
113  Doctor:  - y'know, and he has had trouble (.) for
114           a long time hhh
115  Mother:  Yeah.
116  Doctor:  But we don't see this as something that's
117           just gonna pass.
118  Mother:  Yeah, well, I know that.
119  Doctor:  And - an' go away.
120  Mother:  Right.
```

In this extract, the doctor produces several displays of agreement with the mother's views, such as 'we agree with you' (line 107) and using agreement intonations in saying 'Billy *is* hyperactive' (line 111) and that 'he *has* had trouble' (line 113). Through these remarks the doctor aligns himself with the views previously expressed by the mother. These utterances are placed immediately before a statement of the medical view that Billy's problems are not temporary but permanent: 'we don't see this as something that's gonna pass.' This view stands in opposition to the mother's stated view, and hope, that her son's problems are something he will grow out of. As such, they serve to 'package' the medical view within a sequential context of agreement. In this way, the medical view is presented as a 'modified agreement' rather than a straight disagreement.

Maynard (1992: 355) concludes his analysis of the perspective-display series by saying:

> It seems then, that the perspective-display series is a conversational mechanism that is *adapted* to a clinical environment where professionals must inform patients or parents of highly charged diagnoses. By co-implicating their recipient's knowledge or beliefs (and anticipated reactions) in the news they have to deliver, clinicians present assessments in a publicly affirmative and non-conflicting manner. In short, the series provides a solution to interactive problems that transcend the clinician–parent or doctor–patient relationship.

Managing intimacy in medical examinations

So far, we have emphasized the role of talk in medical encounters. However, important though talk is, it is not the only way in which doctors and patients interact, nor is talk the only source for the information doctors seek from their patients. Medical problems are overwhelmingly, though of course not exclusively, associated with the body. Thus going to the doctor involves being ready and willing to make one's body available to visual and tactile examination. Doctors, uniquely outside the confines of intimate relationships, have the right of access to one's body, including the most private parts of one's anatomy that may be completely off limits in other relationships. As Heath (1986: 99) notes, this was not always the case; as recently as the nineteenth century, doctors 'would often place a small alabaster or marble figure on his desk to enable patients to point to the area of difficulty without having to undergo physical examination'. Nowadays, the doctor may look, touch, poke and probe without any objection being raised on the part of the patient. But not objecting is one thing; managing the challenge to one's demeanor that such exposure involves is something else. In recent years, a number of researchers have begun to look at the physical dimension of doctor–patient consultations using video-recorded data. These studies have emphasized that the process of physical examination is also a social, interactional process and have described the ways in which interactional collaboration between patient and doctor is achieved. They have reported on how physical examinations are managed by doctors and patients so as to sustain a 'detached' definition of the situation. They also have interesting things to say about the relationship between the verbal and the non-verbal in medical interaction, since talk plays a major role in the accomplishment of physical examinations.

As an interactional process, the physical examination can be seen as organized into phases. The first phase, the preparation or setting-up phase, involves managing the shift from purely verbal interaction to the physical kind. This transition can occur in a variety of ways. One typical way in which it is initiated is by the doctor announcing that he or she would like to 'take a look' at some part of the patient's body. This may be taken by the patient as an instruction to make that part of the body available; alternatively, it may be followed by a request to do so. The intial request may be followed by others as the doctor seeks to get adequate access to the part of the body being examined. For example (Heath, 1986: 104):

```
Dr:  Shall we just have a peep at your throat today,
     Rosemary?
     (1.2)
Dr:  Can you open wide?
     (0.2)
P:   hhhh
Dr:  Ooh my word!
     (.)
Dr:  Can you stick your tongue out?
     (1.2)
Dr:  Good.
```

Of course, in some examinations it is required that the patients remove some of their clothing in order to give the doctor access to the relevant part of the body. In these cases the setting-up phase is more complex; the doctor may need to use special equipment (for example, a stethoscope) and the patient has to attend to the business of removing their clothes and putting them somewhere. Heath notes that during this preparation phase the doctor and the patient typically avert their gaze from one another, thus enabling a sense of privacy to be sustained. In some cases this privacy may be ensured by having the patient go behind a screen to undress.

Having attained access to the patient's body, the doctor begins to examine it. It is apparent that collaboration with the doctor during a physical examination involves much finer interactional activity than simply holding out an arm or removing some of one's clothes. Heath reports how patients will spontaneously align their body in a way that facilitates the doctor's access to the relevant part. In this way the patient contributes to the redefinition of themselves as an 'object of inquiry'. As Heath (1986: 113) puts it, patients 'temporarily transform themselves into phenomena under investigation'. Thus patients attend to the need to keep still while the doctor peruses or touches them, being careful not to react to the doctor's touch or do anything that might interfere with the progress of the examination. At the same time, though, the patient will 'read' the doctor's intentions as he or she indicates with pressure of their hands how they wish the patient to change position. Heath (1986: 106) describes the fine physical adjustments made by a patient while undergoing an ear examination; the doctor has his hands on the patient's head and is looking into one of her ears:

> The patient makes a number of attempts to present the complaint to the doctor, each attempt coordinated with the visual action of the co-participant. The patient uses the hands of the doctor and the alignment of his gaze to infer how she should place her body and in particular her head and ears. As the doctor's gaze shifts and his hands move she attempts to infer the presentation they demand and align her body accordingly. As they alter position for the third time the patient once again alters the way she presents herself for examination. In each case the patient uses the doctor's orientation and movements as a way of determining how the doctor wants her to participate during the course to the physical examination.

Although the patient orients to the doctor's movements and attempts to co-operate physically with the examination, this is not usually accompanied by visual attention to what the doctor is doing. In most cases, the patient specifically disattends to what the doctor is doing, by looking away from both the doctor and the site of the doctor's attention. The patient will stare into the middle distance to avoid any show of involvement or interest. However, the extent to which patients disattend in this way is related to the 'moral meaning' of the part of the body under examination. Where the examination involves a part of the body that has low moral meaning, such as the arm or foot, the patient may watch the doctor's actions, but if the examination is of a highly charged body area then the strategy of disattention is followed rigidly. Only if the doctor asks a question will the patient look at him or her, and then only for as long as it takes to answer the query.

The fact that the patient's posture of disattention increases with the moral meaning of the body area under examination, is a clear indication that this disattention is an interactional strategy. Its purpose is to manage the potential moral disruption of the 'impersonal' medical definition of the situation that is created by the exposure of highly morally charged parts of the body to the doctor's touch. On the doctor's side of things, there is attention to the need to maintain a strictly objective and practical orientation. The doctor can display respect for the patient's privacy even while examining highly sensitive parts of the body. This is apparent, for example, in the way that the doctor is careful to remove his or her hands from the patients body once the investigative task has been completed. Since the doctor's hands are diagnostic tools, they have the right to rest upon the patient's body only while diagnostic work is being done. Outside this frame, the moral meaning of the doctor's touch becomes uncertain and potentially subject to other interpretations.

Among the different kinds of medical examination, one that has particular potential for moral uncertainty is the gynaecological examination. Emerson (1970: 77) describes the setting of this medical encounter as follows:

> The examination takes place in a special examining room where the patient lies with buttocks down to the edge of the table and her feet in stirrups … usually a nurse is present as a chaperone, and the actual examining lasts only a few minutes.

For the gynaecological examination to be conducted as a medical activity, non-medical meanings and categorial identities have to be excluded from the situation. The event could be described as involving a 'man' inspecting, touching and probing the genitals of a 'woman'. For the moral implications of this description to be avoided, the activity has to be managed in such a way that the medical definition of the situation – including the medically relevant identities of the participants – is consistently sustained. The man is to be regarded not as a man but as a doctor, and the woman not as a woman but as a patient. Sustaining these medically defined identities takes effort on the part of the participants. Thus, Emerson notes that the doctor takes particular care to display a desexualized matter-of-fact attitude towards the activity and that a corresponding impersonal involvement on the part of the patient also (even more so) involves effort. The doctor makes it clear by his actions that this particular examination is 'just another one' and a routine part of the day's work. Emerson (1970: 81) also notes that the special language of the medical examination contributes to the depersonalization and desexualization of the encounter. The avoidance of sexually implicative language is achieved in several ways, such as the employment of euphemisms such as 'down below' and by the use of the third person to refer to the parts of the woman's body being examined. Thus, for example, the doctor refers to '*the* vagina' and '*the* uterus' rather than 'your vagina' and 'your uterus'. Patient behaviour that could be seen as indicative of embarrassment or sexual arousal either is consciously ignored or is redefined by the doctor in less morally charged terms as, for example, 'fear of pain' or 'ticklishness'.

Approaching medical encounters from the point of view of ethno-methodology, then, enables us to focus on how participants manage the relationship between the moral and technical dimensions of such encounters. Studies of doctor–patient interaction show how participants in medical encounters orient to these expectations as features of their here-and-now practical situation. In particular, they show how the technical demands of medical intervention are configured with the moral demands of personal autonomy and bodily decorum. The medical consultation requires complex and subtle patterns of interaction if the doctor and patient are to get the business of the encounter done while maintaining appropriate normative definitions and respecting one another's moral status. As Talcott Parsons pointed out long ago (Parsons, 1951), the relationship between doctor and patient is a reciprocal one defined by mutual moral expectations. Just how these expectations are realized as such and managed in practice is some-thing we can examine through ethnomethodology.

The professional dominance theory

Not all studies of medical interaction have taken the kind of approach we are advocating. Many studies have interpreted such interaction from a point of view shaped by some general theoretical model of medical encounters, seeking to show how this model reveals hitherto disguised features of the relationship between medical professionals and patients. In this respect such studies adopt what we will call an 'ironic' stance towards medical interaction. The irony consists in the claim that such interaction is not what it seems to those involved in it; medical encounters may appear to be oriented towards the practical business of diagnosing and treating health problems, but 'from the enlightened viewpoint of the sociologist' they can be seen to involve something else entirely. Thus medical interaction as it is conducted by doctors and patients turns out to be about something other than it appears, and other than anyone involved is capable of recognizing.

Along these lines, a number of sociologists (for example, Bloor, 1976; Mishler, 1984; Davis, 1988) have interpreted the asymmetry in questions and answers in medical consultations as evidence of a power struggle based on a fundamental conflict of interests between doctors and patients. Rather than viewing this asymmetry as intrinsic to the instrumental orientation of the doctor–patient consultation, they point to the chaining of question–answer pairs as manifesting the imposition of medical power over the patient.

Clearly, given the adjacency pair organization of question–answer sequences, the party who asks the questions has more control over the direction of the talk than the one who answers. On this basis it is suggested by such sociologists that the monopolization of questions provides the doctor with a means to shape the content and direction of the talk, restricting the flow of information to a one-way process and preventing the patient from moving the talk in directions that might be threatening to the doctor's position.

This argument is inspired by a view of doctor–patient relations first proposed by Freidson (1970), who coined the term 'professional dominance' to describe the imposition of medical power upon patients. A key assumption of his approach is that two distinct and opposing forms of thought confront one another in medical encounters. In contrast to the everyday perspective of the patient, the doctor's perceptions and concerns are said to be governed by a technical perspective deriving from the bio-medical conception of illness. This conception, in essence, is the view that the body is a complex biological machine, one that functions – and malfunctions – in predictable ways according to known biological laws, and that all health problems – all physical ones at least – consist in such biological malfunctioning. Understanding of, and commitment to, this bio-medical model is held by Freidson and others to be asymmetrically distributed: doctors' perceptions are shaped by it in dealing with patients problems, but patients themselves neither understand it nor view their problems in its terms. Furthermore, the bio-medical model, it is claimed, amounts to a legitimating device for the authority of doctors, since it is they, and not patients, who possess the technical, scientific knowledge that alone provides the basis for explaining the health problems that patients may be experiencing.

According to the professional dominance theory, then, by controlling the sequential shape of consultation talk, doctors ensure that patients have little opportunity to question the doctor's knowledge or raise matters that might put into doubt the relevance of this knowledge for understanding the patient's problems. In other words, the asymmetrical organization of doctor–patient talk is a functional device for sustaining professional dominance. However, ethnomethodological studies of doctor–patient interaction such as those discussed in this chapter cast considerable doubt on the claim that patients have an oppressive and alien perspective imposed upon them by doctors, one which systematically negates their own understandings of their problems. On the evidence of such studies, while it might be reasonable to argue that some patients in some medical consultations may find what they are told confusing or hard to understand, to suggest that patients have no awareness or understanding of a clinical approach to illness and find the bio-medical model quite alien to their experience is unsupportable.

In our view, the professional dominance theory is a further example of sociological analysis being driven by pre-defined theoretical commitments rather than detailed observation of social life. Critics of this professional dominance analysis of medical interaction have pointed out that it begs some important issues about the nature of evidence. For example, there is a big difference between, on the one hand, noting that *some* medical consultations can involve tension and conflict and that *some* patients are observably dissatisfied with the information that the doctor offers to them, and, on the other hand, arguing that *every* medical encounter is a struggle for control. Thus Sharrock (1979: 140) argues that:

> The approach in question ... leads us to exaggerate the elements of confrontation in the doctor–patient encounter, when the striking thing about the relevant materials is the sporadic nature of any (even the slightest) *display* of opposition to the doctor's views, and the easy way in which those are overridden.

The professional dominance theory, critics such as Sharrock argue, seems to presuppose the very thing that it claims to establish. Thus, if there is no evident conflict and the patient simply responds to the doctors questions, the theory has it that this shows just how effective the doctor's control strategies are. This leads critics to ask: would anything be accepted as counter-evidence? If not, then the theory is untestable and should be rejected on methodological grounds.

Conclusion

In this chapter we have examined some aspects of the activity of going to the doctor. We began by considering the decision to go to the doctor with a medical problem. We saw how this decision was informed by members' understandings both of the nature of such problems and of the social organization of health care. As in previous chapters, we found that making such a decision involved categorical and sequential structures. We then considered the medical encounter between doctor and patient. We saw that this encounter is conducted in and through talk that displays an asymmetry with respect to the distribution of turn types. The participants to the encounter organize their interaction in terms of a preference for doctor-initiated questions. We also saw that the delivery of diagnostic news in medical encounters may be accomplished by means of a particular sequential structure, the perspective-display series. Finally, we considered the physical aspects of the medical encounter, and more specifically the interactional management of intimacy and detachment. We saw how the physical examination involves co-operative work between the two participants, the doctor and the patient, in order to sustain the appropriate categorical relations for the situation.

One thing that has been clear in this chapter is that talk in a medical setting displays some structural differences when compared with the organization of ordinary conversation. We noted earlier (in Chapter 5) that some ethnomethodological sociologists have coined the term 'institutional talk' to refer to the systematic differences between talk in institutional settings and ordinary conversation. In particular, they seek to draw attention to the fact that talk in institutional settings is pre-structured in various ways. Thus, as we have seen in the previous chapter, talk in the classroom between teacher and pupils often is structured in terms of an 'initiation-response-evaluation' sequence, in which the initiation and evaluation turns are the prerogative of the teacher. Similarly, in this chapter, we have seen how in the medical consultation there is a distributive asymmetry of questions and answers between doctors and patients.

There needs to be caution, however, in conceiving such comparative differences in terms of the notion of the pre-structuring of talk and then generalizing this into an institutionally-specific speech exchange system. As we have seen in Chapter 7, the sequential structures of teacher–pupil talk are emergent and highly contextually sensitive. It is also clear that patients can and do ask questions of the doctor in some cases. Therefore the notion of the pre-structuring of talk as a speech exchange system should not be understood as suggesting that the organization of talk is rigidly pre-specified or explainable in terms of 'external factors' rather than being the ongoing interactional production of the participants. Additionally, we would point out that some sequential structures found in talk in institutional settings are widely prevalent in ordinary conversation. As Maynard points out with respect to the perspective-display series, for example, this structure is borrowed from ordinary talk and put to local interactional use to accomplish a specific medical task, the delivery of diagnostic news. It would be a mistake, therefore, in our view, to regard such sequential structures as definitive of particular institutional interactions, since although one may find such structures characteristically, one may also find exceptions to them and instances of their use in other contexts.

Student Activity

1 Do a self-reflective analysis of a decision to go to the doctor.
2 Take detailed notes of a visit to see the doctor. Consider the sequential organization of the activities prior to entering the doctor's surgery, for example, 'waiting to see the doctor'.
3 Write as detailed an account as possible of the conversation between you and the doctor. What sequential structures and categorical orientations are exhibited in the talk?

Further reading

C. Heath (1986) *Body Movement and Speech in Medical Interaction*. Cambridge: Cambridge University Press.

D. Maynard (1992) 'On clinicians co-implicating recipient's perspective in the delivery of diagnostic news', in P. Drew and J. Heritage (eds) (1992), *Talk at Work*. Cambridge: Cambridge University Press.

G. Psathas (1990) 'The organization of talk, gaze and activity in a medical interview', in G. Psathas (ed.), *Interaction Competence*. Lanham, MD: University Press of America.

D. Silverman (1987) *Communication and Medical Practice: Social Relations in the Clinic*. London: Sage.

P. Ten Have (1995) 'Medical ethnomethodology: An overview', *Human Studies*, 18: 2/3: 245–61.

9

Working in an Organization

In this chapter we turn our attention to work. In doing so we will begin with situations and activities that are familiar to just about everyone and then move towards less familiar, more specialized activities. Of course, the business of working for a living is something that the majority of adults in contemporary industrial societies are massively familiar. Most of us know only too well what is involved in going to work; furthermore, most of us have experience of working in an organization of some kind, be it an industrial, commercial or other kind of business company or a public service organization. Even those who do not literally 'go' to work but instead work at home – nowadays a growing minority thanks to computer technology – typically do so as part of working for or with an organization of some kind. Thus, most of us are familiar with working in an organization and as a result with the following kinds of circumstances: there are tasks to be accomplished, procedures to be followed, deadlines to be met, targets to be achieved, meetings to be attended, decisions to be made, colleagues to get along with, bosses to be placated, assistants to be instructed, clients or customers to be satisfied and so forth. The detail of work activities are what we wish to make observable and available for study in this chapter.

Although much that is involved in organizational work is broadly familiar to anyone who has held down a job in any kind of organization, there is, of course, much else that is specific to the nature of the job one has, the tasks that comprise it and the relations with others that it affords or requires. In examining aspects of organizational work, then, we will endeavour to begin with what is mundanely familiar and then move to consideration of specialized kinds of work that are more distant from most people's experience. Let us start with something universal. One thing all work has in common is its interactional character. All jobs involve, to a greater or lesser extent, interacting with others to accomplish some defined ends. Even homeworkers, sitting in front of their computer screens or working at their sewing machines, are engaged in tasks that are part of a larger enterprise.

Another way of putting this point is to note that what sociologists refer to as 'the division of labour' is fundamental to the organization of work.

This concept directs our attention as sociologists to the ways in which work is structured into systems of activity. Any organization involves a division of labour, a set of arrangements by which tasks are allocated to and performed by persons with differing responsibilities. Traditionally, sociology has tended to view divisions of labour in a static and finished way, as a structure or container within which persons carry out their respective tasks. From this traditional point of view, the question of how organizational personnel co-ordinate their activities is rendered unproblematic and unexplained. They simply carry out their duties and – lo and behold – co-ordination follows. Against this view, interactional studies by ethnomethodologists raise the question of how a working division of labour is accomplished in and through the activities of workers. That is, they seek to describe how workers fit their activities to those of others as an ongoing feature of their work. As a worker one is engaged in tasks that should fit together with tasks being performed by other people, such that the co-ordination of these tasks serves to realize some general purpose or goal within the organization. But co-ordination with others does not 'just happen', nor is it adequately explained by pointing to structural models of the organization. Instead, we must look at the detail of how specific activities actually get done as part of a larger system involving others.

Furthermore, as technology becomes more sophisticated, people's work inevitably becomes more specialized and technical. Also, as technology makes possible more complex activities and achievements, the problem of the co-ordination of tasks within a system becomes more problematic. Therefore the knowledge and skills required of those who work with advanced technology may be different in some respects from that demanded by more conventional forms of work. These facts, in our view, present something of a methodological challenge to ethnomethodological sociology. To explain what this challenge involves, let us remind the reader of the three-step method outlined in Chapter 2:

1 Notice something that is observably-the-case about some talk, activity or setting.
2 Pose the question 'How is it that this observable feature has been produced such that it is recognizable for what it is?'
3 Consider, analyse and describe the methods used in the production and recognition of the observable feature.

Thus the ethnomethodological sociologist wishes to know not just *what* people do in their work, but *how* they do it. Step 2 involves questions such as the following: 'How do workers accomplish the tasks they face?', 'How do they co-ordinate their activities with those of others?' and 'How do they ensure that the purposes or goals of the system are efficiently realized?' Answers to these questions pave the way for Step 3: 'By what interactional methods is such co-ordination and task accomplishment achieved?'

However, to address these Step 2 and 3 questions requires first that one has established what persons are doing in their work: what that work consists of and how 'what is observably the case' is to be described. Such description may be straightforward: the familiarity of many everyday work situations, involving ordinary knowledge and experience, may be such as to enable the ethnomethodological sociologist to make sense of what a given work task amounts to from the point of view of the worker. Understanding the work of, for example, a road labourer might seem not to pose deep methodological difficulties.[1] But what about the work of a radiography scanner operator in a hospital, or the doctor who analyses and interprets the resulting scan? Understanding work such as this – such that one can describe in detail from the worker's own standpoint what it is that he or she is doing – would seem to require more than ordinary, everyday knowledge on the part of the ethnomethodological sociologist. It would seem that the researcher must acquire something of the specialized knowledge that the practitioners themselves possess if misunderstanding of what is being done and how it is being done are to be avoided. We will return to this issue in the conclusion to this chapter.

Organizational work: an initial example

In this chapter we will consider several aspects of working in an organization. First, we will examine some ethnomethodological work on the use of rules in organizations. We will then discuss decision-making in the context of an entrepreneurial organization. Finally, we turn to studies that have observed and analysed how technology is put to work. In this chapter, then, we will once again be drawing primarily upon published studies in ethnomethodological sociology, rather than analysing data collected by ourselves. However, in line with our practice of beginning by considering some observational data of a readily available kind, we start with some data of our own that captures a mundane piece of organizational interaction. The authors of this book both work in universities, in departments of sociology to be precise. One of them (Dave) was sitting in his office not long ago when a colleague (Jane), whose office is just next door, walked in. The following exchange took place:

Jane: Dave, do you have a mark for that combined honours student?
Dave: She didn't turn up to the exam.
Jane: Oh, right (.) Fine, that's all I need to know. I'll tell them that.

As an encounter between two colleagues working in the same organization, we think you will agree that this is about as mundane a piece of interaction as one could hope to find. Nevertheless, it seems to us that in these three brief utterances one can see displayed participants orientations to, and accomplishment of, most of the features of organizational work to which sociologists have sought to draw attention since the pioneering work of Weber on bureaucracy.

To begin with, the exchange clearly demonstrates an orientation to organizational rules and procedures in action. In asking 'Do you have a mark for that combined honours student?', Jane can be heard to be invoking common-sense organizational knowledge about such rules and procedures. That is, she does not, because she does not have to, explain to Dave that it is a requirement of this university, as of every other, that students be assessed by their tutors, such assessments forming the basis for the eventual awarding of a degree or other qualification. She takes it that he knows that such assessments have to be recorded and the records presented for official ratification to a properly constituted academic decision-making body, an examinations board. In replying 'She didn't turn up to the exam', Dave employs his knowledge that both he and Jane know that non-attendance is an adequate explanation for why there is no examination mark for the student.

Furthermore, the exchange displays how local knowledge of organizational structure is employed interactionally. That Dave does not respond to Jane's question by asking, for example, 'Why do you want to know?' can be seen as displaying two things. First, it displays his general knowledge of the organization that the operation of such procedures involves allocation of responsibilities to particular persons, such persons being charged with, among other things, gathering, collating and administering the necessary information. Second, it displays his specific knowledge that Jane is the sociology department representative on the combined honours examination board and, as such, is responsible for ensuring that the assessment results of combined honours students taking sociology options are transmitted to the relevant administrative staff in time for the examination board meeting. Knowing that the examination in Dave's option took place more than a week ago, and not having received a memo from Dave about the student who was taking his option, Jane can be understood as having resorted to face-to-face interaction to get the information she needs. In other words, her actions amount to what is known, locally and colloquially, as 'chasing the bugger up'.

What this small example illustrates is not simply that members of organizations use their knowledge of the organization and its features as a resource to get their work done, but more than this, our analysis of the data shows that the organization is known 'from within' as a taken-for-granted environment of practical and occasioned circumstances. Members of an organization employ their knowledge in 'situated ways' to accomplish organizational activities; in assuming such knowledge members are at one and the same time constituting the organization and its features as everyday realities of their working lives.

Organizations-in-action

Ethnomethodology's conception of organizations as 'accomplished in action' stands in stark contrast to the mainstream sociological tradition. For example, we referred above to the concept of division of labour. One might say that this concept means that each person has a role within a complex, multi-party activity made up of a co-ordinated set of more specific activities; what one person does is dependant upon, and facilitates, what others do. However, to speak of roles might suggest that work activities are clearly defined and that the tasks involved are such that the person charged with fulfilling them – the worker – needs simply to follow instructions in order to get their work done. If this were the case, then explaining how work is done would be a simple matter; if work was a matter of following laid down procedures and nothing more, then explaining it would require little more than stating the rules and instructions given to the worker.

This is precisely how the concept of 'role' was employed by sociologists in the past (and still is by some to this day). This concept was especially useful to sociologists who wished to theorize about organizations as 'social wholes'. An organization could be thought of as a complex structure of roles, with different roles at different levels within the organization. Understanding the organization as a whole, then, meant constructing a description of the role structure that comprised it. This conception gained plausibility from the fact that organizations typically were found to possess a 'plan' of their structure, in which the management positions in the organization were named and the responsibilities attached to them outlined. In many companies such a plan could be found represented in a chart on the wall of the managing director's office. To many sociologists it seemed that describing the organization – explaining what people did within it and how their activities fitted together – required little more than filling out the details of the chart. The assumption was that once one knew what persons in the organization were supposed to do, one had the key to what they did. In other words, organizations were thought of as rational systems in which goals of the organization provided for a set of rules that defined what the members of the organization should do, and these in turn determined workers' conduct.

This rational system perspective gave rise to what has come to be known as the 'two faces' conception of organizations (Hughes, 1984). In this conception organizations are held to consist of two dimensions: one 'formal' and the other 'informal'. The formal dimension refers to those aspects of an organization that have been planned and intended, for example the overall goals of the organization and the structure of departments, positions and lines of responsibility that are represented in a management chart of the kind that is often found in the offices of senior executives. The informal dimension refers to relationships and shared beliefs that arise unplanned among an organization's personnel. The social organization of an organization consists of and is the product of the interplay between these two dimensions.

This rationalist approach dominated sociological thinking about organizations and the work that goes on in them throughout most of the twentieth century. It was not without its critics, however. The most significant of these, from the standpoint of ethnomethodological sociology, was Bittner (1973). His critique centered around two key points. The first is that the distinction at the heart of mainstream organization theory between (formal) structure and (informal) action is a false one. What organizational sociologists call the formal structure is a 'member's version' of the organization. It originates from a particular set of organizational personnel, the 'management technicians' who have designed the organizational chart on which the sociologist relies. By treating this as a theoretically privileged version of the organization, the sociologist cedes to particular parties to the setting 'the authority to organize the field of observation' (1973: 272). The formal managerial chart should not be thought of as a detached description of the organization, but rather as a working document within the setting. As such, it is a scheme of interpretation that can be used in different ways and for different purposes by organizational personnel as they go about their activities. The sociologist cannot assume to know what the features of the formal chart mean in practice in advance of examining how it is used on specific occasions by particular parties.

The second key point that Bittner makes concerns the language of organizational sociology. He notes that the very concept of organization, as well as other essential concepts of organizational sociology such as goals, rules, office and hierarchy are, first and foremost, ordinary concepts used by persons in the society as they go about their daily lives. The point Bittner makes has general application to the relationship between sociological uses of words and ordinary, everyday ones. In appropriating ordinary words for the purposes of sociological analysis, sociologists wish to retain their ordinary sense, since once this is lost it is unclear what the sociological uses of a term could possibly be referring to. For sociological analysis to have any purchase on the ordinary social world in which persons live, its language has to stay close to the language of daily life. The problem is that sociologists typically want to employ these words in a different way – or for rather different purposes – than they are ordinarily used. Starting from the assumption that the task of sociological analysis is to construct objective, context-free descriptions of social life, descriptions that capture general truths about society, ordinary words are treated as though they can be abstracted from the situations of their use in ordinary social life in order to describe objective phenomena that are ill-understood by ordinary persons. Thus, although their meaning seems to be the same it is subtly different, since what these terms now stand for is phenomena-as-seen-by-sociology, phenomena seen from an objective rather than a subjective point of view. But the shift from 'ordinary words as used in ordinary life' to 'ordinary words as used for doing objective sociological analysis' is more than simply a change in viewpoint. Between the ordinary and the sociological usages it is the ordinary common-sense one that is paramount, since it is in and through the ways in which members of society use these words that the phenomena the sociologist wishes to theorize about have existence in the first place.

In the case of organizational sociology, then, it should be recognized that organizational phenomena such as rules, offices, hierarchies and the rest, are constituted in and through the ways in which persons in organizations employ these concepts to organize their daily lives. Instead of thinking of these words as identifying properties of an objectively describable system, sociologists should examine the ways in which they are used in the very activities that make up organizational life. Since the meaning of a word cannot be divorced from the ways in which it is used to say and do things, instead of constructing theoretical definitions sociologists should try to describe the uses to which members of organizations put these concepts. Bittner makes a start towards this by suggesting some ways in which the key concept, 'organization', gets used by organizational personnel. He outlines three typical uses, which he refers to as: the gambit of compliance; as a model of stylistic unity; and as corroborative reference.

The first refers to the ways in which the organization as a set of formal rules and relationships is invoked as a scheme of interpretation to define the meaning and acceptability of specific actions. This may be done prospectively, by members of the organization asserting in advance what an action should be like in order to accord with organizational requirements, or retrospectively, such as where an action that has already occurred is judged for whether and how it is organizationally acceptable. The second use, stylistic unity, involves invoking the organization to give a sense of how actions tie together and form part of a larger picture. Members of the organization can use features of the formal managerial scheme to characterize the organization as a whole, thereby identifying certain features as universally relevant for everyone in the organization. The third use, corroborative reference, refers to how members use the organization to establish the point or purpose of activities or events that otherwise might appear pointless. It may seem to someone that what they are doing has no value or function, but others may 'put them straight' by noting that their action contributes to the organization in ways they had not considered.

Bittner's arguments have important implications for how sociologists should think about and study organizational work. The basic points he is making are first, that organizations should be thought of as 'arenas of practical, situated action' and second, that what the members of an organization do is not to be seen as determined by the organization as some kind of separate entity over and above participants actions. Rather, such actions constitute the organization in the ways they are produced as organizational activities of recognizable kinds.

From the standpoint of ethnomethodology, then, the 'two faces' conception of organizational work is wrongheaded if our aim is to discover what workers actually do and how they do it, since what is neglected in this theoretical conception are the ways that organizational realities are accomplished in and through the work that workers perform. By focusing on what determines how workers behave, conventional approaches deflect attention away from the detail of the work itself.

Making rules work

When we begin to look closely at how organizational personnel carry out their tasks, it very soon becomes clear that rules and procedures play an important part in organizational work, but not in a deterministic fashion. Thus, in many work situations the issue of what it would take to appropriately follow a laid down rule or procedure often is not a simple matter to decide. A rule is by its nature a general statement: it specifies what should be done in the typical or normal situation. The situations that workers in an organization are confronted with frequently are complex and untypical. Indeed, the very notion of a standard, typical situation may seem from their point of view little more than an organizational myth. In line with Bittner's arguments, Suchman and Wynn (1984: 152) note that:

> The operational significance of a given procedure or policy on actual occasions is not self-evident, but is determined by workers with respect to the particulars of the situation at hand. Their determinations are made through inquiries for which both the social and the material make up of the office setting serve as central resources.

Against the notion that work activities simply either conform to or violate the rules, with the meaning of those rules viewed as self-evident, Suchman and Wynn propose that there are prior questions to be addressed. What do the rules mean in practice? What would constitute acting in accordance with them in this situation? Which rules most relevantly apply in this case? These are all questions the worker must resolve before conformity or deviance can become an issue.

Consequently, the ethnomethodologist proposes that rather than assuming in advance that the meaning of a rule is clear and definite, organizational sociologists might be better advised to look at workers actual activities, to see how a rule is interpreted and given an operational meaning in practice. Furthermore, workers know that the rules are themselves part of the organization and are subject to assessment in terms of organizational priorities. In other words, they take it that a rule is there for a purpose, to ensure that a particular aspect of the work gets done in an efficient and effective way. If it is clear that acting in strict accordance with the rule would result in an outcome that detracts from such effectiveness, for example, by having negative consequences for other organizational activities, then workers regard themselves as perfectly justified in applying the rules in an innovative or non-standard way, and will defend such actions, when necessary, as 'acting in the spirit' of the rules. In other words, workers do not treat the literal statement of the rule as the sole and overriding rationale for their actions. Rules are available to be interpreted in various ways, depending on the circumstances. The key question thus becomes one of the use of organizational rules to 'get the work done'. We turn briefly to two studies that have pursued this topic.

This question of how organizational rules are interpreted in practice in a specific work situation was addressed by Zimmerman (1971) in his study of the work of receptionists in the office of a public welfare agency. The receptionist's job is to deal with members of the public who come to the agency as welfare applicants or recipients. This involves the preprocessing of such persons – taking initial details of their identity and their problem – and then allocating them to a caseworker for interview. There is a panel of caseworkers, each in a separate interview cubicle, waiting to receive interviewees. The procedure for allocating applicants to caseworkers is by strict turn order: the caseworkers are numbered (for example, 1–6) and applicants are directed to them in that order. However, other factors frequently override this turn-taking rule. The rule actually is operated by receptionists in an 'all things being equal' manner, and things are often anything but equal.

For example, the strict order rule contains within it the assumption that interviews will be of approximately equal duration. Frequently this is not the case. Zimmerman (1971: 230) details one instance in which a receptionist found herself in the situation of assigning a third applicant to a particular caseworker ('Jones') when that worker was still engaged on her first interview. The receptionist commented that:

> The biggest problem is keeping these people moving. Jones had her first assignment, well, shortly after 8.00 a.m. [It was 10.30 a.m. at this time.] She hasn't picked up her second and here's a third.

In referring to the problem of keeping people moving, the receptionist is acknowledging her responsibility to manage the flow of applicants through the agency interview process. She knows that members of the public are prepared to wait to be interviewed, so long as the waiting time is reasonable. If an interview is prolonged, the queue of waiting applicants begins to back up, leading to complaints and tensions with which the receptionist, as the public face of the agency, will have to deal. Confronted with such problems, the receptionist does not see herself as faced with a stark choice between either conforming to or violating the rule. Rather, she regards the rule as a means for achieving a desired organizational end: the efficient and fair processing of applicants. As a means to this end, the rule has, in effect, an unstated *ceteris paribus* (other things being equal) clause – 'Do it this way so long as that does not undermine the purpose for which the rule was instituted'. Thus in the case above, the receptionist, in consultation with her senior, decided to allocate the next applicant to a different caseworker. In so doing she has interpreted the rule by defining in practice the limits of its proper application. As Zimmerman (1971: 233) notes:

> By deciding to suspend the rule in this instance of its potential application, the intent of the rule was apparently not seen to be violated. Furthermore, in finding such modifications to be 'reasonable', receptionists appear to provide for ways to ensure that the continuing accomplishment of the normal pacing and flow of work may be reconciled with their view of these task activities *as governed by rules*, in this instance, the intake assignment procedure.

Zimmerman goes on to outline other situations in which the intake assignment rule is modified or suspended 'for good organizational reasons', for example, the receptionist's practice of assigning perceivedly difficult applicants to one particular caseworker who is regarded as having special competence in dealing with such persons.

Numerous other studies have documented the flexible ways in which rules are employed in organizational settings and shown how the interpretation of a rule is a contextual matter. A second one that we will mention is a study of retail banking; Harper, Randall and Rouncefield (2000) observe that bank cashiers dealing with customers often find themselves in situations where strict accordance with the laid-down procedures for processing customer inquiries becomes problematic. Such procedures assume a model of cashier–customer interaction in which the customer has 'normal customer competence', in other words is capable of acting in ways that make it possible for the usual procedures to be followed smoothly. They also assume that the cashier will have the normal resources for dealing with customer inquiries. Unfortunately for cashiers, situations often occur in which neither of these assumptions applies. Many customers fail to display 'proper' competence, and the organizational resources on which the cashier relies for dealing with inquiries sometimes break down. In such situations the cashier is faced with the choice of adhering rigidly to the rules, thereby precipitating a serious confrontation with a frustrated, confused or awkward customer, or suspending the rules 'in this instance' in order to solve the problem at hand. Here is one example, taken from Harper et al.'s field notes:

> FEMALE CUSTOMER wishes to cash two cheques but the CASHIER replies 'I'm sorry but THERE'S ONLY Mr. Smith's signature on the passbook … it hasn't got yours … have you got a signature with you?'
> CUSTOMER: 'No'
> CASHIER: 'I'll have to find a signature' … CASHIER searches through card index file of customer details (application forms, etc.): 'I'm just trying to find your signature card … we should have a card for you and I can't find it … I'll just get you to sign your passbook for the next time.

The rule is that customers can only have cheques cashed on presentation of a properly signed passbook. The passbook should be signed in the presence of a bank official when the account is opened and the bank keeps a copy of the customer's signature for security. In this instance both of these signatures are absent, something that can be seen as a failing on the bank's part. This fact, together with the fact that the cashier recognizes the customer as 'Mrs Smith' (thus enabling her to judge that the security aspect of the signature rule is redundant in this instance), prompts the cashier to 'act reasonably in the circumstances'. She allows the customer to sign the passbook and receive the cash.

The studies by Zimmerman and by Harper et al. show that workers orient to organizational rules and procedures in flexible, situationally specific ways. In their work practices, workers show that they understand the nature and limitations of rules; they use their knowledge of the organization to judge what is required of them in this or that situation to fit the rules to the particular circumstances with which they are confronted. Together with Bittner, they make it clear that, as ethnomethodological sociologists, we should eschew decontextualized description of organizational work and instead seek to appreciate that rules and procedures have to be understood in their use rather than in the abstract. Rules and procedures are part of the phenomenon of the workplace, not an explanation of it. Stating a procedure abstractly can tell us little or nothing about what is involved in implementing it in practice. In particular, it does not tell us how workers interact collaboratively to realize the procedure.

Making decisions in an entrepreneurial firm

The second theme we wish to discuss concerns organizational decision making. Ever since Weber, sociologists have taken it that organizational decisions are taken in ways that seek to guarantee the rationality of those decisions. Exactly what the manner of this rational form of decision making consists of has been a matter of theoretical dispute, but the general view has been that wherever possible, management personnel in organizations will attempt to base their decisions on a clearly defined set of goals and will utilize precise and accurate information relevant to achieving these.

If there is one kind of organization where one might expect these sociological assumptions to be confirmed, it is the entrepreneurial commercial firm. In the cut-throat world of commercial competition, surely it is those firms that have the clearest goals, that pursue these goals most single-mindedly, and that employ the most accurate information in deciding upon courses of action that will succeed over their rivals? And it is not just sociology that assumes these things. Theorizing about entrepreneurs and entrepreneurial firms occupies a central role in modern economics, where the basic view has been taken that what sets these economic actors apart from others is precisely their greater degree of rational motivation. Both in organizational sociology and mainstream economics, rationality in general and entrepreneurial rationality in particular is conceived in 'intellectualist' terms, as involving a strictly calculative, non-social relation to reality. For reasons we need not go into, Anderson, Hughes and Sharrock (1989) refer to this approach as 'Cartesian economics'.

However, as we have seen already, theory is one thing, everyday practical reality something else. In light of this, Anderson et al. studied the everyday organization of an entrepreurial firm called Leisure Time Foods (LTC), a small-to-medium sized catering company that specializes in running retail food outlets in public facilities such as airports and leisure centers. This involves the managing of a large number of small, widely dispersed units, each operating with a relatively small budget and a correspondingly small profit level. Perhaps for this reason the ethos of the company, as continually emphasized by its Chairman and Managing Director Lawrence Hunt, is that 'Profit margins are what it is all about'. In other words, profitability is the measure of everything the company does or considers doing. All the company's current outlets are closely monitored for their level of profitability, and should these fall below an acceptable level action must be taken urgently. Every new project or possible development is considered first and foremost on whether it will result in a good profit for the firm. A typical remark by Lawrence was his reply in a meeting to a colleague's comment about the need for the company to develop a more prominent image: 'Image is fine as long as it doesn't cost us money'.

In line with the emphasis on profitability, the senior management of LTC maintain a close and regular check on the monthly operational figures sent in to head office by each food outlet. Lawrence and Sandy, the company's Financial Secretary, prided themselves on their ability to review these sets of figures and see at a glance how any outlet was performing. However, they were aware that figures alone 'don't tell the whole story'. They knew that local managers were capable of producing figures that would 'look OK' but which did not necessarily reflect the true state of an outlet's performance. The real skill of a senior manager lay in knowing how to read between the lines of the submitted monthly reports, interpreting them in the light of other knowledge about the unit concerned. As Anderson et al. (1989: 108) note:

> It is not simply a question of seeing what is 'in the figures' and then working out what should be done. 'What is in the figures' is itself something which has to be worked out. Working that out involves teasing out both the operational complexities of a particular site and the organizational contingencies, the likely knock-on effects, of the case in hand.

A similar reliance on background, non-numerical knowledge to interpret and fill out numerical information was involved in the evaluation and planning of new projects. In assessing such a project, Lawrence and his colleagues would seek out a wide range of information before coming to a decision. Although there were typical questions they would pose, concerning such things as the potential customer population that the new outlet could draw upon and the possible competition from other food retailers, there was no standard checklist of information that was common to all such decisions. Each decision-making situation was treated as having its own special character and each decision was arrived at essentially in a unique way. This *ad hoc* character of executive decisions did not make them irrational in the eyes of Lawrence and his colleagues. Rather, they considered themselves to be giving due and proper recognition to the peculiarities and particularities that marked each separate case. Furthermore, executives did not regard it as an overwhelming obstacle to proper decision making that the information available to them was frequently 'loose and dirty' rather than precise and reliable. They accepted it as an inherent and unalterable feature of their daily work that they had to operate in a less than perfect informational environment, in which 'guestimation' was typically the best that one could do. Lawrence himself was quite scathing (to the fieldworker) about business theories that fail to recognize the 'seat of the pants' nature of decision making in a business such as his. It is not, of course, that such decisions are random or unmethodical, but the methods through which they are made are nothing like the formal reasoning favoured by economic and sociological theorists.

Making technology work

The third aspect of organizational work we wish to consider concerns working with high technology. It has become a sociological commonplace to refer to our contemporary society as an 'information society'. This appellation is intended to mark the increasing role that computer technology plays in our lives. Ever more aspects of our lives are organized through the use of computer technology; indeed, many of our activities, from buying petrol at our local garage to undergoing a medical scan at a hospital, involve the use of computerized technological systems of one kind or another. However, such technology does not work on its own. Every technological system has operatives, technicians and other specialist workers associated with it, not to mention ordinary members of the public. Our key question as ethnomethodologists, then, is: what is involved in working with computer and other forms of high technology? In answering this question, we will show that paying attention to the interactional character of the workplace is no less important with respect to this form of work than it is in relation to any other. The knowledge and competence workers possess is not something individual, as though it is privately locked away in each individual mind. Rather, workers treat their knowledge of the work situation as socially shared; one knows what others know and can rely on this shared knowledge in acting collaboratively with them. Thus workers take it that others who work alongside them know the relevant procedures just as they do themselves, and can make judgements just as they themselves can about what is required in a given situation.

To illustrate these points we will consider two studies of high technology work. The first is Harper and Hughes's investigation of air traffic control (Harper and Hughes, 1993), the second is Heath and Luff's (2000) study of the control room of a London Underground line. Both settings are examples of what is known as 'control and communication systems', that is, systems which involve the structuring of information in order to manage the operation of some environment of objects and activities. We will see that the knowledge and competence involved in operating such systems is embedded in and made available through 'structures of interaction' among groups of workers. In other words, the knowledge required to operate the system effectively is not lodged in any single individual, but consists of a social order of knowledge-in-action. Some researchers have coined the phrase 'distributed cognition' to emphasize the socially shared nature of operational knowledge in high technology work settings. While it is useful for this purpose, even this concept, it seems to us, does not go far enough in recognizing the interactional character of workplace competences in settings where workers employ their knowledge and skill to control objects and events through technology.

In the case of air traffic control, the objects to be controlled are aircraft in flight and the activities involve getting them from the points of departure to their destinations safely. The essence of the problem is that air traffic, unlike, say, pedestrian traffic on the streets, cannot be relied upon to manage itself. The task of air traffic control is to ensure that aircraft are kept safe distances apart in the sky. This involves keeping a constant check on the relative positions of aircraft flying through the same airspace and communicating relevant information and instructions to pilots such that aircraft are in no danger of collision.

Modern air traffic control is based on a system of computer-driven radars, fed by a network of radar beacons that feed information to the air traffic control centre. At the centre, each air traffic controller sits at a console in front of a radar screen showing a given sector of airspace for which he or she is responsible. The controller communicates with the planes in the sector by means of radio-telephone (RT), each aircraft having its own individual call-sign. The information that the controller relies upon in managing the flightpaths of the aircraft in the sector is contained on what are known as 'flight progress slips', or 'strips' for short. These are strips of paper, one per aircraft, on which is printed computer generated information, including aircraft identity and type, departure and destination points, cruising height, planned flight path and next reporting point. The latter refers to the fixed points in an air sector over which the aircraft will pass at a time predicted by the computer, based on the aircraft's current speed and position. The strips are placed in a rack in front of the controller. They are the main information source on which controllers rely in getting a 'picture' of the distribution of aircraft in their sector. The order of the strips in the rack reflects the order in which planes have entered the sector. As a plane passes out of the sector into an adjoining one (and thus becomes someone else's responsibility), the controller removes the strip and discards it.

All of this may make it seem as though the work of air traffic control is entirely individualized, each controller working in isolation, communicating only with the aircraft in his or her sector. If this were the case, there would be some basis for a 'mentalistic' conception of work knowledge, as residing in the mind of the individual controller. However, Harper and Hughes stress that the work of air traffic control is not individualized in this way. Although the air traffic control centre is divided into separate console positions, this does not mean that the work is 'privatized'. Each controller works with other controllers, assistants and a chief controller who is responsible for all the controllers making up a control suite. The interactions between these persons has an important bearing both on how information is constructed and communicated to aircraft, and upon the decisions that are taken in managing the distribution of aircraft in a sector. For example, although the initial information on the strips is computer-generated, further information is written on them by controllers as they deal with each aircraft. Each strip thus serves as a running record of the aircraft's progress through the sky. This record is a public document, available not just to the particular controller concerned, but also to others around him or her. The information is public property, so that written entries will be made by the controller and also when necessary by the chief and by assistants. The meaning and validity of the information on the strips is also a public, collective matter, as Harper and Hughes (1993: 139) note:

> The negotiation of information on the strips by members of the team 'trustably' incorporates them into work activities. Controllers are only too aware of the fact that mistakes are made, errors that can be alarming to the outsider. But the trustability of the strips does not lie in any technical failsafe but in the accessibility to members of the team and the mutual checking that goes on. A routine part of the work is checking information and this begins as soon as a strip is printed.

The checking and recording of information, then, is just one way in which what might appear superficially to be an individualized work situation turns out on closer inspection to be a collaborative, team situation[2] (Harper and Hughes, 1993: 142):

> The controller at the screen is part of a division of labour around the suite and thus part of an embodied collection of courses of action achieved by the working team. It is the team which circulates knowledge, which reproduces the production processes, checks 'how things are going', doing their respective jobs, and so on. It is in the work of the team that the invisible but vital skills, and other resources furnished by the system-in-use, are 'made to hand' for controlling.

Similar observations to these can be made in respect of our second high technology workplace, the control room of a London Underground line. Whereas Harper and Hughes used an ethnographic approach (making observations and fieldnotes), Heath and Luff (2000) are able to focus their analysis on a more detailed interactional level because they were able to use video data of activities in the control room. Consequently, their analysis focuses in far greater detail on what is involved in the co-ordination of activities amongst operatives.

The control room houses a number of people with different roles in the overall control process. These include first the line controller, who is charged with co-ordinating the day-to-day and minute-by-minute running of the rail line and trying to keep the trains running regularly with only brief gaps between them. Second, there is the divisional information assistant (or DIA) whose main tasks are to communicate with station managers and to provide information to passengers through a public address system on the current state of the trains on the line. Finally, there are two signal assistants who oversee the operation of the signaling system that actually determines the movement of the trains. The control system is computerized: signal assistants operate the signals through computerized controls and the position of trains on the line at any given moment is relayed from electronic indicators on the track to an illuminated board in the control room that diagrammatically represents the entire line. This board is continuously monitored by the control room staff who sit at the consoles facing it. The consoles contain monitor screens, some linked to closed-circuit television showing station platforms, others displaying train running times and graphic displays of sections of the line and its traffic. In addition to these electronic resources, the control room staff make use of the written timetable. As well as detailing the routes and running times of trains on the line, this document also contains information on staffing, including crew allocation and shift arrangements, and availability of rolling stock in relation to maintenance and other constraints.

The fact that the control room personnel have named roles and specific responsibilities, a division of labour, might lead one to assume that each person gets on with his or her job independently of the others. But Heath and Luff emphasize that this is not the case. The control room personnel work as a team, with each person co-ordinating with others in carrying out their tasks. While each has access to the paper timetable and the information provided by the electronic systems, using this information involves interacting and co-ordinating with others in the room. For example, with reference to the DIA, Heath and Luff (2000: 96) say:

> While the DIA does have independent access to various forms of information concerning the operation of the service, such as the fixed line diagram and the CCTV screen, the assessments he makes and the various actions he undertakes are often dependant on the actions of his colleagues, particularly the line controller.

Heath and Luff point out that the way that control room staff co-ordinate with one another is not separate from the activities involved in performing their specific individual tasks. Co-ordination occurs at the same time as they are engaged in their own specific work tasks and as part of those tasks. In other words, the structure of interaction in the control room cannot be easily divided into 'own task' work and 'interacting/communicating with others', as though these were distinct and separate kinds of activity. Typically, personnel do not, nor are they required to, break off from what they are doing to provide information or assistance to someone else. Rather, they show in the way that they perform their 'own' tasks that and how they are taking account of others and fitting their own actions to those of others'. What this means is that control room personnel treat the control room as a shared and mutually implicative action scene, where what any one person is doing is available to others for how it should inform their own actions.

The interaction involved is often quite subtle, with individuals being careful to ensure that in monitoring what another is doing they do not interfere with or distract them. Heath and Luff present a detailed analysis of one particular episode to show just how finely ordered these interactions can be. The video data shows the line controller calling up the driver of a particular train and asking him to hold his train for 'a couple of minutes in the platform' because 'we got a bit of an interval behind you'. The DIA, overhearing this conversation with the driver, transforms the controller's request into a relevant announcement to the passengers waiting on the next station platform down the line. The interesting feature of this episode that Heath and Luff highlight, thanks to the video data, is the way that the DIA gathers the information without distracting the controller from what he is doing (2000: 99):

> As the DIA begins to 'track' the call to the driver and prepare to make an announcement, he neither looks at the controller nor watches the activity of his colleague. Moreover, as he changes position and moves closer to the controller, he avoids making his own activity visible or noticeable to his colleague; rather the actions appear to be accomplished independently of the call to the driver, as if the DIA is engaged in some unrelated business. Through his bodily comportment and the ways in which he warily accomplishes his actions, the DIA preserves a careful balance of involvement, overhearing the controller and monitoring his colleagues actions on the 'periphery' of the visual field, whilst avoiding overt attention to the controller's conduct.

Thus collaborative interaction within the control room involves not just explicit co-operative actions but also, as Heath and Luff (2000: 117) point out, 'the ways in which personnel shape their participation in the activities of their colleagues, even whilst they may be engaged in distinct and unrelated tasks.'

What this analysis demonstrates is that the formal duties assigned to control-room personnel and which make up the division of labour in the control room are accomplished in and through subtle, closely ordered interactional practices. Such practices are an essential feature of this and, we suggest, other workplaces, since it is through them that the technological resources available to the workers are constituted as aspects of the practical work environment. In other words, what the technology is, sociologically speaking, is what a given set of workers make of it interactionally. The technology is, in this sense, an 'interactionally realized' phenomenon.

Conclusion

In this chapter we have discussed some aspects of organizational work that are made available to sociology if we adopt an ethnomethodological stance. We have contrasted this with the mainstream tradition of organizational sociology, which is driven by and pursues general theories of organizational environments. Ethnomethodology, contrastingly, eschews theorizing about the organization and instead examines how the activities of organizational personnel are actually produced. From this point of view, an organization simply *is* the activities in and through which it is accomplished by those who comprise its personnel. In this way the concerns of mainstream organizational sociology, with such things as rules, hierarchies, record-keeping, decision-making and so forth, are re-specified as members' phenomena and as situated accomplishments.

The studies discussed in this chapter serve to demonstrate how ethnomethodological sociology can provide a detailed understanding of the nature of organizational work. In addition, they exemplify the various methodological approaches that can be taken in pursuing such understanding. Thus the studies by Zimmerman, Harper et al. and Anderson et al. employed an ethnographic approach, based on observations and notes gathered by a researcher in the field. The study by Heath and Luff, on the other hand, made use of video-recordings to examine the activities of London Underground control room operatives. Both of these approaches has its advantages and disadvantages. Clearly, as we noted in Chapter 5, access to video recordings enables the researcher to analyse activities more systematically and at a far greater level of detail than is possible through ethnographic observation. By comparison with such detailed analysis, ethnographic studies are limited to what Garfinkel (2002) has recently called 'documented conjecture'.

However, video data should not be thought of as self-explanatory. As we noted at the beginning of this chapter, the analytic task of describing the methodical competencies involved in accomplishing work activities becomes more problematic as those activities themselves become more technical and specialized. The methodological problem of description that we outlined earlier can only be solved by the researcher immersing him- or herself in the setting and thereby attaining a degree of practitioner's competence. Such a requirement places considerable demands upon those who would engage in rigorous ethnomethodological research. One cannot seriously aspire to conduct such research in settings that are highly technical and specialized without a thorough grounding in the knowledge that competent practitioners possess. If there is one field of investigation where these methodological issues are raised more sharply than any other, it is the study of laboratory science. Therefore it is to this topic that we turn in the next chapter.

Student activity

1 Either record or take detailed notes on a meeting that you have been involved in.
2 Consider the organization of turn-taking in the meeting.
3 By what means are decisions arrived at in the meeting?

Further reading

R. Anderson, J. Hughes and W. Sharrock (1989) *Working for Profit: The Social Organization of Calculation in an Entrepreneurial Firm*. Aldershot: Avebury.
D. Boden (1994) *The Business of Talk: Organizations in Action*. Cambridge: Polity Press.
G. Buttton and W. Sharrock (1998) 'The organizational accountability of technological work', *Social Studies of Science*, 28 (1): 73–102.
A. Firth (1995) *The Discourse of Negotiation: Studies of Language in the Workplace*. Oxford: Pergamon.
C. Heath and P. Luff (2000) *Technology in Action*. Cambridge: Cambridge University Press.

Notes

1 We note that symbolic interactionist studies of work have found much sociological interest even in manual jobs.
2 An even more seemingly individualized work situation is that of the Underground train driver. But see Heath, Hindmarsh and Luff (1999) for an account of the ways in which this work involves co-ordination of activity between the driver and others, such as passengers and line controllers.

10

Observing Science

In the preceding chapters we have discussed how one takes an ethnomethodological approach to aspects of social life with which any member of society is more or less familiar. We all have had experience of settings of everyday life such as the domestic home, the street, the doctor's surgery and the school classroom and most of us know what it is like to work in an organization of some kind. Such familiarity is an important resource since, as we have emphasized, ethnomethodology begins by adopting an attitude of reflection upon that which is observably the case. Instead of simply taking familiar scenes and activities for granted, the ethnomethodologist poses the question: how are such scenes and activities being produced? The fact that one can see what is being done provides the basis for the question: how is it being done?

In the previous chapter we posed the question: what about activities that are not widely familiar? Can one take an ethnomethodological approach to situations where what persons are doing is strange and/or unknown, to activities that are not everyday ones? For example, there are aspects of contemporary social life in which people are engaged in highly specialized activities that involve expert knowledge. For those who possess relevant knowledge the activities concerned are understandable, but the rest of us rely upon experts to provide us with a 'layman's gloss' of what is happening or has been done and to explain its significance. While the use of such lay versions of specialized activities may, of course, be interesting as a research topic in itself, it is of little relevance for studying those activities in their own right. Since the ethnomethodologist is committed to understanding activities 'in their interactional detail' from the point of view of the participants, glosses for laymen are no substitute for a practitioner's grasp of the phenomenon.

Faced with such unfamiliar and specialized settings, then, the research techniques discussed so far in this book – self-reflection and recording – would seem insufficient to provide the sort of grasp of activities that ethnomethodological sociology requires. The technique of self-reflection has obvious limitations: how can one reflect on activities that one does not comprehend? But so, too, does the technique of recording: without an understanding of what is being done, how is one to know what the activities are that one has recorded? Faced with these methodological difficulties, ethnomethodological sociology demands the addition of a third technique. As already indicated in Chapter 9, we call this technique 'acquired immersion' since it involves the researcher becoming immersed in the setting and activities to be studied. The point of such immersion is to acquire a working knowledge of the activities under study, such that the ethnomethodologist knows what the participants know, can see what they see, recognize the problems that they recognize and understand the implications of events in the ways that they do.

In this chapter we explain this technique, taking as our research topic the settings and activities of natural scientific research. Our discussion will be somewhat different from that in previous chapters. For one thing, we will not start with observational data of our own, for the simple reason that neither of the authors possesses competence in natural science nor access to scientific laboratories. Furthermore, this chapter will seek to contrast ethnomethodological sociology's interest in natural science with another approach, one with which it is often compounded but with which, in our view, it has only superficial similarities. The reason for drawing this contrast is not to engage in sociological point-scoring, but to try to show how carefully thought out is the position that ethnomethodology takes towards natural science. Investigations by ethnomethodologists of natural science are not numerous by comparison with studies into other settings discussed in this book. However, some of the most interesting and original studies in the entire field of ethnomethodological sociology involve investigation of what goes on in scientific laboratories. Such studies seek to show how the findings of laboratory science are accomplishments of situated, locally organized activities. This does not mean, as some have assumed (for example, Wolpert, 1992) that such studies question the status of scientific knowledge as knowledge. Rather, it means that scientific knowledge, like any other kind, is achieved in and through situated social activities.

The sociology of scientific knowledge

The notion that scientific knowledge can be conceived as a social product is not unique to ethnomethodology. This notion constitutes the basic assumption of a perspective known as the 'sociology of scientific knowledge' (SSK). The basic assumption of this perspective is that scientific knowledge is socially produced or, as it is more often expressed, socially constructed. Researchers within SSK use both historical and ethnographic methods to seek to show that scientific knowledge is created in and through social relations and that the objectivity of such knowledge is an artefact of its social construction. A key feature of SSK, then, is the view that studying the scientific laboratory is crucial for understanding the processes by which this social production of knowledge takes place. Consequently, whereas 30 years ago there were no sociological studies of laboratory science, the ethnographic study of laboratories is now well established.

Such studies employ the method of participant observation. The technique of immersion as it is used in ethnomethodology has obvious similarities with this method. Therefore, it might seem that both theoretically and methodologically, ethnomethodology and SSK are closely aligned. However, we will argue in this chapter that there are important analytical and methodological differences between ethnomethodology and the kinds of studies carried out under the heading of SSK. Briefly, our argument will be that ethnomethodology's concern with the situated character of scientific activities is fundamentally different from SSK's view of scientific knowledge as socially constructed, and that immersion is more than simply another name for participant observation. These key differences point towards others: first, that ethnomethodological studies of science, unlike SSK studies, are not concerned with establishing a general picture of what scientific inquiry is really like; and second, that ethnomethodology, while recognizing that doing any given piece of scientific research involves much ordinary social activity, seeks to show what makes activities within laboratories the scientific activities they are. By explaining how ethnomethodologists use the technique of immersion, we will show what makes such studies different in these respects from SSK ethnographic studies of scientific research.

Sociology and the 'problem' of science

To understand the relationship between ethnomethodology and SSK, it is necessary to know something about the intellectual background to the ethnographic study of natural science. Specifically, it is important to appreciate why the study of scientific knowledge was for a long time 'off limits' as a sociological topic. The fact that sociologists took little or no interest until quite recently in how scientific knowledge is created might seem puzzling. Given the importance that sociology has traditionally accorded to science, viewing it among other things as a dominant force shaping modern culture, one might expect that the study of scientific knowledge itself would be a major field of sociological interest. Sociologists, it might be assumed, would want to know just how scientific findings and discoveries are arrived at, just what their claim to truth is based upon. Yet for a long time such investigations were non-existent. Theorizing about the significance of science was not matched by, and certainly not based upon, studies of the practice of science. In other words, while sociologists were concerned about science as a societal institution, they showed little concern with science as an activity.

This neglect of the practice of science was partly due to the fact that, until about the 1970s, sociologists could not conceive that empirical studies of science would reveal anything of interest. What was involved in doing science, it was believed, was already well known. After all, many books had been written about scientific method, and while there were disputes among philosophers over what the essence of scientific method consisted of, the general form of scientific inquiry and the specific methods of investigation employed by scientists, it was believed, were clear enough. Thus, if one wanted to know what was involved in experimental method, for example, one only had to look in a methodology book.

More than this, though, there was a sense that the conduct of science was not really any business of the sociologist. This view was fostered by the assumption that science was different to all other human activities. From the seventeenth century onwards, the view had prevailed that science is unique in producing objective truths about the universe. In its capacity to produce such truths, scientific inquiry transcends mere social life. Science tells us what reality is and how it works; it provides the ultimate foundation of what we know about ourselves and the world around us. The accepted view was that science is able to provide this foundation by virtue of the uniquely rational character of its inquiries. The guarantee of such rationality lies in the autonomy of science: its inquiries are guided by constraints internal to science itself. Science establishes its own standards and polices these rigorously. Thus there is a boundary around science, one which insulates scientific inquiry from 'contamination' by non-scientific factors. Any attempt to conceive scientific knowledge as a social product threatens this boundary. Such a conception would seem to challenge the transcendental nature of scientific knowledge and undermine the foundation on which any belief in truth rests.

In other words, the conduct of science was off limits, sociologically speaking, because it seemed to raise the spectre of 'relativism'. To account for scientific knowledge in sociological terms would be to deny that it had any objective basis and was capable of reflecting objective reality. If science is shaped by its social context, such that scientific knowledge is explained by social factors such as the social backgrounds of the scientists concerned or prevailing values and beliefs in the wider society, then the door is opened to relativism and contingency; scientific knowledge will change arbitrarily as the social make-up of society changes. How, then, could we have any faith in science?

The rationalist, anti-relativist view of science was a *sine qua non* for philosophers of science such as Karl Popper (1963). Popper was prepared to accept that scientific inquiry is a social activity; it is performed by human beings, after all. But this does not mean that scientific knowledge is nothing more than the product of contingent social factors – it *cannot* be this. To Popper and others, it seemed that conceiving of science as socially determined rather than the product of rational, objective inquiry, entailed rejecting some of the most basic and cherished assumptions about what scientific knowledge consists of. One is the notion of cumulative knowledge. For Popper scientific progress is essentially cumulative. Scientific knowledge builds up, through a process of adding new truths to those already established. The key to this cumulative development is the public and rational character of scientific inquiry. Science is governed by impersonal rules and public commitments to critical, rational method. Learning to be a scientist involves learning to follow these rules and respect these commitments. But opening the door to social factors would make it impossible to ensure that the conduct of science is governed by rational standards. Therefore there would be no basis for cumulative knowledge; each scientist (or group of scientists) would formulate their own theories and their own reasons for believing in them.

The second assumption that would have to go if science is socially determined is the possibility of demarcating a clear boundary between science and non-science. Again, for Popper it was essential that the rational standards that must be met for something to qualify as genuine science be clearly spelt out. Only then could one assess the claims of various inquiries that proclaim themselves to be scientific. Many of these claims, especially within the field of human studies, are in Popper's view false – these inquires are pseudo-sciences (Marxism and Psychoanalysis are two prominent cases, in his view). Any undermining of the autonomy of rational standards of knowledge would, in Popper's view, open the floodgates to such pseudo-science.

Opposing rationalism

Given this background, it is little wonder that when, in the 1970s and 1980s, sociologists began to focus their attention on scientific knowledge many set out with a more or less explicit agenda – that of proving wrong philosophers of science such as Popper. Whereas Popper and others had emphasized the special and distinctive nature of science – emphasizing the boundary between science and other human activities – SSK researchers sought to show that much that comprises scientific inquiry is ordinary social action shaped by the same kinds of factors as action of any other kind. Thus their studies were aimed at demonstrating that the very features philosophers had insisted were inimical to scientific knowledge in fact were displayed by even the most successful sciences. By examining instances of scientific inquiry drawn from established sciences like physics and biology, sociologists of scientific knowledge[1] sought to oppose head-on accepted philosophical views of science as impersonal, objective knowledge. Indeed, the defining characteristic of SSK is that it seeks to present a sociological alternative to the rationalist conception of science argued by philosophers.

The fact that SSK studies are geared towards opposing the conception of science promoted in rationalist philosophy of science means that these studies, although varying widely across different scientific disciplines and research topics, display a common pattern of argument. The basic thesis is that scientific knowledge is constructed through social relations – both relations among scientists themselves and relations between the organized institutions of science and other social institutions. In their studies, sociologists of scientific knowledge seek to show that science cannot be regarded as standing in some objective relationship to an independent reality. Rather, what counts as reality is defined socially. Furthermore, these studies seek to show how the rationalist assumption of the autonomy of scientific judgements does not correspond to scientific reality. That which is taken to be knowledge in science is not so taken on 'a-social', rational grounds, but on the basis of social factors such as interests, values, authority and power.

Typically, then, sociological studies of scientific knowledge involve a two-step argument. The first step is to show that some given piece of scientific knowledge (for example, a theory) is only loosely supported by empirical evidence – the relationship between theory and evidence is not a conclusive one. This poses the question: what does explain why a given idea or theory has come to be treated by the scientific community as 'knowledge'? The second step in the argument, then, is to propose that social factors provide this explanation: they fill the gap between theory and evidence. Social interests and cultural values predispose scientists towards certain theoretical accounts of reality and against others. The links between such factors and the findings of scientific research are established in two main ways: historically, by showing that specific scientific decisions and judgements were taken within a predisposing historical context, or ethnographically, by showing that the social relations of the laboratory shape the ways that some findings are defined as facts while others are not. Therefore it is to SSK studies of laboratory science that we now turn.

Ethnography and laboratory science

The laboratory is the natural scientist's work-site: the place where the findings of science are discovered and tested. It is in and through what happens within the laboratory, then, that the facts of science get established. However, since SSK is committed to the deeply problematic nature of scientific facts and the existence of a pervasive gap between a theory and the evidence on which it calls for support, what happens in laboratories is viewed from a position quite different to, indeed in opposition to, how it is understood by practising scientists.[2] Sociologists of scientific knowledge emphasize the uncertainty of experimental results. Although the point of experimental techniques is to set up an experiment so as to produce results about which researchers can be confident, SSK sociologists have insisted that such confidence is always misplaced. Any experiment involves a myriad of factors, only some of which are known about and manipulated by the researcher. Thus Collins (1985) asserts that experimental replication can never enable a researcher to be sure that he or she has emulated the conditions under which another researcher's findings were produced. Yet without such certainty, how does the researcher decide about the significance of the experimental results? Collins refers to this as the 'experimenter's regress'. Given the impossibility of literal replication, the status of a finding as fact must in principle always be open to dispute.

This argument would seem radically to undermine the role of experimentation in science. It also implies that scientists are mistaken, not to say naïve, in the importance they place upon experiments and experimental replication. That there are many things a scientist takes for granted when doing an experiment does not, of itself, mean that experimental findings are necessarily uncertain. This would only be the case if it could be shown that such factors would, if attended to, make a difference to how the experiment was done. For practicing scientists, unlike sociological researchers, the practical difficulties involved in doing an experiment in such a way as to enable confidence in its results are not to be underestimated; but such problems are just that: practical difficulties for which practical solutions are sought and, typically, found.

Some sociologists of scientific knowledge go even further than Collins in their questioning of the notion of facts in science. Latour and Woolgar, for example, in their study of laboratory research conducted in a major biological research institute, argue that facts are representations of reality about which some degree of agreement has been reached among some group of scientists. The work of laboratory scientists, in Latour and Woolgar's view, consists in the production of texts of various kinds: spectrometer readings, data printouts, task schedules, experimental reports and so on. Scientific research, from this point of view, can be seen as literary work in which textual inscriptions are created and deployed to define scientific facts. What makes a textual representation a fact, then, is not that it correctly describes a thing or event that has occurred, but rather that the representation is persuasive from the point of view of a particular scientific collectivity – for example, the group of researchers working in a laboratory. This persuasiveness is marked by the way that the representation is referred to verbally, whereas representations that have an uncertain status are marked by what Latour and Woolgar call 'modalities'. These are qualifying expressions or markers of subjective reference such as 'I believe that ...', 'A possible X ...', 'Y appeared when we increased the ...', and so on. A fact, then, they assert is 'nothing but a statement with no modality – M – and no trace of authorship' (Latour and Woolgar, 1986: 82). The work of laboratory scientists, therefore, is to create as many as possible (non-modality) statements in the face of a variety of pressures to submerge assertions in modalities such that they become artifacts. In short, the objective was to persuade colleagues that they should drop all modalities used in relation to a particular assertion.

The factual foundation of science, in Latour and Woolgar's view, is no foundation at all, but simply a series of agreements that scientists reach between themselves to speak in a certain way and to treat certain texts as authoritative. In reaching these agreements, scientists construct scientific reality through the shared language they use to describe it. Thus, for example, in agreeing to speak of quarks, neutrinos, X-rays, pulsars and so forth as real things (that is, without modalities) scientists thereby are 'constituting the reality' of these things. Conversely, by speaking of such things as phlogiston as a scientific myth or mistake, they are constituting these things as unreal. Scientific reality, then, for Latour and Woolgar, consists of nothing more than what scientists agree to say and how they agree to say it.

The claim that facts are nothing more than ways of speaking and that scientific reality is determined by what scientists happen to agree to say gives a picture of science that most practicing scientists would find it hard to recognize, let alone accept. In fact, several eminent scientists have raised strong objections to the social constructionist thesis.[3] What these scientists mainly find unacceptable is the claim, made implicitly if not explicitly by many sociologists, that scientific knowledge has no reference to anything outside itself, and that science is just a collection of social relations and practices. In other words, they object to the anti-realism of the constructionist view of science. Surely, these critics assert, if science had no reference to a reality beyond itself but was simply social relations among scientists it would be of no use to us, since it would not enable us to act upon the world in a successful way?

The debate between sociologists of scientific knowledge and their critics has been fierce and heated, and we are not going to review here the various points made on both sides of this debate. However, while we would not endorse everything that the critics assert, it seems to us that their objections are motivated by a legitimate sense that something significant about science has been missed by sociologists of scientific knowledge. In their desire to demolish traditional conceptions of science as objective knowledge, such sociologists have assumed that doing so requires an alternative theory, one that severs all links between scientific knowledge and reality. Such a disconnection is achieved by focusing upon the symbolic dimension of science – to emphasize that science is made up of ideas, beliefs and representations, and the symbolic or textual forms that give expression to these ideational elements. Science is made up of these symbolic or ideational things – and only these. Science, then, under this approach, becomes symbol work, and scientific activity nothing more than disputes and/or agreements about this or that symbol.

But for scientists, of course, their activities are not exclusively symbolic, do not consist of simply exchanging ideas and assessing the merits of this or that representation. These things are done, certainly, and play an important role in science, but that and how they are done is premised upon something else – the activities in and through which scientists access the aspects of the natural world that their investigations are directed towards. It is by virtue of these activities that scientists treat their ideas as being grounded in and informative of an objective world. Through these activities scientists come to regard some representations as real and valid and others as misleading or false, and thus are sure that they know what the natural world is like in this or that particular aspect. By leaving these activities out, sociologists of scientific knowledge present a version of science that conceives it as 'just words'. The very things that, from a scientific point of view, ensure that these words are attached to the world is missing from their studies.

Let us now return to the relationship between SSK and ethnomethodology. The constructionist approach of SSK ethnography is non-observational in two (related) senses. First, it denies that there can be any such thing as observation in science, at least as this is ordinarily understood and taken for granted by practicing scientists (and pretty much everyone else). Scientists construct the natural world rather than observe it, since there is no way they can get at a world that exists beyond social meanings and relations. Consequently, the ordinary language of science, which speaks of discoveries, observations, facts and so forth, is regarded by the constructionist as a 'realist ideology'. To avoid being taken in by it, one has to understand it in a radically different way from that of the scientists themselves. The constructionist approach is predicated upon an ironic stance towards science: scientific knowledge cannot be the sort of thing its practitioners think it is. Scientists may assume that they know what science involves and how it arrives at what it knows, but they are wrong in this assumption.

SSK ethnography is also non-observational in a second, related sense. The constructionist sociologist's ironic view of scientific knowledge is not a product of a close examination of how science actually gets done. Rather, once the ironic stance is adopted, then close, informed observation is rendered sociologically dangerous. It is significant, for example, that Latour and Woolgar explicitly acknowledge their ignorance of the scientific character of the research activities they witnessed. Despite the emphasis they place on the role of documents in laboratory work, they admit that Latour, who did the fieldwork on which the book is based, could not understand the scientific papers produced for publication by the laboratory researchers (1986: 75):

> Alas, it was all Chinese to him. Many of the terms were recognisable as the names of substances, or of apparatus and chemicals which he had already come across. He also felt that the grammar and the basic structure of sentences was not dissimilar to those he used himself. But he felt entirely unable to grasp the 'meaning' of these papers, let alone understand how such meaning sustained an entire culture.

They further note not only that he began the fieldwork as a scientific ignoramus, but also that he intentionally took steps to avoid 'going native' by becoming too knowledgeable about and involved in the scientific issues that informed laboratory activities. Their argument is that over-familiarity with the scientific detail of what was being done would have obstructed their ability to focus on the social relations of laboratory activities. They assert that the distance thereby sustained between sociological observer and scientific subjects was important for maintaining a sociological perspective on the laboratory and its participants. However, as Slezak (1994: 336) has noted:

> The idea that the inability to understand one's human subjects is a positive methodological virtue is surely a bizarre conception even for anthropology. For Latour and Woolgar, however, it is intimately connected with their doctrine of 'inscriptions'. The meaninglessness of the 'traces, spots, points' and other recordings is a direct consequence of Latour's admitted scientific illiteracy.

These two non-observational features of SSK ethnography thus are intimately connected. The practice of science allegedly is informed by a realist ideology strongly related to the rationalist view of science promulgated by philosophers. Under the sway of this realism scientists (naïvely) assume that their activities give them direct access to reality. The outsider stance exemplified in Latour and Woolgar's study is necessary – from an SSK viewpoint – in order to avoid the sociologist becoming incorporated into the culture of laboratory science and thereby accepting uncritically the realism that is the working conception of scientists about the relationship of their inquiries to the phenomena they investigate.

The ironic stance characteristic of SSK ethnography, therefore, arises out of a predefined theoretical commitment: the perceived need to oppose the realist/rationalist conception of scientific knowledge. By attributing this conception to scientists themselves, ethnographers such a Latour and Woolgar place themselves in a position in which they are forced to treat participants as theoretically motivated rivals to their own sociological project. Consequently, whatever meanings are to be attributed to laboratory activities, it cannot be those that the participants themselves attribute to them. The sociology of scientific knowledge thus is constituted as a confrontation between two general theories of science: realism and constructivism. Ethnographic observation is little more than a device for championing the latter against the former. As Michael Lynch has stated, '[constructionist] studies do not empirically demonstrate that "scientific facts are constructed", since this is assumed from the outset' (Lynch, 1993: 102). Similarly, the assumption that practicing scientists are professionally committed to philosophical realism as their working ideology and understand their laboratory activities through the lens of such an ideology is just that: an assumption, and a highly questionable one. Furthermore, it is an assumption that has undesirable methodological consequences that impact upon the kinds of studies that are done. It means that constructionist sociologists have little incentive to look closely and in detail at the activities in and through which scientific discoveries are made and scientific facts arrived at.

It is significant that constructionist studies tell one about disputes and disagreements but invariably have little to say about the routine, day-to-day work of doing scientific investigations. In the terminology of Thomas Kuhn (1962), they are very interested in the 'revolutionary' aspects of science but have far less interest (arguably, none at all) in its 'normal' activities. If one wants to know what ordinary science involves, then, there is little point in looking to the studies of SSK constructionists. And if one wants to examine ordinary scientific activities from a point of view that takes seriously what scientific knowledge is for scientists, then the constructionist sociology of scientific knowledge does not provide a clear route towards such an examination.

Doing ethnomethodology of science

The approach to science taken by ethnomethodology differs in two important ways from the non-observational approach discussed so far. The first is that ethnomethodological studies will not be shaped by any theory about what scientific knowledge really is. As we have seen throughout this book, ethnomethodology is committed to studying social activities in their situated and lived detail. Therefore the activities that comprise scientific investigation are also approached in this way. However, this does not mean that ethnomethodology has a theory of what the activities of scientific inquiry are: that they are just 'situated action' and not what they appear to be. Showing that the activities in and through which natural scientists establish findings about the phenomena they study are situated, locally organized activities in no way undermines the status of those findings. How could it, when the very thing that is accomplished in and through those activities *is* those findings? This leads to a second, methodological difference: it means that ethnomethodology studies of science cannot adopt the kind of outsider stance taken by Latour and Woolgar. The ethnomethodological researcher must engage with the activities of science in their own terms. Since the aim is to examine such activities in their lived detail, researchers will favour the use of data that preserves the detail of such activities, such as tape recordings or field notes based on participant observation. But equally importantly, the researcher will immerse him- or herself in those activities and seek to attain a competence in the scientific work that will give access to the detail of scientific judgement and decision.

The interaction work of astronomical discovery

These features of an ethnomethodological approach to science can be illustrated by considering two studies of scientists at work. The first is a study by Garfinkel and his associates (Garfinkel, Lynch and Livingston, 1981) of astronomers. This study focuses on the work of a group of astronomers at the Steward Observatory in the US, led by John Cocke and Michael Disney. On the night of 16 January 1969, these scientists made a momentous astronomical discovery: the first empirically documented optical pulsar. By chance, a portion of the discussions among the team during the night's work in which this discovery was made was captured on a tape recorder. Garfinkel et al. use this (transcribed) tape recording to consider the activities in and through which the pulsar was discovered. Specifically, their question is 'What does the optically discovered pulsar consist of as the "night's work"?' of this group of astronomers. More specifically still, they seek to recover what they call the 'local historicity' of the discovery.

As ethnomethodologists, Garfinkel et al. view the discovery of the optical pulsar as a course of social action within the laboratory on that night. Thus their concern is not with the status of the pulsar as an astronomical object, but with the actions in and through which that status became apparent to the observatory team. Thus they take no position on what the pulsar is really as an object of astronomical discovery. In their view, this is not a sociological question but a question for, and within the discourse of, astronomical science. Whether the apparent pulsar was a real one or simply an artifact of a set of data was the issue that the astronomers themselves had to resolve, and did resolve as the night progressed. Consequently, and in contrast with the constructionist approach, Garfinkel et al. are not setting out to explain why the astronomers involved came to believe that they had discovered an optical pulsar, as though that discovery is really nothing more than a collective belief on the part of the scientists. To imply this is to take a position on an astronomical question. Rather, they wish to elucidate what the discovery of the pulsar consisted of sociologically, as a course of concerted action in a particular place at a particular time. In other words, what was this discovery in and as situated action?

In one sense, then, what Garfinkel et al. seek to do is 'tell the story' of how the pulsar was discovered in the observatory on that night. But there is a danger in thinking about it in these terms. The very notion of a 'story' suggests an outcome towards which events in the story are progressing. The danger is that, knowing the outcome, one tells the story as the way that that outcome was achieved, as a series of steps that explain how the discovery was made. However, this misses the most fundamental feature of their night's work from the point of view of Cocke, Disney and their colleagues. At no point in the course of their night's activities did the astronomers in the observatory *know* what the outcome of their night's work would be. That outcome could only be known by them when it had come about; they could only know what they had found once they knew it. Thus, although they were following an established procedure – using their equipment to make a series of observational runs across a portion of the heavens – at no point did they know (could they know) 'what will happen next', including such things as 'what the instruments will show this time', or 'what adjustments we need to make to the alignments after this run'.

Above all, to describe the night's work in terms of a success story would be to lose its character as 'first time through'. Cocke and Disney may have been following a procedure and in that sense they were 'doing something they had done previously'. But their activities were not simply a rehearsal of something done before. They were also, crucially, doing something for the very first time: the observational procedure was being realized 'this time', 'in these circumstances' and (most importantly) 'with these consequences'. Each observational run was a new one, different to those before and with potentially different results. Thus standard procedure, while it might describe what, in general terms, a run should be like, could not tell one just what to do to make this run follow from yet be usefully different from the previous one.

A key feature of 'first time through' is that the astronomers had to make sense of what the instruments were showing, and do so in real time, here and now. They had to see that something was being shown, and decide what to do to respond to that something within the constraints that the equipment imposed in order to make it less vague, more concrete and so forth. Above all, they had to assume a shared 'vulgar competence' among those present, including the abilities to 'see the same thing' and 'know what can be done', such that remarks like the following could be (and were) made by members of the team at various points during the night (Garfinkel et al., 1981):

> 'We've got a bleeding pulse here!'
> 'You don't suppose that's really it, do you?'
> 'It really looks like something (from here) at the moment.'
> 'It's moved over.'
> 'It should be in the same place.'
> 'Let's move off that position and do somewhere else and see if we get that same thing.'

In and through remarks like these the astronomers assembled the witnessable phenomenon of the pulsar, at the same time co-ordinating their perceptions as persons witnessing the same things. But such co-ordination of perception was accomplished spontaneously in and as the unfolding course of social interaction; it was not managed according to any plan. Garfinkel et al.'s stress on the 'first time through-ness' of the astronomers' activities emphasizes the fact that the pulsar emerged as a phenomenon over time in and through the ongoing interaction between the members of the team.

The sociological phenomenon to be described, then, is not how the team of astronomers came to agree that they had made a discovery, but rather how they accomplished the kind of co-ordination of perception that is misdescribed if we think of it simply as an agreement. In other words, how was it interactionally that they came to see that their instruments were showing them a new object in the sky? Discovering an astronomical object in the sky involves coming to see it as a phenomenon in its own independent right. As such a discovered object, the pulsar becomes, in Garfinkel et al.'s words, an 'independent Galilean pulsar', something properly to be treated as independent of the circumstances of its discovery, something that can *and should* be extracted from the particulars of the night's work that made it available. Discovering the pulsar means perceiving it as a phenomenon whose locally socially accomplished character not just can, but *must* legitimately be disregarded. However, such a perception is, of course, integral to that local social accomplishment.

These points should be sufficient to make it clear that there is an analytical gulf between Garfinkel et al.'s study and the constructionist studies of science discussed earlier. It would be a gross misreading to believe that Garfinkel et al. are saying that the optical pulsar was not discovered but 'socially constructed'. Their point is not that science does not give us access to the natural world, or that scientific discoveries are not really discoveries. Rather, their concern is to show how it is that scientists, in going about their work, knowing that their inquiries are locally and contingently ordered, none the less can find that these very features of their activities provide adequate grounds for treating the events they are engaged in as amounting to the discovery of (in this case) a new celestial object. Cocke and Disney, then, did not 'construct' the pulsar. They *found* it in their instrumental results, and since correctly reading and interpreting those results was a locally accomplished interactional activity, we can say as sociologists that this finding was achieved in and through the very activities that made it available.

Studying brain scientists

A second study that illustrates an ethnomethodological approach to scientific inquiry is Lynch's investigation of a brain research laboratory (Lynch, 1985). Much of the work of the scientists in this laboratory centred around the study of brain plasticity and brain regeneration processes. The key research issue concerned whether, and by what means, the brain has the capacity to repair itself after some kind of injury or damage by re-adapting its functional organization. This question was pursued through various projects in the laboratory, all requiring the use of sophisticated equipment and drawing upon advanced biological knowledge of the make-up of the brain. As a lone sociologist, Lynch could not study all of these projects, at least not if he wished to examine in close detail the daily work that constituted the research process. Therefore, after the initial period of being shown around the laboratory, given introductory instruction in its work and getting to know some of the staff, he focused his attention upon one project, which involved the use of electron microscopy to study a brain process known as 'axon sprouting'.

Axons are nerve fibres that carry electrochemical impulses from and between neurons (nerve cells). Each axon terminates in a synapse (a kind of information port), through which impulses flow connecting one neuron with another. The brain as a whole is essentially a complex mass of neurons structured into various regions or parts, each with distinct sensori-motor and cognitive functions. The experimental work Lynch studied was concerned with the hippocampus, which is located beneath the cerebral hemispheres and towards the mid-brain. The function of this part of the brain is not fully known, but it is believed to be involved in processes of learning and attention. From the brain scientists' point of view, however, it was a useful site for research because its anatomical layout was instrumentally observable to an extent not found in other parts of the brain.

The phenomenon of brain regeneration is a scientific puzzle, basically because brain cells once destroyed cannot be renewed. How is it, then, that the brain has been proven to sometimes recover functions that have been lost due to damage to the area of the brain from which such functions originate? Neurological theory tells us that this can only happen as a result of some functional reorganization of existing brain tissue, with healthy areas adapting to compensate for the damaged ones. But by what mechanism does this happen, and what are the limits of such regeneration? In other words, how 'plastic' is the brain?

One possible mechanism through which regeneration might occur is axon sprouting. It was theorized that one system of neurons could adapt to the destruction of another system by expanding its territory of synapses. This expansion, the theory proposes, results from the sprouting of new branches from existing axon fibres and the consequent forming of new synapses to make new neural connections. Previous research had established that such axon sprouting did occur elsewhere within the body's nervous system. The question was: did it also occur in the brain?

To pursue this question, the scientists used samples of brain tissue taken from laboratory rats. These samples were examined using electron microscopes. The procedure consisted of taking a cohort of rats, treating each one surgically to create an identical lesion in the hippocampus of the brain, and then sacrificing each rat in turn according to a strict timetable. In this way a temporal series of brain samples was produced, and by comparing these the researchers hoped to discover whether a process of continuous regeneration by axon sprouting could be documented. The micrographs (electron microscope photographs) would be arranged in a montage reproducing the temporal order of the samples. These montages would then be closely examined by the research team to see what (if anything) they revealed about the axon sprouting process.

What we have given up to now is a reasonable account of the brain research work in the laboratory. It is an account specifically constructed for the layman and provides an 'idiot sense' of what that work was about. As such, it is akin to the kinds of descriptions to be found in sociological ethnographies. But, as Lynch points out, such an account *about* the research must be distinguished from an account *of* the research. The former goes nowhere towards revealing what the activities of the researchers involved in their own terms, as their familiar, 'known from the inside', work. For example, the laboratory is not just the site of scientific activity, but also a place of daily work in which persons engage in social intercourse. Constructionists, of course, have emphasized the latter aspect and sought to explain scientific knowledge in terms of the social relations between scientists. However, Lynch makes the point that acquaintance with what goes on in the laboratory quickly establishes that the scientific and the social cannot be separated from one another, such that the one could explain the other. The researchers are not now 'doing science' and then 'doing social relations'; there is no clear segregation between serious scientific activity here and non-serious activity over there. Rather, the serious and the jokey, the practical and the personal were seamlessly interwoven in and as the ongoing interactional activity that comprised the laboratory. Furthermore, everything that went on in the laboratory was available to the setting's participants to be understood and assessed for its 'why that now' character. In other words, as co-participants to the laboratory setting, persons were entitled to orient to anything that was done for its implicativeness with reference to the ongoing stream of activities that constituted working in the laboratory.

We do not have space here to consider all aspects of Lynch's study. We will summarize just one, his analysis of the phenomenon of 'artifacts'. The business of producing electron micrographs of brain tissue for study was a complicated and skilled task. After a rat had been sacrificed at the predefined time and its brain removed, it was necessary to separate the hippocampus and then cut small cross-sectional portions from it. These portions were then placed in shallow dishes of a liquid plastic and baked to harden. The next stage was to cut ultra-thin slices from the portion, using a microtome. These slices were so tiny that they had to be viewed through a microscope while being picked up on a strand of hair and placed onto a copper grid less than 1 millimetre in diameter. The sample would then be immersed in liquid compounds in a series of staining and rinsing operations. Staining is necessary in order to render neural material susceptible to the electron photography process. Only when all this is done can the sample be photographed using the electron microscope.

One important consequence of this complex series of technical tasks was that many – indeed most – finished micrographs turned out to be less than perfect from the point of view of the researcher's interest in observing the presence of axon sprouting processes in the samples. The scientists regarded this fact as an inevitable and intrinsic feature of their work; no matter how carefully and skilfully the samples were prepared, obtaining a perfect micrograph remained a matter of lucky chance. Where these imperfections were perceived as consequential for the use of a sample in the research process, the scientists referred to them as 'artifacts'. An artifact, then, is anything that 'should not be there' in terms of the ideal that the researchers orient to as their procedural goal. This ideal presupposes that the natural phenomena under study – axons, synapses, dendrites and the rest – can be accessed in such a way as to render them visible to anyone with the proper scientific competence, such that what are the objects of study can be clearly distinguished from what are not. But given that this visibility is an instrumentally and practically accomplished visibility, the researchers must (and do) orient to the ever present possibility that what they are seeing is not an axon or dendrite but something else.

These 'something else's', artifacts, can be described as coming in various typical forms, a shared knowledge of which is part of the work culture of the laboratory. Thus, for example, laboratory workers can point to such things as the following:

1 Knife marks: observable features of a photograph that can be attributed to the failure of the micrometer to make a clean cut when slicing the brain portion.
2 Staining errors: patches on the micrograph that result from spillage or running of the staining fluids.
3 Folds: linear features similar to knife marks but caused by folding of the tissue sample during its transfer from the microtome to the copper grid.

These first three types are 'external artifacts' in that they are purely products of the preparation process and do not represent the brain phenomena that are of interest to the researchers. In addition to these, however, are:

4 Distortions: different to the above in that these are representations of the brain phenomena themselves, but are where the features of a neural object have not been reproduced accurately or clearly on the micrograph. Distortions can take the form of fused membranes, blurriness, fringes and so forth.

By elaborating artifact types the impression could be given that such features of micrographs were immediately and unproblematically identifiable, such that researchers would have little or no difficulty in deciding which ones to disregard for research purposes. Lynch emphasizes that this was far from being the case. The classification above is an 'after the fact rationalisation' of the representational problems that micrographs pose to researchers seeking to treat them as research data. The 'lived experience' of viewing micrographs as research data is often far messier and more *ad hoc* than this neat typology suggests.

The brain researcher's problem is that the phenomena under investigation cannot be accessed other than via the technical procedures of the laboratory, yet that same technology standardly generates images that are in various respects puzzling and indeterminate. As Lynch (1985: 98) says:

> How 'natural structures' could be found to have been violated by means of the very technical procedures that made them visible in the first place is a very curious matter.

In other words, given that the technology and procedures of the laboratory cannot be relied upon to produce clear, literal representations of neural objects, how do the brain researchers decide that anything shown on a micrograph can be treated as data? How can they be sure that even clear pictures are what they seem and are not distortions that misrepresent the objects under study? This problem could be regarded epistemologically;[4] as an insoluble one, thus making micrographs questionable as the basis for any claim on the part of the researchers to empirical knowledge of the brain and its processes. Adopting such skepticism as a general attitude would cause the research process to come to a rapid halt. But the fact is that researchers do not adopt an attitude of generalized skepticism about micrograph images. Instead they take a practical attitude – they simply take it that *some* images can be relied on as constituting clear and accurate representations, and that these can be distinguished from other, more problematic images.

Thus, instead of a generalized view about all images, the brain researchers orient to their micrographs in a particularistic fashion, approaching each one for what it can or cannot reveal about phenomena of interest. Interestingly, Lynch notes that artifactual problems do not necessarily disqualify micrographs from being usable in the research. Given the routine presence of artifacts of one kind or another and the comparative rarity of absolutely clean images, researchers make practical, situated judgements about whether and how less than perfect micrographs can be made use of. One feature of these practical judgements is a distinction between 'lookers' and 'users'. The latter are micrographs that are good enough to be treated as data, even though they may contain various artifacts. However, researchers know that these images are not acceptable – that they may give rise to negative reactions from the wider community of scientific colleagues – when it comes to publishing articles in scientific journals or giving conference presentations reporting their findings. For these purposes, then, they seek (and, on finding them, put on one side) 'lookers'; micrographs that offer clear, artifact-free representations of this or that specific neural phenomenon. Needless to say, the discovery of a 'looker' was the occasion for some celebration among the research team.

Conclusion

We began this chapter by asking what is involved in taking an ethnomethodological sociological approach to a non-familiar sphere of life. Can one do ethnomethodological sociology in settings where the activities are strange and exotic, as well as highly technical and specialized? The ethnomethodological studies of science that we have outlined show that the answer to this question is 'yes'. By contrast with SSK constructionist studies, which are more concerned to argue for the socially constructed nature of scientific knowledge than to look in close detail at the practical work of doing scientific discovery, the studies by Garfinkel et al. and Lynch demonstrate two main things: that the technical procedures that make such discovery possible are treated through and through as matters of practical competence; and that the outcomes of such procedures are accomplishments of situated reasoning by laboratory researchers. Both constructionist and ethnomethodological studies confirm the remark by an eminent natural scientist that 'scientists rarely follow any of the scientific methods that philosophers prescribe for them. They use their common sense' (Perutz, 1995: 56). But ethnomethodological studies go further than this: they make available the concrete ways in which a shared common sense operates within laboratories, observatories and other sites in which scientists go about their discovering work.

It is clear, however, that taking an ethnomethodological approach to something as far removed from everyday life as the business of scientific discovery poses its own methodological problems. If the sociologist wishes to engage with the concrete activities of doing science then, at the very least, he or she will have to develop a 'vulgar competence' in those activities. Take, for example, the situation of Michael Lynch, wishing to understand just how brain researchers employ micrographs of brain samples as scientific data. Such understanding required Lynch to go some way towards learning how to use an electron microscope and how to read micrographs of neural matter. He states (1985: 2) that:

> Even within the narrow area I studied, my competence with electron microscopic work never approached a practitioner's skills with preparing brain tissues for microscopic photography. I was unable to participate in the lab's researches, though I achieved a competence in some of the analytic skills used in assembling and interpreting microscopic displays of brain tissues. These limited competencies gave me considerably more access to the talk and conduct which I witnessed in the lab than would have been possible had I relied solely on the analytic skills of a social scientist while observing members' activities.

Thus, to understand what was involved in using micrographs, Lynch had to learn for himself how to view and make sense of a micrograph of brain tissue. He had to acquire the ability to 'see' a micrograph as a practitioner could, recognizing in it what they could recognize and able to find problematic what they found problematic. Lynch could only study the activities he wished to study through developing a vulgar competence in laboratory practices. Given that the knowledge and skills of the laboratory are highly expert and technical, it follows that the ethnomethodologist has to make a big investment of time and effort in acquiring such competence. He or she cannot simply rely on a 'tourist's guide' around the setting and a few interviews in which interviewees, practicing scientists, talk to the researcher like a stranger. Not, at least, if the study is to get to grips with the detail of scientific work.

We can now see what is involved in doing ethnomethodological investigation of specialized activities in unfamiliar settings. In some respects the problem is the very reverse of that with which one is faced in studying more familiar activities. The familiar activities of ordinary life involve knowledge and competencies that are possessed by pretty much anyone. With reference to such activities – reading the newspaper, watching television, having a family meal, travelling to work and so forth – we have emphasized the need to approach the familiar in such a way as to make it, in a sense, less familiar. In this way one is able to reflect upon and question the features of ordinary scenes that we typically take for granted. In relation to unfamiliar activities, the way to proceed is the opposite: here the unfamiliar and strange has to become familiar. Only then can one begin to reflect upon how these activities are done.

A final point. The need to acquire vulgar competence illustrates that, in an important sense, the phenomenon the ethnomethodologist seeks to elucidate and the method by which that phenomenon is made available to be studied sociologically are one and the same. This is a key methodological point. Sociologists standardly regard methods as something distinct from the phenomena with reference to which those methods can be employed in order to generate data. Methods, it is supposed, are the province of the sociologist, such that he or she can decide which method to use to maximize adequate and useful data on the matters under study. Thus the typical methods of qualitative research are described in methodology textbooks: standardized and non-standardized interviewing, participant observation, documentary analysis and so forth. But ethnomethodological studies of science bring home a quite different perspective on methods. A researcher such as Lynch has no choice about the method he uses, at least in this sense: if he wishes to gain access to and understanding of the real-world competencies of laboratory scientists, then he must learn to do what they do to a very considerable degree. What this involves is not simply learning about some idealized, textbook version of scientific method, but mastering what is necessary to bring off *this* experimental work in *this* laboratory concerned with *these* scientific problems. This is what acquiring vulgar competence means.

What this shows is that, against the idea that methods are external to the phenomena one studies, the methods the ethnomethodologist employs are already in place in the setting being studied. They are the methods that anyone in that setting must use to do what is required to get the business of the setting done. Lynch (1993: 273) puts the point like this:

> As should be obvious to anyone who has attempted to read specialized scientific journals, a mastery of disciplinary techniques is required for making adequate sense of the prose, graphics and mathematical expressions. To comprehend the unique 'what' at the core of each coherent discipline requires a reciprocally unique method for coming to terms with it. Such a method is inseparable from the immanent pedagogies by which members master their practices.

Learning how to be a competent brain scientist, then, involves acquiring not a textbook knowledge of methods, but a practical mastery of the *in situ* methods by which brain research is done. It is those very same methods, of course, that the ethnomethodological sociologist seeks to describe. By learning these methods for him- or herself, the ethnomethodologist thereby is equipped to tackle the task of describing them sociologically. Garfinkel, for example, made it a policy to insist that his doctoral students variously enrolled on advanced courses in mathematics, law, medicine and the martial arts prior to conducting ethnomethodological research in these fields. Clearly, however, it is unrealistic to expect this of the undergraduate readers of this book. Here, then, we come up against the limit of what beginning students in ethnomethodological sociology reasonably can be invited to do. To undertake rigorous observational research using the acquired immersion approach as outlined in this chapter, you will have to wait a while.

Further reading

H. Garfinkel, M. Lynch and E. Livingston (1981) 'The work of a discovering science construed with materials from the optically discovered pulsar', *Philosophy of the Social Sciences*, 11 (2): 131–58.

M. Lynch (1985) *Art and Artefact in Laboratory Science*. London: Routledge and Kegan Paul.

M. Lynch and K. Jordan (1995) 'Instructed action in, of and as molecular biology', *Human Studies*, 18 (2/3): 227–44.

Notes

1 Such as David Bloor (1976), Barry Barnes (1977) and Harry Collins (1985).
2 This is one reason why SSK has been subjected to fierce criticism by some practising scientists.
3 For example, Lewis Wolpert (1992).
4 Indeed, it is just this general problem of scientific research that the constructionist, Steve Woolgar, labels the 'methodological horrors' (Woolgar, 1988: Ch. 2).

11

The Primitive Character of Ethnomethodology

In this book we have introduced the reader to the field and practice of ethnomethodology. In Chapter 1, we set out our vision of social life as consisting of social activities accomplished in and through language and social interaction. In Chapter 2, we traced the methodological implications of this vision in terms of a set of principles and investigative practices. In the subsequent chapters we have sought to demonstrate how this vision, and these principles and practices lead to studies whose yield is an understanding 'from within' of the production of social life in its situated detail. Such studies presuppose immersion; either the researcher is already immersed in the field of inquiry or has to become so. Our demonstrations have been ordered in terms of three different modes of analysis in ethnomethodological sociology: self-reflective analysis, the analysis of talk-in-interaction and analysis through acquired immersion. In illustrating the sorts of studies made possible by these modes of analysis, our aim has been to encourage and enable the student to engage in this kind of sociology for him- or herself. It is a kind of sociology that anyone can do, since the basic 'equipment' is already at hand and is possessed by anyone who is a member of society. We hope that the reader will have developed an appreciation of this through the student exercises earlier in the book. Of course, whether you take any further our invitation to try ethnomethodology for yourself is entirely up to you.

As we hope our readers will be aware of by now, our invitation, like any other, is the first part of an adjacency pair and as such projects the production of a second pair part. As inviters, we would hope that our invitation will receive an acceptance as its second-pair part. In this conclusion we want to make sure that exactly what our invitation amounts to is fully understood and to address some arguments emanating from other sociological perspectives that might inhibit some of you from accepting our invitation. Indeed, we have to confess that in writing this book we wondered, given the reception that ethnomethodology had received from some mainstream sociologists, whether we should refer to what we were doing as ethnomethodological sociology at all, instead proffering our work under an altogether more innocuous and less controversial name such as 'observational sociology'. After all, in many ways, and as we hope we have made clear, ethnomethodological sociology is a rather special kind of observational sociology. However, in the end we chose not to do this. Nevertheless, the arguments against ethnomethodology are still around, however misguided they may be, and they therefore need to be addressed if ethnomethodology is to be undertaken with confidence in the context of the discipline of sociology as a whole. We are well aware of the difficulties that many of our colleagues and indeed students of sociology have perceived with it. They have found the approach it names strange and inaccessible. Not only that, but because ethnomethodology's concerns seem at variance with those of mainstream sociology, it has seemed to many that its contribution to the discipline is marginal at best. In what follows, then, we will consider the grounds of these perceived difficulties, and in so doing will explain more fully the nature of our invitation. We will discuss three areas of difficulty associated with ethnomethodology. The first concerns issues of accessibility. The second involves the apparently partial nature of ethnomethodology's interests. The third consists in a perceived methodological naivety.

The accessibility of ethnomethodology

The first perceived difficulty concerns issues of accessibility. One reason why we toyed with the term observational sociology rather than ethnomethodology was our awareness that the latter frequently has been regarded as a rather obscure, difficult and inaccessible mode of sociological inquiry. We could have chosen the name observational sociology in order to make it clear that at the heart of ethnomethodology lies a commitment to a rigorous observational approach to the detail of social life. As Rawls (2002: 6) puts it:

> Ethnomethodology is not itself a method. It is an attempt to preserve the 'incourseness' of social phenomena. It is a study of members' methods based on the theory that a careful attentiveness to the details of social phenomena will reveal social order.

However, to have referred to what we are doing as observational sociology would have sounded as if we were proposing that ethnomethodology change its name, and for no good reason other than some mainstream sociologists have found it rather unpalatable. In our view, it was far better, even if there was a case for viewing ethnomethodology as a special kind of observational sociology, to keep the name ethnomethodology and then seek to confront the grounds of the difficulties with it that have been voiced by mainstream sociologists.

Our own personal history bears witness to the problem of accessibility. We recall the time when, as undergraduates, we first encountered Garfinkel's *Studies in Ethnomethodology*, just after it was first published in 1967. In the opening few pages we encountered strange concepts like accountability, indexicality and reflexivity, concepts that we hadn't come across before. We were puzzled to say the least. Clearly, we were not alone in such initial puzzlement. For example, Lemert (2002: xi) remarks that:

> I can remember, as if it was last year, the day I sat down with *Studies in Ethnomethodology*. Like others, I was at first confused, then alarmed. But unlike much of what I read in those years, the book and subsequent writing by Harold Garfinkel and his colleagues or students stayed with me.

Obviously it stayed with us also. However, whilst we were sufficiently intrigued despite our initial puzzlement, it would seem that for others the strangeness of Garfinkel's ideas was sufficient to dissuade them from serious engagement with those ideas. Our puzzlement was in part to do with the words themselves and what they meant. Even more so, however, the difficulty concerned the radically different vision of social life that these concepts seemed to express. For example, in relation to the concept of indexicality, even when one had grasped its sense, that is, how the meaning of words and actions is tied to the particular context of their use, it was still not entirely clear what the significance of this concept was. The same could be said for many of the other concepts introduced by Garfinkel.

In our view, an initial sense of strangeness and obscurity should not be permitted to inhibit the work involved in coming to terms with intellectual innovation. However, attempts to clarify these ideas and the overall programme of which they form part were hindered by the climate of controversy that developed around ethnomethodology. From its very inception, ethnomethodology was received with both puzzlement and hostility, often in equal measure. This has meant, it seems to us, that its ideas and its studies have hardly been appreciated, let alone understood, by many sociologists. We were aware in writing this book that the legacy of accumulated puzzlement and suspicion had meant that ethnomethodology had rarely been given a fair hearing. Accordingly, we have sought to explicate and illustrate the ideas and interests of ethnomethodology in as clear a manner as possible. We have simply tried to present its key ideas and methods and to illustrate its studies as accessibly as we can, to bring it to a wider audience who may hitherto have been dissuaded from studying it seriously. In the end, we believe that as a programme of inquiry, ethnomethodology is no more and no less difficult than any other form of sociology; it is just different. Of course, we leave it to the reader to judge whether we have been successful in making its approach available, but even if we have been able to assist with ethnomethodology's accessibility, it remains the case that mainstream sociology has objected to it on rather more serious grounds. We will accordingly consider them in what follows.

Ethnomethodology's 'partiality'

Beyond accessibility, the first serious perceived difficulty with ethnomethodology involves the partial nature of its interests *vis-à-vis* those of mainstream sociology. This perception has been fuelled by ethnomethodology's variance from and apparent indifference to mainstream sociological topics and, perhaps more than anything else, has contributed to ethnomethodology's marginalization within sociology. In this regard, there are a number of standard objections that repeatedly have been laid at ethnomethodology's door. Most notably, its focus on activities has led to the charge that it neglects social structure. While it may describe social interaction in great detail, say its critics, ethnomethodology tells us little or nothing about the wider social contexts within which that interaction takes place and by which it is constrained. It focuses exclusively on the 'micro' level of social life, thus neglecting the 'macro' level.

Of course, from the standpoint of ethnomethodology and its focus upon social activities, the wider context to which other sociologists make reference consists in yet more social activities. What, then, is it that ethnomethodology is guilty of neglecting? A representative conception of what this allegedly neglected social structure comprises can be found in Wilson (1983: 47), who argues that:

> Structural relations are not obvious on the surface. They are not immediately detectable in social interaction. For example, if we wish to explain why one factory has higher productivity than another, we might find out if the level of satisfaction that workers have with the performance of their fellow workers varies form one factory to another. In this case we would be studying social relations within each factory. But there is a structure beneath these relationships. The structure is the way work is organised in the factory. We need to study the structure before we can make sense of the relations within it.

We note that what this statement asks one to accept is that there is a structural dimension to social life that is only detectable through the methods of sociological research, and that this hidden dimension is critical for explaining such matters as why productivity levels vary between different factories. The first question to ask about this concerns Wilson's assumption that 'the way work is organised in the factory' is undetectable. If this means that the organization of work has no observable bearing upon what workers do in carrying out their work tasks, then such a claim would seem to render the very notion of work organization incoherent; if such a phenomenon is not apparent in the way workers work, then in what sense is it work organization?

The second question concerns the clear implication in Wilson's statement that, despite the lack of 'obviousness' about work organization, there is one category of observers to whom structural relations are apparent, that is, professional sociologists. But one is entitled to ask: how is it that such things as structures of work organization are apparent to sociologists and to no-one else? By what means does the sociologist perceive the undetectable? Presumably, the answer to this question involves sociology's methods of research and analysis. Through its methods sociology reveals what otherwise remains hidden, in a similar way, perhaps, as the methods of subatomic physics reveal a dimension of physical reality that is otherwise unknown. Unfortunately for such as Wilson, this analogy between physics and sociology does not hold. The research methods of sociology consist in variations on quite ordinary social practices: interviewing, observation, reading documents and so forth. How such ordinary practices can give access to a realm of social life that is ordinarily undetectable is a puzzling contradiction, one that writers like Wilson seem not to recognize as such, let alone convincingly resolve.

Wilson's conception of 'undetectable social relations' is representative of a widely held view that social structure refers to something that can only be accessed through the technical and theoretical practices of sociology. We discussed in Chapter 1 the dominant role accorded to theory in sociology. We will return to this topic later in this chapter, when we discuss ethnomethodology's alleged 'methodological naïvety'. At this stage we note that the assumption of professional sociology's technical and epistemological distinctiveness lies behind the view that ethnomethodology must be guilty of neglecting social structure since it has little, if anything, to say about collective phenomena such as demographic and economic patterns that are not reducible to interaction between individuals. Sociology's capacity to describe such phenomena is proof positive, in the view of some, of its epistemological transcendence. Conversely, ethnomethodology incapacity to take such phenomena into account confirms the limitations of its sociological grasp.

Furthermore, this argument typically continues, by concentrating entirely on what actors do in interaction with one another in this or that social setting, ethnomethodology is not even able to provide a full account of social conduct even at the micro level, since the structured nature of such conduct is explained, at least in part, by the structuring of social life at a macro level. Such settings form part of larger institutions, which are patterned sets of norms, roles, identities and attitudes whose character is more or less fixed. Thus, for example, a person may enact the role of parent in a particular way, but not in *any* way. According to mainstream sociology, his or her role-making is limited by the socially sanctioned norms and attitudes that define the institution of the family (and thus parenthood) in our society. Such norms and attitudes transcend the particular circumstances of any given parent; they are institutional facts with a socio-historical origin.

In response to these arguments, ethnomethodologists point out three things. The first is that social structure is not a hidden phenomenon, detectable only through professional sociological analysis. Rather, the organized nature of social life is known by and apparent to any member of society. As we have seen in this book, members continually employ their common-sense knowledge of social structures in producing the very activities that make society what it is. Second, it should be remembered that the dichotomy of 'micro–macro' is a theoretical conception that has its place within a certain conception of sociology. To view social life in these terms is to accept that conception. However, theoretical conceptions are matters of choice; as a sociologist one may entertain whatever theoretical conception one wishes, providing that grounds can be given for holding it. That ethnomethodologists reject this particular conception, therefore, does not mean that they are guilty of rejecting a universal truth. It simply means that they find a different way of conceiving social life to have, for them, greater utility. The third point is that it is no part of an ethnomethodologist's goal to explain the institutional order of society in the sense usually intended. If one wished to know about the origins of, say, modern conceptions of family life, the place to turn is the writings of social historians. That commonly held conceptions of the family and of the proper relations between parents and children are socio-historical products is undoubtedly true. However, this is irrelevant from the point of view of ethnomethodological concerns, focusing as these concerns do upon how such things as family activities are produced by members of society.

From ethnomethodology's point of view, then, socio-historical generalizations serve little analytic purpose; what is of interest is how persons involved in the activities under study treat normative conceptions as having situated relevance for those activities. In other words, institutional facts are relevant only in so far as they form part of the member's situated point of view. What interests the ethnomethodologist is how members of society, in their interactions with one another, draw upon their common-sense knowledge of the society, including its institutional realities, in producing and managing those interactions. This means that the ethnomethodologist has no interest in describing institutional realities from a sociologist's, as opposed to a member's, viewpoint. In other words, the phenomena that ethnomethodologists are interested in are members' and only members' phenomena. If something is not a phenomenon for those under study, it is not a phenomenon for ethnomethodology.

The same point applies with reference to macro or 'supra-individual' phenomena such as patterns of population and economic inequality. Measuring rates of population change and levels of wealth distribution are themselves social activities undertaken by sets of persons within society. Like other social measures, such as crimes rates and levels of educational achievement, what the existence of such activities demonstrates is that much that goes on within contemporary society consists in treating society itself as an object of inquiry in various respects. This is an interesting fact about the kind of society we nowadays live in, but it does not mean that these sorts of descriptive practices have to be accorded a different status conceptually from other descriptive practices that members of society routinely engage in. Why should one treat the activity of constructing statistical accounts of relative income levels as of a different order (that is, as having a different conceptual status) to that of giving a description of what one witnessed in a traffic accident? That such descriptions are different in all sorts of practical respects does not mean that they have to be regarded differently from a sociological standpoint. From the point of view of ethnomethodology, both are members' practices.

Rejecting the agency–structure dichotomy

It is ethnomethodology's refusal to entertain the idea that there can be a distinctive sociological view of society's organizational features that marks a major difference between it and more mainstream approaches. The criticism that ethnomethodology neglects social structure actually reflects mainstream sociology's commitment to the idea that there is a level of social life that transcends the knowledge and actions of society's members, and that description of this structural level is possible only through the theory and methods of sociology. The usual way in which this idea is expressed is in terms of a (supposed) dichotomy between 'agency' and 'structure'. Members of society, it is said, possess 'agency'. Roughly, this means that they possess knowledge of their circumstances and act on the basis of that knowledge. Overwhelmingly, social conduct is action rather than mere behaviour, since persons understand their situation and have reasons for acting as they do. Accepting this, mainstream sociology goes on to argue that the circumstances in which actors find themselves to be located and which they may have knowledge of are not, in important respects, created by them. Therefore, while some aspects of their actions may be explainable with reference to their own intentions and motives, other aspects can only be explained with reference to social structures that are built into their circumstances and which are beyond their individual control. Such structures are said to *predetermine* conduct in certain respects and, in the view of some at least, do so regardless of whether the individual member is aware of them or not.

It would seem, then, that sociology explains social conduct in two quite different kinds of ways. Running through the history of sociology is a debate concerning which of these two kinds of explanation is the correct one for the discipline to adopt. In other words, should persons' actions be explained either in terms of their knowledge and intentions (that is, agency) or by virtue of their location within a nexus of social forces (that is, structure)? However, opting for either of these to the exclusion of the other seems to deny something fundamental about social conduct. On the one hand, it seems undeniable that what persons do is shaped by the organized nature of social life, which organization is a collective phenomenon that pre-exists those persons and their actions. On the other hand, it appears equally undeniable that persons act as they do because of how they interpret their situation in relation to the interests and purposes they hold. Given the compelling nature of both insights, mainstream sociology has tended to opt for a 'have the cake and eat it too' position. This amounts to the view that some (aspects of) conduct are to be explained in terms of the knowledge and intentions of actors, while other (aspects of) conduct are due to the effect of forces beyond the actor, of which he or she has little or no knowledge. However, this solution to the problem of sociological explanation raises the obvious question: how much (and just what aspects of) conduct is due to the former and how much to the latter? Mainstream sociology's failure to provide any clear answer to this question has prompted an enormous amount of theoretical effort in recent years. Much of it has been geared towards trying to find some acceptable way of bridging the gap between the 'voluntarism' of agency explanations (that is, people decide for themselves what to do) and the 'determinism' of structuralist ones (that is, people do what is predetermined by social structures.).

Ethnomethodology often is identified with the agency side of the agency–structure dichotomy. According to this interpretation, it is committed to explaining social conduct entirely in terms of the knowledge and intentions of individual actors. However, this interpretation is mistaken and betrays a failure to grasp just what distinguishes ethnomethodology from mainstream sociology. As we have already noted, ethnomethodology is concerned with how social activities are produced and managed by those engaged in them; it seeks to describe the methods by which this is done. Furthermore, it undertakes to ground such descriptions in 'the point of view of the member of society', that is, in the knowledge and understandings upon which members of society base their actions. However, the phrase 'the point of view of the member of society' has the capacity to mislead – one has to understand what is *not* being said by its use. First, it is important to realize that in speaking of the members' point of view, ethnomethodologists are not presuming that knowledge and action are 'individual' phenomena. The member in this phrase is, of course, one who inhabits a common social world with others and collaborates with them on the basis of shared, as well as socially distributed, knowledge. Ethnomethodology's point is that members of society treat much of their knowledge as shared knowledge – they know that in all sorts of ways others know what they know and can recognize the same things that they can recognize. In other words, the world that the member inhabits is a public, commonly known and socially organized inter-subjective world. Second, in referring to a 'point of view', it may be seen to imply that the member's viewpoint is one among several or many possible viewpoints (one of which is the sociologist's viewpoint). But this idea is firmly rejected by ethnomethodology. There is no other viewpoint upon social life than that of the member of society, for the simple reasons that we are all – sociologists included – members of society and that our ability to understand social life at all derives from that membership.

Furthermore, it is no part of ethnomethodology's project to claim that members of society can 'act as they please' for the simple reason that members of society themselves do not assume this. As participants in social settings, members know that there are limits to what they can or should do – how could it be otherwise? The form these limits take depends on the particular circumstances at hand, what kind of situation it is and what has happened in the situation up to now. Thus parents know that being a parent means being responsible for one's children in various ways, and they can use that knowledge to see that what has happened in *this* situation up to now requires them to exercise those responsibilities in *this* way. As we have emphasized repeatedly throughout this book, generalized, decontextualized versions of social norms and rules fail to account for how they are applied in practice. Members of society do not simply follow internalized norms or rules in the manner of 'cultural dopes' (Garfinkel, 1967) but rather practically analyse situations in terms of the relevance of such norms and rules. In any given situation, they have to decide just how they pertain, that is, what the implications of such norms and attitudes are for what they should do 'here and now in this particular context'.

The distinction that underpins the agency–structure dichotomy is the common-sense one between doing something because one wants to for personal reasons and doing it because one is in some sense required to by virtue of one's social identity. However, since this is a common-sense distinction it is one that members of society are familiar with and which they can employ in situationally appropriate ways, when they need to, to account for why something has been done. As we have seen throughout this book, members' common-sense knowledge is categorially organized. Members of society use this knowledge both to recognize actions that are puzzling and in need of explication and in constructing situationally appropriate accounts of such actions. The key problem of sociological analysis turns out to be a decontextualized version of a commonplace problem that is the meat and drink of ordinary social life. For ethnomethodology, then, social structure is nothing more than a gloss that refers to the multitude of ways in which members take into account their social circumstances in accomplishing their activities.

Putting activities before outcomes

It is ethnomethodology's insistence upon focusing its attention on situated activities themselves that is one of the main things that makes it distinctive in contrast to other sociological approaches. The usual view is that the task of explaining social conduct is to be achieved by conceptualizing activities as resulting from forces or factors that are located outside the activity itself. For example, according to mainstream sociology, if one wishes to account for how, say, the legal processes of courtrooms work, one must consider the nature of such things as the 'professional ideology' of lawyers or the 'structural inequalities' of the law. It is important to be clear about how such concepts as these are employed within sociology. The phenomena to which they refer are invoked in order to account not for activities themselves, but for the *outcomes* of activities. The archetypal sociological question is 'Why did things turn out like *this?*' rather than like *'that'* – where the 'that' in question often is an idealized outcome that exists nowhere except in the imagination of the sociologist. The preferred answer to this question is to identify some factors that predisposed the outcome in a particular direction. Given this style of analysis, sociologists have little incentive to examine closely the activities themselves. They are even less inclined to ask how the activities are produced so as to be the activities they are. The 'outcome bias' and the assumption of predisposition that are characteristic of much sociological analysis means that the activity itself is analytically uninteresting and can be taken as read.

It is mainstream sociology's practice of treating outcomes as separate from the activities in and through which they are defined as outcomes that forms the basis of the macro–micro dichotomy. The notion that social life consist of two distinct levels is sustained by the analytic strategy of taking the outcomes of activities out of the circumstances of their creation and conceiving them as having some free-standing objective status. In essence, this is the same kind of mistake that was made (and still continues to be made) within philosophy concerning language. Ethnomethodology's sociological stance has much in common with the philosophical view taken by Wittgenstein (1967) and expressed in his famous maxim regarding language: 'Don't ask for the meaning, consider the use.'

From the point of view of ethnomethodology, then, it is the situated activity itself that matters. As we have seen, ethnomethodology conceives of social activities as 'productions'. In saying this, we do not mean that there is something else going on than the activity itself; production does not refer to some other activities that are responsible for 'these ones here'. Rather, to describe activities as productions is to emphasize that people produce activities in their course. Thus it is persons engaged in courtroom trial (the judge, lawyers, clerks, the accused, the witnesses and so on) who produce the trial as a social activity in and through their actions. In the interactions between the participants the work of conducting a trial gets done. This work is collaborative, in the sense that what any one participant does has implications for other participants. The actions of this or that participant have to be responded to by other participants as 'actions in the courtroom'. Another way of putting this is to say that courtroom actions are produced as structured actions – they display their character as courtroom actions and are responded to as such by others. Courtroom interaction is collaborative, then, because participants produce their actions so as to fit together with the actions of others in contextually specific ways.

To act within a setting such as a courtroom, then, involves understanding the actions of others and what those actions imply for one's own participation. The understandings that persons possess, and which they display in and through their actions, are not arrived at randomly or arbitrarily. Rather, they are methodical products of the ways in which persons analyse social situations and thereby find them to be orderly in various ways. It is commonplace in sociology to speak of 'the problem of order' – how and to what extent social life displays orderly features – as a (or even *the*) sociologist's problem. However, it is members of society, first and foremost, who operate on the assumption that social life has an orderly, intelligible character.

We trust that these considerations should suffice to undermine the commonly held view that ethnomethodology is a form of micro sociology that needs to be combined with the macro dimension of sociological analysis and that it emphasizes agency over structure. We have indicated that in our view these arguments are spurious. Whilst some sociologists may treat them as solid grounds for doing mainstream sociology, they actually provide about as much foundational security as a hill of sand. Furthermore, they are incapable of undermining the validity and internal coherence of ethnomethodology because the criticisms are both misconceived and irrelevant. Indeed, were ethnomethodology to accept from mainstream sociology an invitation to slip into a comfortable micro-niche within its embrace, then its *raison d'être* would be utterly negated. For the above reasons, then, this standard objection to ethnomethodology's alleged partial character is unconvincing under close scrutiny and fails to provide good grounds for declining our invitation to engage in ethnomethodological sociology.

Ethnomethodology's 'empiricism'

We can now turn to the third perceived difficulty with ethnomethodology. This is ethnomethodology's insistence on descriptive studies of the details of social activities. As we have already noted, the focus of ethnomethodology's interest is in how such activities are produced in their course by those who engage in them. Therefore, ethnomethodological studies have insisted upon grounding their descriptions in data that captures such activities in their naturally occurring state. This methodological stance has led to charges of naïve empiricism from some quarters. The basis of this charge is that ethnomethodology assumes that description of its phenomena is possible without recourse to sociological theory.

As we pointed out in the first chapter of this book, one of the key tenets of sociology is the primacy of theory. Thus, it is widely assumed within sociology that description is secondary to and dependant upon theory. Underlying this assumption is the view that sociological analysis is essentially a kind of sorting exercise: the task of the sociologist is to sort those features of social life that are more significant from those which are less so. The problem he or she faces in tackling this task is the sheer vastness and complexity of social reality. Given this vastness and complexity, where does the sociologist begin in order to try to sort out social phenomena? This task is made possible by the possession of a theory. The theory provides the sociologist with a guide or set of criteria by means of which to begin to assess the relative significance of phenomena. Only by being armed with a theory can the sociologist hope to tackle the sorting and significance task in a rational way: the theory suggests both what to describe and how to describe it. In other words, the role of theory is to provide the sociologist with resources for understanding social life.

Without theory, the argument goes, social life simply cannot be understood in a systematic, sociologically adequate way. Faced with the confusing complexity of social life, theory comes to the sociologist's rescue, since theory provides just the 'outside' perspective that is required in order to view the entirety and thus be able to see what is significant in terms of the whole and what is not. Through theory, then, the sociologist can sort the wheat from the chaff, focusing attention and effort on matters that promise to reveal social order. The underlying assumption is that social order is restricted to certain locations in society. Look in those places and it will be found; look elsewhere and all there is to be seen is the sociologically uninteresting behaviour of individuals. In other words, as Sacks (1984: 21) has pointed out:

> The important theories in sociology have tended to view society as a piece of machinery with relatively few orderly products, where, then, much of what else takes place is more or less random. Such a view suggests that there are a few places where, if we find them, we will be able to attack the problem of order. If we do not find them, we will not.

As we noted in Chapter 1, one thing that follows from the sociological assumption Sacks describes is that theoretical understanding must be utterly different from ordinary members' understandings. Theory stands over against common sense, differing from it in fundamental ways and having a different epistemological character. Sociology transcends members' ordinary common sense knowledge, revealing the orderliness of social life that is unavailable 'from within'.

Ethnomethodology, in contrast, has long insisted that its investigations of social life do not require any theory of its general nature. The problem for which general theory is a solution, the ethnomethodologist argues, is a non-problem. The idea of unmanageable complexity, thus requiring theoretical simplification before anything can be adequately grasped, derives from the notion that sociology should seek some overall and all-embracing account of social life. Furthermore, the dilemma of sociological understanding, according to the accepted view, is between, on the one hand, adopting a stance 'from within' ongoing social life and, on the other, seeking a viewpoint 'from without'. Between these two alternatives the choice is clear. Viewing social life from within – adopting the stance of the member of society – leads the sociologist to become lost in the detail and provides no means by which to put that detail into perspective. The very closeness of the sociologist to the activities that make up social life means that 'the wood cannot be seen for the trees'. If this choice is taken, it is alleged, sociological accounts are no different from members' accounts because they provide no more insight into social life than members of society already possess.

Against this entire line of thinking, ethnomethodology argues that there is no genuine choice to be made between viewing social life 'from within' and 'from without'. The sociologist is first and foremost a member of society, and his or her ability to describe social life in any way at all is made possible by that membership. In making any sense of social life, the sociologist employs the same kinds of resources as other members of society. Furthermore, the assertion of complexity does not legitimate an 'outside' viewpoint. Social life is complex, certainly, but its complexity is not such as to necessitate or justify some epistemologically different kind of knowledge. To say that social life is complex is to make an ordinary, common-sense observation. Thus, for example, to say – correctly – that politics is a complex business is to refer to such ordinarily known things as that political decisions involve many different individuals and groups, not all of whom will agree or have interests in common, that political problems frequently have no simple or straightforward solution, and that those charged with making such decisions often have to act on the basis of incomplete or inadequate information. Similarly, to say that a given course of action by a particular actor or group is complex is to say nothing ontologically momentous. Actions are complex in so far as, for example, it is not clear to the members of society involved what is the best way to proceed in order to achieve their goals, and it is less than apparent what the potential consequences are of acting in this way rather than that. Such complexities are not philosophically profound discoveries (only capable of being made by sociologists), but rather are frequent and mundane features of daily life experience.

Furthermore, it is not clear in what the overview of social life that sociologists assume to be necessary could conceivably consist. The object of this overview is society; but is society the kind of thing that one could have an overview of? For example, it is true that the term 'society' is used by persons in ordinary speech. However, it is a mistake to assume that such uses are attempts – still less failed attempts – to make reference to the whole of social life in some transcendental, metaphysical sense. When an expression such as 'British society' is used in everyday social life, one needs to look at the circumstances in which and purposes for which that expression is being employed to see what sense it has in this particular usage. It may be, for example, that the speaker is making a contrast between the 'British way of life' and the way of life in other countries; alternatively, the speaker may be invoking our common national identity to claim that we share common interests *vis-à-vis* some public problem. Whatever the particular circumstances of use may be, the point is that collective expressions such as 'society' (culture, institution and so on) are ordinary terms that have everyday uses within ongoing social life. They do not refer to some overarching reality, the nature of which is unavailable to the ordinary person and whose adequate understanding is the unique prerogative of the sociologist. Of course, some sociologists might claim that when they use such terms as 'society' or 'culture' they are using them in a different, more technical sense than they are employed in ordinary language – one whose meaning has little or nothing in common with ordinary use. After all, they insist, sociologists are doing sociological analysis, not ordinary action. But this claim does not stand up to examination. Whether the sociologist speaks of, say, American society, Yanamamo culture, rural society or police culture, the description makes sense only in so far as it can be understood as referring to a collectivity who are ordinarily and commonsensically recognizable as such.

If one accepts that there is no special, technically definable or ontologically distinct social reality for which a special kind of knowledge – a theoretical overview – is required, then the question has to be asked: what need have we for sociological theory of a generalizing kind? From the point of view of ethnomethodology, the answer is that it has no need for sociological theory at all. As we trust we have made clear, the members of society do not engage in their activities on the basis of any systematic theory. Rather, they analyse social events in their course; they do so with methods and it is the task of ethnomethodology to identify, describe and analyse those methods. Of course, whilst ethnomethodology is disinterested in theory as a resource for understanding social activities, it is interested in theorizing as an activity in its own right. Members of society frequently engage in theorizing, and since this is so ethnomethodology may adopt an investigative attitude to this activity, just as it does to others. Rather than displaying methodological naïvety, then, ethnomethodology's eschewal of theory is essential to its programme of investigation.

Ethnomethodology's primitive inquries

The eschewal of theory marks one side of the coin of ethnomethodology's alternate status *vis-à-vis* other kinds of sociology. We suggest that the effect of 'leaving theory behind' is profoundly liberating. The other, more positive side of the coin of ethnomethodology's alternate status is its appreciation of, and attention to, the detailed orderliness of social life. Such appreciation and attention affords new insights into foundational questions. As we stated in Chapter 1, society is made up of activities constituted through language and social interaction. By focusing on their methodical production, ethnomethodology demonstrates, in the words of Sacks, that there is 'order at all points' in social life. As we have sought to show, the discovery of such orderliness is not difficult and certainly does not require recourse to heights of theoretical speculation. Rather, understanding that orderliness requires shifting one's gaze towards the mundane activities of those members of society and what they know and use to accomplish those activities.

We trust that the contents of this book have sufficed to convince the reader that there is much to be gained sociologically from close attention to the detail of social activities. We would go further and argue that this is so even for the kinds of questions that mainstream sociologists wish to pose. After all, one can only begin to raise questions about outcomes and speculate on predisposing factors if there is an activity from which such outcomes emerge and to which such predisposing factors might apply. Thus, how an activity is produced 'so as to be the activity it is', is not a side issue but a fundamental one. Therefore it is not out of perversity or theoretical naïvety that ethnomethodology rejects the idea that the sociologists should look outside an activity for an explanation of how that activity is conducted. To repeat the point, where other sociological approaches might invoke concepts such as culture, socialization or ideology to explain how persons are able to understand situations and thereby act in appropriate ways in them, ethnomethodology regards these predispositional concepts as of little use in answering the question: how do persons make sense of a situation as it unfolds, such that they can gear their own actions to those of others and thereby bring off the activity? The ethnomethodologist does not deny that persons have background knowledge acquired in and through their membership of the society, but the question that is posed is: how do they put such knowledge to use in making sense of what is happening here and now? Extra-situational explanations that simply appeal to a body of knowledge or belief that the person supposedly possesses fail to answer this question, since they do not explain just how this knowledge is employed in the ongoing interaction that constitutes the situation.

The focus on activities themselves means that members' knowledge, understandings and relevancies are available in what people say and do, since it is in and through their actions (including speech) that persons make available to one another their understandings of what is going on. As we stressed in Chapter 1, understandings are not private things locked away inside persons' heads, they are public, in the sense that it is through what we say and do that we display to others around us our grasp of the situation and sense of our place in its unfolding character. The public nature of understandings has an important methodological consequence: it means that understandings are available to be studied sociologically, since they are visible in the data acquired by the ethnomethodologist. This places an important constraint on what can qualify as data. Data must be such that it *does* display the understandings and relevancies of the participants in the activity under investigation. This means that the ethnomethodologist will seek to employ forms of data that capture the detail of activities as they actually occur. A further methodological point follows from this. Forms of data that capture social action, in so far as they make participants' understandings available, do so not just for the ethnomethodologist him- or herself, but also for the reader. Through the provision of the data in which members' understandings and relevancies are displayed, the reader can then assess the analyst's descriptions.

Having dealt with the difficulties that might inhibit an acceptance of our invitation, we can now turn to what we believe are its full implications for the discipline of sociology. We have indicated why we reject the conventional conception of the relationship between ethnomethodology and mainstream sociology. How then do ethnomethodological studies stand in relation to other sociological inquiries? It seems to us that such studies address questions and investigate phenomena that are both preliminary to and presupposed by mainstream topics of inquiry. In this sense, then, ethnomethodological studies have a 'primitive' character with reference to sociology. Their concern is with matters that lie at the beginning of sociology's attempt to understand social life. In this respect, if sociology were able to free itself from the confusing clutter of prejudice that currently characterizes it, then it would become apparent that ethnomethodology provides the most promising prospect to date of adequately answering sociology's foundational questions. In short, an acceptance of our invitation to take up ethnomethodology will empower its practitioners to revolutionize the discipline and fully realize its promise. Such a revolution will involve giving up certain things that sociology holds dear. It is for this reason that we realize that our invitation to take up ethnomethodology may be rather more momentous than it might initially appear. Thus, if you decide to take ethnomethodology seriously, then you will quickly realize that the conventional sociological frame of reference will have to be set aside. However, any sense of loss that you might experience in this respect will, in our view, be more than outweighed by the discovery that there is a realm of phenomena – the situated detail of social activities comprising social life – that is now available to be studied.

Epilogue

If the reader is still with us, he or she will now have some idea about what ethnomethodology involves and how to do it. You will also by now have some appreciation of the differences between this kind of sociology and the more usual kinds that you may have come across. If, instead of declining our invitation, you have decided to accept it, then we hope that you will find much to enjoy in undertaking ethnomethodological investigations. More than that, we trust that you will experience, as we have done, a sense of wonder at the sheer enormity of the detailed orderliness to be found in social life and the range of phenomena that are opened up for investigation. The pleasures to be gained from this experience may be sufficient in themselves to justify engaging in observational studies of the ethnomethodological variety. However, as our discussion in this concluding chapter hopefully has made clear, such engagement may also help to contribute towards a reorientation of sociology itself, away from theory driven inquiries that perpetuate mainstream sociology's opaque vision and false dichotomies and towards a sociology that takes seriously the task of exploring how social life works.

Further reading

H. Garfinkel (1967) *Studies in Ethnomethodology*. Englewood Cliffs, NJ: Prentice Hall.

H. Garfinkel (2002) *Ethnomethodology's Program: Working out Durkheim's Aphorism*. Lanham, MD: Rowman and Littlefield.

J. Heritage (1984) *Garfinkel and Ethnomethodology*. Cambridge, Polity Press.

H. Sacks (1992) *Lectures on Conversation*, Vols 1 and 2. Oxford: Basil Blackwell.

Bibliography

Anderson, R.J., Hughes, J. and Sharrock, W.W. (1989) *Working For Profit: The Social Organisation of Calculation in an Entrepreneurial Firm*. Aldershot: Avebury.

Atkinson, J.M. (1984) *Our Masters' Voices: The Language and Body Language of Politics*. London: Methuen.

Atkinson, J.M. and Heritage, J. (eds) (1984) *Structures of Social Action: Studies in Conversation Analysis*. Cambridge: Cambridge University Press.

Barnes, B. (1977) *Interests and the Growth of Knowledge*. London: Routledge and Kegan Paul.

Becker, H. (1963) *Outsiders: Studies in the Sociology of Deviance*. New York: Free Press of Glencoe.

Bernstein, B. (1975) *Class, Codes and Control*. London: Routledge & Kegan Paul.

Bittner, E. (1973) 'The concept of organization', in G. Salaman and K. Thompson (eds) *People and Organisations*. London: Longman (also in R. Turner (ed.) (1974), *Ethnomethodology*. Harmondsworth: Penguin).

Bloor, D. (1976) *Knowledge and Social Imagery*. London: Routledge and Kegan Paul.

Bloor, M. (1976) 'Professional autonomy and client exclusion: A study in ENT clinics', in M. Wadsworth and D. Robinson (eds), *Studies in Everyday Medical Life*. London: Martin Robertson.

Boden, D. (1994) *The Business of Talk: Organisations in Action*. Cambridge: Polity Press.

Button, G. (1993) *Technology in Working Order: Studies of Work, Interaction and Technology*. London: Routledge.

Button, G. and Sharrock, W. (1994) 'Occasioned practices in the work of software engineers', in M. Jirotka and J. Goguen (eds), *Requirements Engineering: Social and Technical Issues*. London: Academic Press.

Buttton, G. and Sharrock, W. (1998) 'The organizational accountability of technological work', *Social Studies of Science*, 28 (1): 73–102.

Chomsky, N. (1965) *Aspects of the Theory of Syntax*. Cambridge, MA: MIT Press.

Chomsky, N. (1975) *Reflections on Language*. London: Temple Smith.

Cicourel, A., Jennings, K., Jennings, S., Leiter, K., MacKay, R., Mehan, H. and Roth, D. (1974) *Language Use and School Performance*. New York, NY: Academic Press.

Collins, H. (1985) *Changing Order: Replication and Induction in Scientific Practice*. London: Sage.

Cuff, E.C. and Francis, D. (1978) 'Some features of "invited stories" about marriage breakdown', *International Journal for the Sociology of Language*, 18: 111–33.

Davis, K. (1988) *Power Under the Microscope*. Dordrecht: Foris.

Duranti, A. and Goodwin, C. (eds) (1992) *Rethinking Context: Language as an Interactive Phenomenon*. Cambridge: Cambridge University Press.

Eglin, P. and Hester, S. (1992) 'Category, predicate and task: the pragmatics of practical action', *Semiotica*, 88 (3/4): 242–68.

Eglin, P. and Hester, S. (2003) *The Montreal Massacre: A Story of Membership Categorisation Analysis*. Waterloo: Wilfrid Laurier University Press.

Eglin, P. and Wideman, D. (1986) 'Inequality in service encounters: Verbal strategies of control versus task performance in calls to the police', *Zeitschrift fur Soziologie*, 15 (5): 341–62.

Emerson, J. (1970) 'Behaviour in private places: Sustaining definitions of reality in gynaecological examinations', in H.P. Dreitzel (ed.), *Recent Sociology, No. 2: Patterns of Communicative Behaviour*. London: Macmillan.

Firth, A. (1995) *The Discourse of Negotiation: Studies of Language in the Workplace*. Oxford: Pergamon.

Frankel, R. (1990) 'Talking in interviews: A dispreference for patient-initiated questions in physician–patient encounters', in G. Psathas (ed.), *Interaction Competence*. Lanham, MD: University Press of America.

Freidson, E. (1970) *Professional Dominance*. Chicago, IL: Aldine.

Garfinkel, H. (1967) *Studies in Ethnomethodology*. Englewood Cliffs, NJ: Prentice Hall.

Garfinkel, H. (2002) *Ethnomethodology's Progam: Working out Durkheim's Aphorism*. Lanham, MD: Rowman and Littlefield.

Garfinkel, H., Lynch, M. and Livingston, E. (1981) 'The work of a discovering science construed with materials from the optically discovered pulsar', *Philosophy of the Social Sciences*, 11 (2): 131–58.

Garfinkel, H. and Sacks, H. (1986) 'On formal structures of practical actions' in H. Garfinkel (ed.), *Ethnomethodological Studies of Work*. London: Routledge.

Goffman, E. (1963) *Behavior in Public Places*. New York, NY: The Free Press.

Goffman, E. (1971) *Relations in Public: Microstudies of the Public Order*. London: Allen Lane/Penguin.

Gold, R. (1973) 'Janitors versus tenants: A status-income dilemma', in A. Birenbaum and E. Sagarin (eds), *People in Places: The Sociology of the Familiar*. London: Nelson.

Goodwin, C. (1994) 'Recording human interaction in natural settings', *Pragmatics*, 3: 181–209.

Harper, R. (1998) *Inside the IMF: An Ethnography of Documents, Technology and Organisational Action*. San Diego, CA: Academic Press.

Harper, R. and Hughes, J. (1993) '"What a f—ing system! Send 'em all to the same place and then expect us to stop 'em hitting": Making technology work in air traffic control', in G. Button (ed.), *Technology in Working Order: Studies of Work, Interaction and Technology*. London: Routledge.

Harper, R., Randall, D. and Rouncefield, M. (2000) *Organisational Change and Retail Finance: An Ethnographic Perspective*. London: Routledge.

Have, P. ten (1995) 'Medical ethnomethodology: An overview', *Human Studies*, 18 (2/3): 245–61.

Have, P. ten (1999) *Doing Conversation Analysis: A Practical Guide*. London: Sage.

Heap, J. (1979) 'Rumpelstiltskin: The organisation of preference in a reading lesson', *Analytic Sociology*, 2 (2):

Heap, J. (1980) 'What counts as reading: The limits to certainty in assessment', *Curriculum Inquiry*, 10 (3): 265–92.

Heap, J. (1982) 'The social organization of reading assessment: reasons for eclecticism', in G. Payne and E. Cuff (eds), *Doing Teaching*. London: Batsford.

Heap, J. (1989) 'Writing as social action', *Theory into Practice*, 28 (2): 148–53.

Heath, C. (1986) *Body Movement and Speech in Medical Interaction*. Cambridge: Cambridge University Press.

Heath, C., Hindmarsh, J. and Luff, P. (1999) 'Interaction in isolation: the dislocated world of the London underground train driver', *Sociology*, 33 (3): 555–75.

Heath, C. and Luff, P. (1993) 'Explicating face-to-face interaction', in N. Gilbert (ed.), *Researching Social Life*. London: Sage.

Heath, C. and Luff, P. (1996) 'Convergent activities: collaborative work and multimedia technology in London Underground Control Rooms', in D. Middleton and Y. Engestrom (eds), *Cognition and Communication at Work*. Cambridge: Cambridge University Press.

Heath, C. and Luff, P. (2000) *Technology in Action*. Cambridge: Cambridge University Press.

Heritage, J. (1984) *Garfinkel and Ethnomethodology*. Cambridge: Polity Press.

Hester, S. and Eglin, P. (1992) *A Sociology of Crime*. London, Routledge.

Hester, S. and Eglin, P. (eds) (1997) *Culture in Action: Studies in Membership Categorisation Analysis*. Lanham, MD: University Press of America and International Institute for Ethnomethodology and Conversation Analysis.

Hester, S. and Francis, D. (2001) *Local Education Order: Ethnomethodological Studies of Knowledge in Action*. Amsterdam: John Benjamins.

Hopper, R. (1992) *Telephone Conversation*. Bloomington, IL: Indiana University Press.

Hughes, J. (1984) 'Bureaucracy', in R.J. Anderson and W.W. Sharrock (eds), *Applied Sociological Perspectives*. London: Allen and Unwin.

Hustler, D. and Payne, G. (1982) 'Power in the classroom', *Research in Education*, 28: 49–64.

Hutchby, I. and Wooffitt, R. (1998) *Conversation Analysis: Principles, Practices and Applications*. Cambridge: Polity Press.

Jayyusi, L. (1984) *Categorisation and the Moral Order*. London: Routledge and Kegan Paul.

Jefferson, G. (1990) 'List construction as a task and resource', in G. Psathas (ed.), *Interaction Competence*. Lanham, MD: University Press of America and the International Institute for Ethnomethodology and Conversation Analysis.

Jefferson, G. and Lee, J.R.E. (1981) 'The rejection of advice: Managing the problematic convergence of a "troubles-telling" and a "service encounter", *Journal of Pragmatics*, 5 (5): 399–422 (also in P. Drew and J. Heritage (eds) (1992), *Talk at Work*. Cambridge: Cambridge University Press).

Kuhn, T. (1962) *The Structure of Scientific Revolutions*. Chicago, IL: University of Chicago Press.

Latour, B. and Woolgar, S. (1986) *Laboratory Life: The Social Construction of Scientific Facts* (2nd enlarged edn) London: Sage.

Lee, J.R.E. (1984) 'Innocent victims and evil doers', *Women's Studies International Forum*, 7 (1): 69–73.

Lee, J.R.E. and Watson, D.R. (1988) *Plan Urbain: Final Report*. Unpublished.

Lemert, C. (2002) 'The pleasure of Garfinkel's indexical ways', in H. Garfinkel (ed.), *Ethnomethodology's Progam: Working out Durkheim's Aphorism*. Lanham, MD: Rowman and Littlefield.

Levine, J., Vinson, A. and Wood, D. (1973) 'Subway behaviour', in A. Birenbaum and E. Sagarin (eds), *People in Places: The Sociology of the Familiar*. London: Nelson.

Liazos, A. (1972) 'The poverty of the sociology of deviance: Nuts, sluts and perverts', *Social Problems*, 20 (1): 103–120.

Livingston, E. (1987) *Making Sense of Ethnomethodology*. London: Routledge and Kegan Paul.

Lynch, M. (1985) *Art and Artifact in Laboratory Science*. London: Routledge and Kegan Paul.

Lynch, M. (1993) *Scientific Practice and Ordinary Action: Ethnomethodology and Social Studies of Science*. Cambridge: Cambridge University Press.

Lynch, M. and Jordan, K. (1995) 'Instructed action in, of and as molecular biology', *Human Studies*, 18 (2/3): 227–44.

Macbeth, D. (1990) 'Classroom order as practical action: the making and un-making of a quiet reproach', British Journal of Sociology of Education 1 (1): 49–66.

Macbeth, D. (1991) 'Teacher authority as practical action', *Linguistics and Education*, 3: 281–314.

Manning, P. (1992) *Erving Goffman and Modern Sociology*. Cambridge: Polity Press.

Maynard, D. (1991) 'The perspective-display series and the delivery and receipt of diagnostic news', in D. Zimmerman and D. Boden (eds), *Talk and Social Structure*. Cambridge: Polity Press.

Maynard, D. (1992) 'On clinicians co-implicating of recipient's perspective in the delivery of diagnostic news', in J. Heritage and P. Drew (eds), *Talk at Work; Interaction in Institutional Settings*. Cambridge: Cambridge University Press.

McHoul, A. (1978) 'The organization of turns at formal talk in the classroom', *Language in Society*, 7 (2): 183–213.

McHugh, P. (1968) *Defining the Situation*. New York, NY: Bobbs-Merrill. Ch.2.

Meehan, A.J. (1989) 'Assessing the "police worthiness" of citizen's complaints to the police: accountability and the negotiation of "facts"', in D. Helm, W. Anderson, A.J. Meehan and A. Rawls (eds), *The Interaction Order: New Directions in the Study of Social Order.* New York, NY: Irvington.

Mehan, A. (1991) 'The school's work of sorting students', in D. Boden and D. Zimmerman (eds), *Talk and Social Structure*. Cambridge: Polity Press.

Mehan, H. (1976) 'Assessing children's school performance', in M. Hammersley and P. Woods (eds), *The Process of Schooling*. London: Routledge and Kegan Paul.

Mehan, H. (1979) *Learning Lessons: Social Organisation in the Classroom*. Cambridge, MA: Harvard University Press.

Mishler, E. (1984) *The Discourse of Medicine: Dialectics of Medical Interviews*. Norwood, NJ: Ablex.

Parsons, T. (1951) *The Social System*. London: Routledge and Kegan Paul.

Payne, G. (1976) 'Making a lesson happen', in M. Hammersley and P. Woods (eds), *The Process of Schooling*. London: Routledge and Kegan Paul.

Payne, G. and Cuff, T. (1982) *Doing Teaching*. London: Batsford.

Payne, G. and Hustler, D. (1980) 'Teaching the class: The practical management of a cohort', *British Journal of Sociology of Education*, 1 (1): 49–66.

Perutz (1995) 'The pioneer defended', *New York Review of Books*, 42 (December 21): 54–8.

Pollner, M. (1974) 'Sociological and common sense models of the labelling process', in R. Turner (ed.), *Ethnomethodology*. Harmondsworth: Penguin Books.

Pomerantz, A. (1984) 'Agreeing and disagreeing with assessments: Some features of preferred/dispreferred turn shape', in J.M. Atkinson and J. Heritage (eds), *Structure of Social Action: Studies in Conversation Analysis*. Cambridge: Cambridge University Press.

Popper, K. (1963) *Conjectures and Refutations: The Growth of Scientific Knowledge.* London: Routledge and Kegan Paul.

Psathas, G. (1990a) 'Methodological issues: Recent developments in the study of naturally occurring interaction', in G. Psathas (ed.), *Interaction Competence.* Lanham, MD: University Press of America.

Psathas, G. (1990b) 'The organization of talk, gaze and activity in a medical interview', in G. Psathas (ed.), *Interaction Competence.* Lanham, MD: University Press of America.

Psathas, G. (1991) 'The structure of direction-giving in interaction', in D. Boden and D. Zimmerman (eds), *Talk and Social Structure.* Cambridge: Polity Press.

Randall, D. and Hughes, J. (1995) 'Sociology, CSCW and working with customers', in P. Thomas (ed.), *The Social and Interactional Dimensions of Human-Computer Interaction.* Cambridge: Cambridge University Press.

Rawls, A. (2002) 'Editor's Introduction', in H. Garfinkel (ed.), *Ethnomethodology's Program: Working Out Durkheim's Aphorism.* Lanham, MD: Rowman and Littlefield.

Ryave, A.R. and Schenkein, J. (1974) 'Notes on the art of walking', in R. Turner (ed.), *Ethnomethodology.* Harmondsworth: Penguin.

Sacks, H. (1967) 'The search for help: No-one to turn to', in E. Schneidman (ed.), *Essays in Self Destruction.* New York, NY: Science House.

Sacks, H. (1972) 'An initial investigation into the usability of conversational data for doing sociology', in D. Sudnow (ed.), *Studies in Social Interaction.* New York, NY: The Free Press.

Sacks, H. (1974) 'On the analysability of stories by children', in R. Turner (ed.), *Ethnomethodology: Selected Readings.* Harmondsworth: Penguin Books.

Sacks, H. (1984) 'Notes on methodology', in J.M. Atkinson and J. Heritage (eds), *Structures of Social Action.* Cambridge: Cambridge University Press.

Sacks, H. (1992a) *Lectures in Conversation,* Vol. 1. Oxford: Basil Blackwell.

Sacks, H. (1992b) *Lectures in Conversation,* Vol. 2. Oxford: Basil Blackwell.

Sacks, H., Schegloff, E. and Jefferson, G. (1974) 'A simplest systematics for the organization of turn-taking in conversation', *Language,* 50 (4): 696–735.

Saussure, F. (1983) *Course in General Linguistics.* London: Duckworth.

Schegloff, E. (1968) 'Sequencing in conversational openings', *American Anthropologist,* 70 (6): 1075–95 (also in P.P. Giglioli (ed.) (1972), *Language and Social Context.* Harmonsworth: Penguin).

Schegloff, E. (1987) 'Between macro and micro: Contexts and other connections', in J. Alexander, B. Giesen, R. Munch and N. Smelser (eds), *The Micro-Macro Link.* San Francisco, CA: University of California Press.

Schegloff, E. (1988) 'On an actual virtual servo-mechanisms for guessing bad news: a single case conjecture?', *Social Problems,* 35 (4): 442–57.

Schegloff, E. (1991) 'Reflections on talk and social structure', in D. Boden and D. Zimmerman (eds), *Talk and Social Structure.* Cambridge: Polity Press.

Schenkein, J. (1978) *Studies in the Organisation of Conversational Interaction.* New York, NY: Academic Press.

Schutz, A. (1962) *Collected Papers,* Vol. 1. The Hague: Martinus Nijhoff.

Schwartz, B. (1975) *Queuing and Waiting: Studies in the Social Organisation Of Delay.* Chicago, IL: University of Chicago Press.

Sharrock, W.W. (1979) 'Portraying the professional relationship', in D. Anderson (ed.), *Health Education in Practice.* London: Croom Helm.

Sharrock, W.W. and Anderson, R.J. (1986) *The Ethnomethodologists.* London: Tavistock.

Sharrock, W.W. and Turner, R. (1978) 'On a conversational environment for equivocality', in J. Schenkein (ed.), *Studies in the Organisation of Conversational Interaction*. New York, NY: Academic Press.

Silverman, D. (1987) *Communication and Medical Practice: Social Relations in the Clinic*. London: Sage.

Silverman, D. (1998) *Harvey Sacks: Social Science and Conversation Analysis*. Cambridge: Polity Press.

Silverman, D. (2001) *Interpreting Qualitative Data: Methods for Analysing Talk, Text and Interaction*. London: Sage.

Slezak, P. (1994) 'Sociology of scientific knowledge and science education, Part 2: Laboratory life under the microscope', *Science and Education*, 3: 329–55.

Speier, M. (1973) *How to Observe Face-to-Face Communication: A Sociological Introduction*. Pacific Palisades, CA: Goodyear.

Speier, M. (1976) 'The child as conversationalist', in M. Hammersley and P. Woods (eds), *The Process of Schooling*. London: Routledge and Kegan Paul.

Suchman, L. and Wynn, E. (1984) 'Procedures and problems in the office', *Office: Technology and People*, 2: 133–54.

Sudnow, D. (1965) 'Normal Crimes: sociological features of the penal code in a public defender office', *Social Problems*, 12 (3): 255–76.

Sudnow, D. (1972) 'Temporal parameters of interpersonal observation', in D. Sudnow (ed.), *Studies in Social Interaction*. New York, NY: The Free Press.

Tannen, D. (1990) *You Just Don't Understand: Men and Women in Conversation*. New York, NY: Morrow.

Watson, D.R. (1978) 'Categorisation, authorisation and blame-negotiation in conversation', *Sociology*, 12 (1): 105–113.

Westley, W. (1970) *Violence and the Police: A Sociological Study of Law, Custom and Morality*. Cambridge, MA: MIT Press.

Whalen, M.R. and Zimmerman, D. (1987) 'Sequential and institutional contexts in calls for help', *Social Psychology Quarterly*, 50 (2): 172–85.

Whalen, M.R. and Zimmerman, D. (1990) 'Describing trouble: Practical epistemology in citizen calls to the police', *Language in Society*, 19: 465–92.

Wilson, J. (1983) *Social Theory*. Englewood Cliffs: Prentice Hall.

Wittgenstein, L. (1967) *Philosophical Investigations*. Oxford: Blackwell.

Wolpert, L. (1992) *The Unnatural Nature of Science*. London: Faber.

Woolgar, S. (1988) *Science: The Very Idea*. London: Tavistock.

Zimmerman, D. (1971) 'The practicalities of rule use', in J. Douglas (ed.), *Understanding Everyday Life*. London: Routledge and Kegan Paul.

Zimmerman, D. (1974) 'Fact as a practical accomplishment', in R. Turner (ed.), *Ethnomethodology*. Harmondsworth: Penguin.

Zimmerman, D. (1992) 'The interactional organization of calls for emergency assistance', in P. Drew and J. Heritage (eds), *Talk at Work: Interaction in Institutional Settings*. Cambridge: Cambridge University Press.

Index